Reaching For The Crescent Moon

The Michael and Mary Cawthorne Story
told by
Helena Rogers

Christian Focus Publications

© 1995 Helena Rogers
ISBN 1 857 92 123 2
Published by
Christian Focus Publications
Geanies House, Feam, Ross-shire,
IV20 1TW, Scotland
Printed and bound in Great Britain by
Cox & Wyman, Reading, Berkshire.

Contents

Milestones

1933	Michael is born
1934	Mary is born
1967	Mary becomes Head Teacher of Westland's Girls' School
1968	Michael is appointed to post at Westland's Girls' School
September 1st 1969	Michael and Mary are married
June 1970	Ruth is born
September 3rd 1971	They set off for Pakistan
September 1973	Sarah is born
October 1974	They move into Pathan village
April 1978	Overland journey to England
July 1981	Michael begins working for the Bishop of Peshawar
January 1982	Mary is appointed Principal of Police Public School
December 1983	Three month furlough during which Mary and Michael are accepted as Partners with the Church Missionary Society
January 1987	Return to Pakistan where Mary is appointed co-ordinator to the Christian schools
January 1991	Mary returns to England to care for her father
August 1991	Ruth and Roy are married Michael and Mary's employment with the Church Missionary Society ends

Foreword

Not many people have the opportunity to visit Pakistan. Fewer still have the pleasure of viewing the Khyber Pass, and far smaller in number are those blessed folk who have travelled through the Khyber Pass to the ancient land of Afghanistan.

Mary and Mike Cawthorne are numbered in that blessed few.

Their home in Pakistan at times served as a refuge for some of the lost souls my wife and I were reaching out to in Afghanistan. Michael and Mary visited us when they came to Afghanistan, and their presence always brought joy and encouragement.

This book will take you back over many years to visit with Michael and Mary as they journey to the land of Pakistan. You will walk with them in the market places and the bazaars, and your heart will join with theirs as they reach for the crescent moon, and the people who live in the shadow of that crescent.

I commend this book because it is about two of God's servants who gave their lives on the front lines for Him. Join with me now as we turn the page, and travel to that distant land.

Floyd McClung
(International Director, Youth With a Mission)
April 1994

Preface

Trust and obey, for there's no other way
To be happy in Jesus, but to trust and obey.

The words above are so often thought of as simply a children's hymn, but they contain such profound truth that we had this hymn at our wedding, little dreaming how literally we would be called on to practise it a mere two years later! After many sermons about Abraham and Sarah going out into the unknown in faith, believing that they had heard God's call to them, we found ourselves journeying to Pakistan in a similar manner. The wonderful thing is the way we proved God's faithfulness from day to day as He led us about in a strange land.

It was to be after twelve years that we did eventually join a Mission, and as we shared the true stories of how we saw God at work in everyday events in Pakistani villages, people often urged 'Do write it all down in a book'. When David and Helena Rogers from our home church in Tankerton visited us in situ, they not only said the same, but Helena offered to write this book.

But why should there be a book written about us? Are we remarkably successful partners in Mission? No! Did we get it right all the time? No! Have we founded a prestigious institution or a church? No! We are ordinary, fallible human beings - but obeying God works, and we have been privileged to 'see the salvation of our God' in everyday living.

Therefore this book is written to motivate other Christians to 'trust and obey'. It tells of adventures and hard times; of brick walls and open doors; and is as honest as the avoidance of misrepresentation or embarrassment of others will allow.

We have learned that God does not require us to be perfect, but that He delights in His children's willingness and obedience.

If it also shows that as well as a call, faith and certain skills, you also need a sense of humour, the ability to keep on trying, perseverance, patience and the determination to put the past behind and press onward, it will have served its purpose - remembering that it is Christ alone who can accomplish anything.

It is dedicated to those who have helped and encouraged us along the way: our parents who gave us each such good, though different starts in life; the DeHart family of 'TEAM Mission' - outstanding examples of what Mission partners ought to be like; and the Church Missionary Society - a wonderful family of caring, supportive Christian folk whose wise and practical care made enjoyable, as well as possible, our latter years of service in Pakistan.

We pray that our readers may be inspired to new heights of dedicated service to our Lord and Saviour, Jesus Christ.

Mary and Mike Cawthorne

1. God's Olive Branch

Michael turned his car on to the A2 road towards Sittingbourne, Kent. He was not particularly nervous about this job interview. He had waited for God to show him the right place to apply for his first teaching post, and he was certain that Westlands School for Girls in Sittingbourne was the right place.

He had been told about this job by the head of Religious Instruction at the school where he had spent his last teaching practice. She was a friend of Miss Bogg, the Head Teacher of Westlands, and she had told Michael that Miss Bogg was looking for a Christian teacher to teach Science. Apparently, the school was soon to go co-educational, and there was every chance that a male teacher would be appointed.

The A2 opened up into a dual carriageway, and Michael dropped in behind a lorry for the last leg of the journey. He was in no desperate hurry. He had plenty of time, he knew he was within the Lord's will. All would go according to plan.

With horrifying suddenness, the lorry in front braked so fast that its drive-shaft gouged into the road, and the bed of the lorry lifted about eight feet into the air. With split-second reactions, Michael jammed on his brakes, prayed instantaneously, and found himself underneath the towering lorry.

Once more in his life, he had the uncanny sensation that he was the object of demonic action.

It was not the first time Michael had been within a hair's breadth of death. As he looked back he could see a series of calamities snaking through his life as though some unseen influence begrudged his right to live. It was only when he became a Christian that he was sure he was right.

He put it all down to the 'Wheatley Connection'. His grandmother was a Miss Wheatley before she married - a distant cousin of Dennis Wheatley, the eminent occult writer. It seemed as though tentacles of evil emanating from the writer's fascination with the occult insidiously permeated the family like an invisible parasitical vine seeking to ensnare further willing hosts.

Strangely - or, as he came to understand later, *necessarily* - there seemed to be Christians dotted about the family - as though God continually sustained an olive branch of love to draw the unsuspecting away from the evil towards Himself.

The link was continued when the troubled Miss Wheatley eventually married a devout Christian from whom she grasped the olive branch and found peace through Jesus Christ; thus holding the next olive branch to reach out to her young grandson. The foundation of Michael's life's work was begun therefore, when, as a little boy, he used to creep into grandma's bed, and she would open up her big 'King James' Bible, paraphrasing the stories for his young mind to understand.

When it came to education, Michael's father and grandfather wanted the best for him. It was therefore at nearly twelve years of age that Michael found himself at the prestigious King's School in Canterbury, reputedly the oldest school in England. It was at King's that he discovered a lifelong love of the sea as he joined the Naval Cadet Section, sailing at Whitstable Yacht Club and serving in H.M.S. St. James, where nights were spent in hammocks, and blaspheming was more or less obligatory. But it did not come easily to the boy. He was not the healthy outdoor type who might be expected to have an interest in the Navy.

Michael had never enjoyed good health. He was asthmatic, and at best, a seven-stone weakling who was not allowed to play rough games or even go near the horses which his friends so eagerly learned to ride. But the need to compete with his fellow students was very strong, and he refused to be excluded from anything the others did.

Each weekend, therefore, since he had no horse, he would push himself to the limit as he *ran* after the hounds. At the end of the chase he would relax with 'county' society and consume copious pints of Guinness with the best of them!

Gradually, however, the determination which was to become increasingly apparent in his character began to assert itself. He would beg or borrow a horse until he mastered the method and the horse, and went on later to greatly enjoy fox-hunting. The result of all this exercise in the open air was that by the time he left school, he had put on weight and his health had improved substantially.

His father's firm of chartered accountants had been the obvious place to begin work on leaving school. He took his place there as an articled clerk, being the last of those who were obliged to pay £750 for the privilege. This, in 1949, was a large sum of money, when his weekly wage was around £2!

However since his health had improved so much, he could now liven up his off-duty hours by joining the 'rugger' team of the Royal Naval Volunteer Reserves. It was during an important match that disaster threatened.

During the first half, he found himself at the centre of a scrum with what seemed like the rest of the hefty team on top of him. He felt a pain, but had no time to dwell on it. He played on through the second half, the pain increasing until, at the end of the match, his neck began to feel strangely awkward.

One of the members drove him to St. George's Hospital for an X-ray. Immediately sandbags were placed each side of his head and he was told to lie absolutely still.

'Don't move an inch!' He was told firmly. 'Your neck is broken, and the break is serious.'

The doctor went on to explain that a little 'peg' had fractured and the dislocation above it gave the same effect as a hangman's knot. One movement could mean death. 'We will give you an injection as soon as possible, but do not move until you have had it,' he was warned.

Michael managed to remain motionless for the rest of that day and on into the night, but at some time, as he lay there, he heard a fire engine go past the window. It reminded him of the fire at his home only a week before.

Something within him just could not let it go by without looking. So he pushed the sandbags aside, and rushed to the window as fast as cramp from being in one position for so long, would allow him. The last thing he remembered before he passed out was the promised injection.

When he came round some time later, his aunt, who was actually an eminent consultant at Great Ormond Street Hospital, was sitting beside him, accompanied by a brain specialist whom she had contacted and rushed down from Oxford. He was to advise regarding the manipulation which was to be necessary to reset Michael's neck. He was deep in conversation with medical students about the intricate case before him.

'His neck can't be moved this way or that way,' he demonstrated with his hands, as Michael's aunt frowned in thought.

'Why not?' chipped in the patient, involuntarily turning his head in the direction the consultant was indicating.

Incredulous stares met this 'impossible' movement, and then when he had recovered from the shock, the consultant's eyes opened wide.

'This is fantastic! It isn't possible!' he exclaimed, 'It's a miracle!' He went on, amazed, as Michael continued to prove that he had regained all the original movement in his neck.

Some time later, Michael heard that his case had been reported in the British Medical Journal with two others who had survived this type of injury. All he knew at this point was that when he got out of bed to look at the fire engine, his neck had clicked back perfectly. He was convinced that he was now completely well, and argued with the doctors who insisted that he must be put into plaster until the fracture had healed.

This was a great nuisance because it would interfere not only with his studying, but with his tennis - and in addition he was soon to take the Intermediate Examinations for the Institute of Chartered Accountancy. He did not want his future jeopardised by what he considered to be an unnecessary lump of plaster. That he may have been miraculously healed by the power of God did not occur to him. He simply had a deep conviction that his neck was now better, and that further treatment was pointless.

The doctors insisted however, and Michael was encased in the white restraining plaster. Soon his neck began to itch. Several times he begged to be rid of the plaster nuisance, but the consultant insisted that it must remain. The accountancy examinations came and went and Michael's future had to wait, but he constantly exercised his neck until the plaster was loose and it was finally removed early after six months!

He was to remain with his father's firm for the next two years, but his passionate interest remained with the sea, and he decided that he could have the best of both worlds by joining the Royal Naval Volunteer Reserves as an ordinary seaman on H.M.S. President in the evenings.

When National Service loomed for him in 1954,

Michael was quite determined to go into the Navy. The fact that he was excluded because he had suffered a broken neck was quite irrelevant to him. There may well have been suggestions that he could easily get into the Army, but Michael was adamant.

'I am going into the Navy - and that's final!' He insisted, and swung into action. First he wrote to the surgeon in Oxford with the argument that if a neck is broken and it heals, then it could be stronger than it was before. This, he argued, should not therefore be any barrier to joining the Navy.

He managed to acquire an interview, but the struggle was not over. He battled on, insisting that he was determined to be admitted. Eventually, a doctor was called to assess the situation. Michael waved a piece of paper in front of him.

'I tell you I'm all right!' he remonstrated. 'There is absolutely nothing wrong with me at all - now!'

'All right,' the doctor acquiesced, 'I'll pass you, but you may be turned down later.'

Having won his first Naval battle, Michael went in as an able seaman to HMS Victoria Barracks, where he was made a class captain straight away because he was from the RNVR and found to be good at organising.

He went on to take his sailing certificates and he was eventually offered promotion. However, he failed his first interview because he was asked impossible questions like 'what actions he would take about ships coming in to the North Sea from Murmansk?'

'I haven't the faintest idea!' admitted Michael without a qualm.

The next interview was more reasonable. He was asked to describe 'ice' for five minutes. This he could manage, and as he had had five year's experience in accountancy, he was duly commissioned in the Supply and Secretariat branch of the Royal Navy for his National Service.

Michael's aim was to be an Executive Officer of some kind, but he seemed to be thwarted again. It was thought that he had a problem with colour vision, but Michael persevered, insisting that as he had no problem with the coloured lamps at sea he should therefore be perfectly fit for promotion. He was refused however, but finally acquired a watch keeping certificate. Being firmly convinced that the Navy would now be his career, he signed on for further training.

It was only one short year later, with the government short of cash, that cuts were implemented, and Michael's hopes of a Naval career were dashed. He had to leave, and find some other kind of work, although he stayed in the Reserves for the rest of his life as a Lieutenant Commander.

As his financial position on leaving the Navy consisted of nothing but an overdraft, Michael was obliged to find work quickly.

He was soon, therefore, to be found on a building site earning the grand sum of six shillings an hour - which was good for his overdraft, since in the Navy he had entered at six shillings per *day*! His wage in the building trade should have been *five* shillings an hour, but he gained the extra shilling because he said he could drive a digger. He had never actually tried, but was sure he must be able to, and soon proved himself to be right! However, the job did not last too long, because Michael could not get along with the dishonesty and crookedness which he saw there. He did not see how he could change matters, so he left to look for more congenial employment.

Next he tried landscape gardening and loved every minute. Michael's parents, however, had not spent a small fortune on his education to let him 'waste his time' being a gardener. They told him so, and Michael looked once again for a 'proper' job.

Several were suggested, but at last Michael opted for the position of postal clerk with a Bristol firm. He told himself that although this was humble work, it at least promised prospects of a career, and since he was denied his responsible position in the Navy, then this job was as good as any.

It all started well. Michael was keen to get on, and did his best to comply with all requests. However, his superiors had not taken into account his Navy training when they urged upon him the importance of delivering a particular letter one day.

'Get this to the other factory as fast as you can!' they impressed upon him. Then in case he had still not grasped the urgency of the situation, they added, 'No matter *how*!'

Michael did not need to be told twice. He had not reached the position of Lieutenant in the Navy through dithering. Rather he had got there through his ability to act promptly in any situation. He thought quickly and chose the fastest and most available way of delivering the letter - he took the Director's car!

When he returned, having delivered the letter successfully, of course, Michael faced the music. There was a lot of it. It was made quite clear to him that the Director's car was not 'available transport' to office juniors, and that if he ever did such a thing again, he would be carrying the ladder - not climbing it - in this company! But when it was thought that he was sufficiently chastened and cut down to size, they promoted him to the sales division - for his initiative!

Michael worked well for some time, but eventually he began to feel restricted, not only in the job, but in the attitude of the Directors to their employees. There had, after all, been a spot of bother about his beard.

Michael satisfied his need to be in the open air by going rock climbing at weekends. His custom, at these times, was to leave his razor at home and let his beard grow freely. He maintained that the wind made his shaved face sore, but he would revert back to the 'company image' when he got home.

On one particular occasion he returned home at midnight after a gruelling expedition, and in his exhausted condition, sleep was more important to him than shaving. He arrived, therefore, at work the next morning with a good growth of ginger beard to go with his shock of fiery hair. It was not long before he was summoned to the Boss's office. 'What,' said the Boss sternly, 'is this *fungus* around your face?'

Michael was tired and irritable, and took exception to the remark. He stood up, clenched his fists and said angrily, 'You'd better retract that.'

The Boss had not been spoken to like this before. He was of the 'old school', and expected the deference of any employee - especially juniors - as his right. He too, brought himself up to his full height and responded with the only answer that came to him at that unique moment in his life: 'I am your Boss!'

This did not impress Michael one bit, and he snapped back, 'You can be what you like. I won't have anyone speaking to me like that! If I want to wear a beard I will.'

The Boss was non-plussed. This kind of treatment to one's superiors was outside his experience. He had no tried and trusted responses to such outspokenness. He floundered. 'No-one in our company wears a beard,' he offered weakly.

'You know what you can do about that!' said Michael, enjoying the success of the battle, but ignoring the consequences, and he walked out.

Bristling with anger, he recalled his paternal grandfather, whose spirit he seemed to have inherited. He, too, had been reprimanded by his superiors for what he considered was a trivial matter. And also regardless of the consequences, he had stood up for himself - small though he was. He had grabbed the tyrant by the lapels and heaved him into the Manchester Ship Canal!

His father had been so incensed by his son's wayward behaviour that he had cut him off with only a shilling. Michael recalled that shilling. It had become a symbol of achievement to him.

His irascible grandfather had not despaired at the injustice dealt to him. He went on to use the shilling and his wits to form a company which packed tea for the grocer's owned by one Tommy Lipton. It did not stop there, however. His inventive mind soon came up with a neat little package called the 'tea-bag', which was snapped up by Tommy Lipton's organisation. Unfortunately, Michael's grandfather did not think to take out a patent on his invention, and missed out on the fortune which Lipton's went on to make from it. Still, the shilling had gone a long way.

Michael ached to achieve something worthwhile as he continued to work in the sales department of the Bristol company - for in spite of his outburst, he was not sacked. The Directors had not become a successful company by ignoring ability in their employees, and they had no wish to lose an able one. But Michael was not content to remain on the same rung of the ladder. He wanted to climb higher. Once more he was driven to action. At an appropriate moment he went to the Directors.

'I have enjoyed my job,' he told them, 'but I am ready for advancement. You gave me a lovely apple and I've chewed it to the core. Now I want a new one.'

They were rather taken aback, and said they would think about it. But Michael was not convinced. That contretemps over the beard could not be forgotten lightly. He was sure they would not promote such a rebel further, so he handed in his notice.

Once again he was obliged to take whatever jobs were available, but he was to find another job from an unexpected quarter.

For some time, Michael had been organising a 'Gentlemen's Dinner Party' - a monthly event of sheer nostalgia, which involved half-a-dozen guests and a dinner of eight or nine courses. The object was to create the kind of occasion which the Victorians enjoyed - liveried waiters, silver service, beautiful table settings and everything which the modern world could no longer advocate.

It was at one of these dinners that he met John Collins, who was using the same restaurant. Mr. Collins told Michael that he was just the kind of person he was seeking to help start a new company.

Before long Michael found himself the first of three salesmen for Robinson's Building Techniques Limited. He found the work stimulating and quite fascinating, and it looked like the beginning of a bright future.

About a year after Michael had been working for the new company, he was invited to a cocktail party on Christmas Eve. During the evening he met a man who worked for a firm who specialised in Educational equipment. As they chatted, the man seemed impressed by Michael.

'You shouldn't be a salesman, you should be in education,' he said earnestly.

'There's no money in it,' responded Michael, 'and anyway, I'm not qualified.'

The man persisted. 'But there are schools who will accept an unqualified teacher if he has a gift for teaching. I'm sure that's what you should be doing. You come and see me, and I'll set you on the right road.'

It was not long afterwards that Michael found himself out to lunch with his new acquaintance, and he left afterwards with a list of six or seven schools who were advertising for staff. He had no intention of giving up his lucrative job, but - just for the fun of it - he applied to one of the schools, a preparatory school in Scotland.

In no time at all, it seemed to Michael, he was on his way to Scotland to be interviewed for the job. 'Why am I doing this?' he thought. Here he was, earning not far short of four thousand pounds a year, and going to an interview for one which offered only three hundred and twenty per year because he was unqualified. It was madness!

The school impressed Michael. It was in beautiful surroundings and had an aura of peace. He was shown around, and interviewed, and then the Headmaster mentioned that there was to be a special dinner that night, because they were sending their son off to Durham University the next day.

'Why not stay the night here?' the Headmaster invited, 'then you can share in the dinner with us.'

As Michael was only a potential junior teacher, he hardly spoke to the Headmaster's son, and he did not learn until a long time afterwards that the son was a Christian. Neither did he discover that the young man had experienced a strong urge to pray for the intending new teacher. As he had left to go to university, he had spent earnest hours in prayer for him on his train journey.

On his return from Scotland, Michael told one of his directors about the interview. Mystified, the director asked, 'Why do you want to go into education?'

'The Lord knows!' answered Michael instinctively.

As soon as he had uttered the words, he felt stricken. He was totally confused. That phrase was a common, innocuous sort of remark. He had used it often. In fact it was one of the least offensive kind of remarks which, as a sailor, he had used. Why, then, should he suddenly feel as though he had blasphemed in the worst possible way? He was terribly upset and couldn't get the incident out of his mind, but had no real idea why it should affect him this way.

One of the subjects which Michael was asked to teach at the school in Scotland was Religious Instruction. He considered that with his grandmother's training, and with what he had learned at King's, he would be able to cope adequately.

It was with confidence, then, that he set about explaining the teaching of the Beatitudes to his class during his first term in Scotland. 'Blessed are the pure in heart, for they shall see God,' he quoted, and then he explained, 'that means God will bless the good people in this world because they will go to Heaven one day.'

One of the boys had a question. 'Do you really believe that, sir?' he enquired.

Michael was annoyed. Who was this child to question a teacher? 'Of course I do,' he responded irritably, 'what else could it mean?'

The boy continued. 'Well, I don't think it means *that*, sir. I have only been a Christian a short time, but I believe it means that only those whose sins have been forgiven through faith in Jesus will see God.'

Michael was now angry. 'Shut up, Peter!' he retorted, having no wish to discuss the matter further.

In the next class was Peter's brother. He was therefore listening and watching with interest when Michael read the story in Genesis, where Abraham is asked to sacrifice his very important son, Isaac. Towards the end of the story, Michael read, *since you have not withheld your son, your only son ...* (22:15).

In consternation, Michael felt tears falling down his cheeks. He wiped them away quickly, but more fell. Each time he pictured the faith and resolution of Abraham, tears flowed unbidden. He was dreadfully upset.

The two brothers knew what was happening to Michael. They had both been touched by the love of God, and recognised the signs in their irritable teacher.

If he was to earn a reasonable salary in teaching, it was necessary for Michael to acquire a teaching certificate. To this end he left the school in Scotland and returned to the South to attend Redhill Technical College where he studied for 'A' level Physics as the first step towards qualifying.

While there, he was asked to show films about mountaineering to young people in a school in Sussex. Michael loved the mountains and, as a qualified instructor, tried to foster a love of nature and creation in the children he taught.

The film show had been organised by a Mrs. Sheppard who was a volunteer worker with underprivileged children. Interestingly, she happened to be the mother of the famous cricketer, David Sheppard, who later became the Bishop of Liverpool. She watched with interest as Michael showed a film called *The Love of the Mountains*, but the young people seemed to Michael to be looking at him blankly, having no understanding of what he was talking about.

Indignantly, Michael burst out, 'You'll never know the love of the mountains unless Mrs. Sheppard and these other people here provide a bus for you and take you to experience the mountains for yourself. You can't have any enthusiasm unless you've actually seen them and know them for yourself!'

In the silence which followed his outburst, a voice, heard only by Michael, spoke from the back of the hall, '*And you'll never know Me or love Me, until you've met Me and experienced Me.*'

Michael knew unequivocally that the voice was God's. He was overwhelmed. Being near to tears and shaking with emotion, it was all he could do to close the talk and leave. He drove from the village in Sussex until he came to a roundabout where he saw a man in a raincoat indicating that he wanted a lift. Michael stopped and asked the man where he was going.

'Anywhere,' answered the man.

'Well I'm going to Dorking,' said Michael.

'That'll be fine,' said the man, 'drop me anywhere.'

In conversation, Michael asked him what he had been doing, and the man told him that he had been baptising Gypsies.

'Oh, no,' responded Michael in exasperation, 'I suppose you are a clergyman.' And then, still smarting from his recent experience which seemed to be the culmination of a kind of 'harassment' from God, he went on to attack his passenger verbally.

The man listened patiently, and then said, 'Michael, you don't know God.'

It went from bad to worse. Michael was furious that in the first place this man was defying the usual conventions and had the temerity to call him by his Christian name, and in the second place he was telling him he didn't know God! The man was insolent, and would have to go. Michael stopped the car and ordered the man out.

As he drove on, he felt the same confusion he had felt in the school. The voice he had heard and the man's presumptuous statements jostled each other for meaning in his mind. In desperation he called out in anguish,

'God, if You're real I must know You. Please help me.'

Then, as he turned a corner into the village where he was living, he saw with stunned recognition, the unmistakable figure of Jesus standing on the village green in all His glory!

In great distress, Michael somehow drove the final yards to his home, and went to his room where he wept uncontrollably. But he was aware that Jesus was still there. The same figure was standing just beside him on Michael's right! There was no feeling of fear, only one of deep contrition, and as he wept, Michael experienced that love of God which had been missing in his life up to this point.

There was a Bible on the bookshelf above his bed. He had not used it for years, but tonight Michael felt compelled to open it. He wanted to read from John chapter one, but he couldn't see through his tears. He just sat there holding the Bible, knowing irrevocably that God was real. He had no further doubts. From this point on his life would be totally changed because he now knew that God was definitely and indisputably real.

2. Life of Surprises

For the next few days Michael walked on air. He thought back over his life, and pieced together the times when God had intervened to teach him something that would bring him to this point. There had clearly been times when the devil had the upper hand, but there could have been no doubt about the final outcome. God had won the victory over Satan when Jesus died and conquered death, and now Michael realised that he had been called of God to become one of His beloved children.

He considered the time when his neck was broken. Now he could quite clearly see that the healing was miraculous! God's hand had been on him all the time!

It was all so amazing! The Bible which he had not opened for so long was now read avidly, and in it Michael began to gain a deeper understanding of the gospel message. He had known it before, but now it struck him with glittering clarity. This was news that everyone should hear. The gospel was for everyone!

He read John 3:16 again and again: 'God so loved the world that He gave his *one and only Son* ...,' here the tears began to fall again, '... that *whoever* believes in Him, shall not perish but have eternal life.' He paused to take in the incredible significance of it all, and then read on: 'Whoever believes in Him is not condemned, but *whoever does not believe stands condemned already* because he has not believed in the name of God's one and only Son.'

'*Condemned already* ...'. Michael meditated on the words. People everywhere - millions of people - condemned because they do not believe. How could he tell them, when most people would not take his experience seriously?

As each day went by, he began to realise that God was

prepared to do crazy things with anyone - if they would let Him. He therefore determined to do nothing without checking it out first with God. He would pray, 'Is this Your will, Lord?' when faced with a crossroad, and if he did not have clear direction otherwise, he would go ahead. It was to lead him into all kinds of adventures.

There was the Friday morning during a vacation, when Michael was due at an interview for a temporary job. As he was getting ready, it seemed to him that God was saying, 'I want you to come with Me today.'

Michael was a bit puzzled, but responded in his spirit, 'Well, Lord, if this is true, You will have to provide me with transport.' With that, he went on out, and stood at the roadside. 'Which way, Lord?' he said.

He was supposed to be going to Reigate, but instead he crossed the road. He then thumbed down the first car he saw, and said, 'Where are you going?'

'Weymouth,' answered the accommodating driver.

'Excellent!' said Michael, and jumped in.

The weekend that followed was an experience in obedience for Michael. At Weymouth he joined up with some Christians who were running the annual Beach Mission for children. Each day they would have a lively meeting in which they sang, told stories, and taught the youngsters about God - often in the loudest possible way!

It just so happened that they were one man short that weekend, and Michael told them how God had led him to them. He was received with gratefulness, and Michael pitched in and helped eagerly.

On the Monday, when he returned, he telephoned the builder who had offered him an interview. He was just about to apologise for not turning up, when the builder cut in with, 'I am very sorry that I wasn't there on Friday, Mr. Cawthorne ...'.Michael got the job, and learned that being led of the Lord was great fun!

It was soon time for Michael to apply for teacher training college, and he gained a place at the college of S. Mark and S. John in Chelsea.

Being rather older than the average student, Michael was chosen to be 'floor rep.', and was therefore in the position where he could talk to many of the students about God. One young man to whom he spoke was sceptical. He was not at all sure that he could believe in God.

At one o'clock the next morning, however, he came charging into Michael's cubicle saying, 'Yes! Yes! God is real! He was there! He is real!'

When Michael could calm him down, he discovered that the man had been praying for hours and trying to find the Lord, when at last he got out a Bible. Suddenly he saw something which seemed to stand out in brilliant letters: '*You will seek Me and find Me when you seek Me with all your heart*' (Jeremiah 29:11). He was instantly touched, and he said that the Lord came into the room - he felt His presence there greater than anything ever before.

He was so totally convinced of the reality of God, that dressed only in pyjamas he had chased down six flights of stairs, run across the quadrangle and up another six flights of stairs, in order to tell Michael all about it! And all this in the depths of winter at one o'clock in the morning! They were to remain friends for many years.

And so Michael set to working towards his important teaching certificate, but he became increasingly aware of the fact that God could suddenly teach him something new at any time.

He had been to a conference and had returned exhausted. All he wanted to do was sleep. He dismissed his fellow students, and fell into bed. Almost immediately he woke up again, and so it continued every half-hour, until Michael was cross and irritable. 'What is going on?' he remonstrated with the Lord. 'Why can't I sleep?'

The answer was brief. 'Praise Me.'

That was all very well, thought Michael, but how should one praise in the middle of the night? He couldn't sing adequately and he didn't think the other students would appreciate it even if he could. Then the thought came to him that he must get out of bed, kneel down in the cold, put up his hands and praise with his thoughts.

As he praised he understood. Whenever he awoke he would praise God. Then, if the devil was attempting to disturb his nights, he would be frustrated in his efforts and give it up, but if God was awakening him to tell him something, then he certainly would not want to remain asleep! From that time on, Michael never had any trouble in sleeping.

And one night he did awake to hear something from God. He had fallen into his usual deep sleep, but after some hours he woke up. As his eyes opened, they focused on the wall of his study. What was it he could see? He peered into the darkness. There on the wall he could see colours - purple, yellow and white. Was it a picture of some kind? He asked the Lord.

'It is a map,' came the answer.

When he awoke the next morning, Michael knew that he had to acquire a solid copy of that map. As he went down to breakfast he discussed it with the Lord.

'Lord, I'd like to try to get a copy of that map today, but I have a lecture which I ought not to miss.' His route to the dining room took him past the notice board and he saw a paper pinned there. The lecture had been cancelled.

The best place Michael could think of to acquire a map was at Stanford's, the prestigious London store which dealt in every kind of map imaginable. He walked into the shop and told them he wanted a map.

'Oh, yes,' said the mystified assistant, waiting for a little more information. Michael tried to elaborate.

'Well, it's purple and yellow and white.'

The assistant was patient. 'What part of the world is it from?'

'I'm afraid I don't know,' responded Michael, suddenly feeling that this was not going too well. If only he had been able to get more information about it from the Lord.

'Well,' said the young man, not giving any sign that he thought his customer a hopeless eccentric, 'if it's purple, do you think it would be an aircraft map?'

Michael hadn't a clue, but just as he was wondering what to say next, the young man's brow creased and he peered closely at Michael.

'Just a moment,' he said, 'aren't you Mike - Mike Cawthorne? I'm in the RNVR - I know you, don't I?'

'That's right,' grinned Michael, 'we met on HMS President, didn't we?' They shook hands and began again. The young man's memories of the forthright character began to fall into place. It accounted for a lot.

'Now,' he continued. 'Let me think. We had some aircraft maps which were taken by an American called Gary Powers. They were withdrawn at the request of the Russian Government, and went back to the Ordnance Survey Depot. However, there is one downstairs which has not been replaced - I saw it yesterday. It should have gone back, and it's a bit of an embarrassment to us now. As naval personnel you are allowed access to restricted maps, so I don't see any problem. I'll get it for you - maybe that's the one you are looking for.'

It was a map of Pakistan, Afghanistan and part of Russia, and one look told Michael it was exactly the right map, except that it had no yellow on it. He soon altered that by taking a yellow marker and adding the line he had seen in his vision on the bedroom wall. It went all round an area including Kabul in Afghanistan, the town of Peshawar and the state of Swat in the North West Province of

Pakistan, almost to Rawalpindi. With very grateful thanks, he took his precious map and returned to college.

He pinned the map on the wall of his room, and after a few enquiries from the Worldwide Evangelisation Crusade regarding missionaries in the area, he simply began to pray for them, and the Pathan people who lived there. He had no further instructions from the Lord, so continued to pray on a regular basis.

Later in his time at college, Michael was 'promoted' to House Representative of the Student Body. How proud he was as he was taken to the election ceremony along college corridors in a canoe. He was carried aloft while all the students sang the popular song, 'Michael, Row the Boat Ashore'! It was a great privilege to represent his fellow students .

He was firm, however, when it came to singing rugger songs in his car. He often had to transport some of the team, and the custom was to sing lustily on the journey. The nearest to rugger songs he would allow, were the ones which he now discovered originally had hymn words. It therefore became a phenomenon of the college of S. Mark and S. John that theirs was the only rugger team who arrived at matches singing hymns!

Michael himself was not allowed to play rugger. He had promised his mother after he had broken his neck that he would never play it again. He did not make promises about any other kind of sport, however, so he took up Judo instead!

He did not reach any great heights in the sport, but one night he took on a 'blue belt'. By some fluke he managed a superb throw which landed his opponent flat on his back. The opponent now revised his opinions. He had been told that this fellow was not very experienced, and he had made allowances. Obviously he had been told wrong. He made no more allowances. When Michael hit the floor, he knew he had broken his arm. He was taken to Hammer-smith Hospital where they put him in a splint in preparation for adding the plaster when the swelling had gone down.

As he was walking back across Wandsworth Bridge, a group of 'Teddy Boys' swaggered up, bent on trouble. Michael feared the worst, and as they began to attack, he raised his arms to demonstrate the love of God. 'You can do what you like with me,' he said, 'it's nothing to what you are doing to the Lord Jesus.'

Suddenly he was aware that his arm was totally healed. At the moment when he had spread out his arms, the injury had gone! He hardly noticed the 'Teddy Boys' go without further trouble, and when Michael attended the hospital the next morning there was pandemonium!

Another X-ray proved that the arm was perfect, but the picture of the day before clearly showed the break. As the doctors scrutinised them, they were mystified. They searched for an explanation but found none. Michael explained that God had healed him when he tried to tell some louts about God's love, but the doctors did not understand.

Just before he qualified as a teacher, Michael went on his last teaching practice in a school in South London. During a biology lesson, he remarked strongly to the children that anyone who smoked was a fool. The boys apparently reported with a certain amount of glee that this student teacher was calling all the staff in the school 'fools', since every one of them smoked!

When Michael next entered the staffroom, he was appalled at the revolting smoke-filled atmosphere, but even more annoyed by the challenge he received from one of the teachers.

'Are you the young student teacher who says all the staff are fools because they smoke?' demanded the angry man. Michael affirmed that he was, and went on, 'Not only the staff, but *anyone* who smokes!'

'That is not the kind of attitude which a student should bring to a school,' said the teacher, seething with anger.

'I don't care what you think,' retorted Michael, equally angrily, 'the truth has to be told. I don't like to see these kids deceived by people who smoke in staffrooms but not in classrooms.'

The row that ensued convinced Michael that he would never be appointed to a position in this school - or maybe any other if the word got around that he was a fervent and outspoken anti-smoker.

It was all the more welcome, therefore, when one of the lady teachers came to him afterwards and congratulated him. 'Well done, Michael,' she grinned, 'I was so pleased about that!'

They chatted for a while, and Michael discovered that she was a Christian.

'We're going to pray for you,' she said. And then she had another thought. 'I know a Christian head teacher in Sittingbourne who is looking for a science teacher. The last one was an agnostic, so she now wants someone who will give the Christian view. You must apply for the job.'

And so Michael set out confidently along the A2 road to Sittingbourne for his interview, and for his narrow brush with death.

As he backed his car from beneath the lorry, he took a moment to survey the situation. Such an accident should have meant at the very least, horrific injuries, and at worst, death. Yet here he was, alive and unhurt, and even his car had not been seriously damaged. He considered that God must have some purpose for his life. That persistent finger of evil had pointed once again to Michael, but God had preserved him for something special.

Perhaps his new appointment at Westlands Girls' School would be the start of it - for he had no doubts that he would be appointed to the vacant post.

3. Learning to Trust

Mary Bogg had no intention of becoming a Headmistress. She enjoyed teaching the children too much to relinquish the classroom for a study. True, her Christian upbringing had evoked thoughts about becoming a missionary, and these persisted, but one needed qualifications even for that, and teaching became her instinctive choice. She found herself quite satisfied to live out her career as a class teacher, changing schools now and then in order to retain freshness and to gain experience - and a Deputy Headship had undoubtedly helped financially since her parent's illness had made her the family breadwinner - but the Headship had not been a welcomed step.

Mary believed that the chasm between selected children of the Grammar Schools and non-selected children of the Secondary Modern Schools could be reduced considerably with encouragement and inspired teaching. She aimed, therefore, to remain a class teacher and devote her career to helping those largely forgotten children of the Secondary Schools.

Mary knew a little of what it was like to feel 'different'. Not that she had been unhappy when she was a child. No, indeed. In fact she looked back on her childhood with gratefulness and love towards the father and mother who had cared for her so faithfully and lovingly. But it might not have been like that.

****

Little Joan appeared as a sickly scrap when Mr and Mrs Bogg had first seen her in the children's home. At one year old she weighed just twelve pounds. The paediatrician to whom Mr and Mrs Bogg took her after her adoption expressed outrage at her condition, and made steps to have the 'home' investigated, but before this could be put into effect, all records were destroyed in a fire ....

The Boggs were not happy with the name 'Joan'. She had a new life now, and a new name would be appropriate. They favoured 'Mary', but were reticent about naming her 'Mary Joan' in case it should become 'Mary Jane' - like the popular character in Enid Blyton's books. 'Joan Mary' would be better, but they decided they would always refer to her as 'Mary'.

'Little Mary' began the slow progress towards health and strength. She soon came to realise that she was dearly loved, and before long the subconscious memories of 'the home' disappeared.

When she was old enough to understand, her parents told her that they had adopted her, explaining sensitively that they had chosen her especially from all the other children because she was the only one who smiled! Mary loved the feeling of being especially chosen, and grew up to feel happy and secure in her loving home. It was some years before she became aware that being adopted might have a negative aspect to it.

At last Little Mary had a family. She had no brothers and sisters, but she had grandmothers and grandfathers - one of whom shared the same birthday with her on April 3rd - and she had uncles, aunts and cousins. There were also many friends who were customers of her father's greengrocery business in a busy part of Herne Bay in Kent, and on Sundays there would be the children at the Sunday School at Sunnyhill Road Evangelical Church of which Mary's father was the Superintendent.

She loved the Sunday School and the wonderful Bible stories her teacher Miss Minnis told her class week by week. One day Miss Minnis told them that the little chorus they had learned could be repeated as a prayer:

'Into my heart, into my heart,
Come into my heart, Lord Jesus.
Come in today, come in to stay,
Come into my heart, Lord Jesus.'

Mary decided that she would like to do that very much, and told her mother and father when she got home from Sunday School. They were very pleased indeed, and encouraged her childlike faith in their Heavenly Father.

Some things were difficult to understand, however. For instance, how could a two-year-old - even a very bright two year old - grasp what happens to grandmother when she goes to Heaven? Grandmother seemed such a large lady. Only when Mary grew old enough to learn some history at school did she realise that her plump grandmother, in her black, long dresses, reminded her exactly of Queen Victoria.

To the two-year-old Mary, grandmother simply seemed very imposing. That she had gone to Heaven was never in doubt of course, but after the old lady's funeral, Mary was puzzled. 'How can the angels manage to carry grand-mother up to Heaven? She must be very heavy!' she asked innocently. The explanation proved hard to understand, but her simple faith was unshakeable, and it steadily strengthened as she grew up.

Her introduction to day school began ominously. Her parents had no doubts that she would learn easily and grow up to be a credit to them, but they were unprepared for another setback in little Mary's development. Her early time of deprivation had left her constitution still rather weak when she was admitted to school, and it could only be expected that she should pick up any childhood illnesses which might be circulating. But to catch measles, chicken pox and whooping cough all at the same time, and almost immediately on entering school, took them entirely by surprise!

When after six weeks in bed she recovered enough to be able to begin school once more, Mary fretted because all the other children had already started to learn to read and write, and she would have to catch them up. By this time they had reached 'E for Egg', and she couldn't tell how many letters she must have missed.

She worked very hard, and discovered that learning to spell and write the words proved no problem, it was having to *draw* them which taxed all her abilities and left her wondering if she would ever be able to learn to read!

Then it seemed to Mary that just as she had caught up with the other children, everything changed again. It was exciting at first.

It all began on her uncle's birthday, September 3rd, 1939. Her aunt and uncle, and cousin Margaret, had all come to visit at her home, when suddenly a raucous whine which rose and fell in the most alarming manner, ripped into their lively celebration. Then, to her astonishment, everyone squashed together under the table! She soon discovered that the air-raid siren heralded the start of nearly six years of war and disruption which would change her family's life substantially for ever.

The dismal depression which hung over the usually light-hearted Herne Bay as the pier was dismantled was bad enough, but with the mining of the beach, the days of walking happily along the promenade and looking at the waves gently tumbling over the shingle ended menacingly.

A move to London curtailed her carefree childhood even more. An uncle who was beyond the call up age worked out his war years with the Woolwich Borough Council, and as help continued to be requested, Mary's father decided to join him. Plumstead then became home for eighteen months until the bombing increased, when it was decided that the female members of their families should be voluntarily evacuated. So for the next two years Mary heard the sound of the sea once more in Lancashire, near Lytham St. Annes.

Pleasant though Lytham St. Annes seemed to be, the two fathers who were still working in Woolwich were sadly missed by their distant families. The girls' mothers found separation very hard to bear, and the news from their menfolk heart-rending. Having heard that her husband had been bombed out of his accommodation three times, Mrs Bogg could bear it no longer, and resolved to return to London to share the discomfort with him. Their return meant they would have to begin all over again to collect a home together, since the bombings had robbed them of everything they owned.

At school in Plumstead, Mary discovered that this time she soared ahead of the other children. Her school days in Lancashire had been largely undisturbed, but in London it was a different story. Lessons were frequently punctuated by air-raid warnings, and the damp, uncomfortable shelters became tedious accommodation during the days, and offered uneasy protection for the nights.

After the air raids, spaces would appear from time to time at desks where children used to sit, but those remaining were carefully shielded from the horrors of the war and mercifully did not think to ask what had happened or where friends had gone.

An inclination that something very bad was happening came sometimes at nights for Mary when her father, a driver for the Fire-Watch with the Woolwich Borough Council, would awake with nightmares.

He would never talk about his experiences, but when she grew up, Mary could imagine what he must have gone through as an ambulance driver who had to dig people out of bombed houses. The bad dreams continued for the rest of his life.

The long, dreary days at last drew to a close, however, and Mary's family set about rebuilding their shattered lives. With VE day approaching, they optimistically moved back to Herne Bay, and as Mary took the Scholarship examination and looked forward to going to the Grammar School in Faversham, so her father began all over again to build up his greengrocery business.

The years that followed were good years for Mary. She loved learning and study, and worked at school with a will. Her parents looked on proudly as she passed her examinations with ease, and although her education meant a good deal of struggle to them, they considered the effort well worth while as they watched their beloved daughter achieving all they had hoped.

When Mary finally took the 'Matriculation and School Certificate', they glowed with pride at her seven distinctions and one credit, and the subsequent three Advanced Level successes. She was now set to spend one more year in the sixth form in order to prepare for the place which she had been offered at Oxford University to study French.

But amid the euphoria of success, Mary's parents were forced to admit that no matter how hard they tried, it might well prove impossible for them to finance her way through University.

They had put all their energies into trying to build up the greengrocery business, but it was difficult for anyone to make ends meet after the war, and it had become a drain on Mary's mother's health. So in spite of constant effort, they had to admit defeat - the shop would have to go.

Then came the task of finding alternative work, and for a time Mary's father gratefully accepted a job with a promising Christian Holiday and Conference Centre which had been recently opened in Herne Bay. Unfortunately it did not offer a very realistic wage since most of the staff lived-in and accepted a low wage, with their board making up the rest, and there could be no increase for those who lived out and had families to support.

The Holiday Centre proved interesting to Mary, however, because in the summer extra help was welcomed on a voluntary basis, and she willingly offered her services, along with other local young people, so that they could enjoy the opportunity of listening to the excellent speakers who ministered to the holiday-makers.

One such speaker was the well-known and revered Gladys Aylward whose inspiring story was told in the film *The Inn of the Sixth Happiness,* through which she became famous in her own lifetime.

It was natural, then, that there should be a missionary call to the listening people at Herne Bay Court. They were challenged as to what they were doing for God in their lives, and to find out if he could be calling them to distant places to tell of his love to those who had not yet heard. Mary listened avidly. What a wonderful calling! Could it be that God would send her - perhaps as a teacher - to some distant land? She was filled with enthusiasm at the prospect.

After the talk, someone spoke about the need for evangelism, not only in far-flung places like China, but nearer to home in Europe. They asked anyone who felt that God might be calling them to this kind of work to stand up, and wait afterwards for further information. Mary stood up immediately. Yes, she was sure that God was speaking to her.

The information she was given afterwards did not deter her, but it certainly meant that she would have to delay any call to the mission field for a few years. She was told that the missionary societies would only send *married* couples out on to the European mission field. Travel was too dangerous for a woman alone. She needed the support and care of a husband to help in the work.

Mary understood the advice, and sensibly recognised also that she might be of more use to God's purpose if she went on to university and became a qualified teacher to begin with. So although she did not forget what she had heard, she set it to the back of her mind, and resolved to take her call one step at a time.

But the speakers were not the only attraction at Herne Bay Court. The son of a local minister from the town of Tankerton, five miles along the coast, also took advantage of the fun that the summer employment offered, and before long he and Mary found themselves enjoying a firm friendship.

Although Mary's father enjoyed the work too, it could never be more than a lifeline, and the day came when he was forced to look for better paid employment. A new job beckoned in Tankerton, and the family decided to move there and begin again.

The move also meant that they would attend a new church, and so Mary found herself attending the church of which her young friend's father was the minister.

By the time Mary reached the age of nineteen, her friendship with the minister's son was well established, and the future looked promising.

Then another blow fell. Just as Mary prepared to accept a place at St. Anne's College, Oxford, to study French for four years, her father was made redundant, and their finances dried up. The university education faded into oblivion.

With regret, they all agreed that Mary would need to leave school and work for six months in order to accumulate a little finance, then she could go on to Homerton College in Cambridge for two years, instead of the university's four, to study instead for an Advanced Teaching Certificate.

Her time at college did not disappoint her. She revelled

in the teaching she received, recognising and appreciating the excellence of the instruction. But there was more to college life than study.

In those days Homerton College was not affiliated to the University, but the students were allowed to join in all the extra-curricular activities. The Christian Union and the choir therefore soon dominated her social life, and she fell into a routine of study and recreation which promised to make these college years some of the happiest of her life.

Her friendship with the minister's son was not neglected amid the euphoria of her new life, however. They had been friends for four years by now, and they wrote to each other every day, sharing their new interests and experiences, and their hopes of a future together. Life was necessarily taking each in a different direction - his with two years National Service in the RAF - but Mary had no other thoughts than that one day, when they had both finished their training, their lives would merge again to go on into marriage.

It was, therefore, all the more shattering when she received his letter one morning saying that he felt they should have a trial period of several months in which they would have no contact at all with each other. Mary could hardly believe what she was reading. She was totally unprepared for the suggestion, and was completely shocked.

She wrote one more letter to her lost love. It was never answered, and she then learned that he had moved camp, and since his father had moved to another church in the South West of England, all contact was lost. She never saw him again, but shadowy repercussions permeated her life in an unexpected direction when she returned home and explained the situation to her parents.

'Did you tell him you were adopted?' they asked.

'Yes,' said a mystified Mary.

'Well, that's the problem,' they answered, 'his parents would probably not want an adopted child as their daughter-in-law.'

For the first time in her life, Mary felt that there might be something disadvantageous in being adopted. She reasoned that this might not be the true or only reason for the rejection, but she had to admit that now she came to think about it, adoption was not a subject which was widely discussed. In fact, it seemed to be generally avoided in most conversations.

She had no problems with it from her own point of view, however. Her parents had always treated her as a dearly loved and fully accepted member of the family, and it had never occurred to her to think that there could be a negative side to being adopted. But now, perhaps ....

Friends at college rallied round to ease Mary out of her sorrow, and she threw herself into her studies and social activities.

At one point during this time, a large mission outreach was staged in Cambridge. It had for its focus the fact that when there had been only seventy members of the University Christian Union, seven had volunteered and gone off to answer the missionary call overseas. They were called 'The Cambridge Seven'. Now there were seven hundred students, and the challenge was that perhaps there should be seventy people responding for work on the mission field.

As a result, a volunteer unit was set up of those who would be willing to work towards becoming missionaries, and 'The Cambridge *Seventy*' was born. Mary willingly became involved together with her friend, Grace Isaacs, who was the president of the Christian Union at Homerton, and whose father was the secretary of the Ruanda Mission of Africa. They met to pray about the project, and together asked God to show them definitely one way or the other whether they should be seriously considering becoming missionaries. Their leading would naturally include direction from their everyday reading of the Bible.

'What are you reading at the moment?' asked Grace, one day. 'I am revising the prophet Ezekiel and I'm just about to begin chapter three. Shall we study it together and see what God says to us?'

When they next met together, there could be no doubts about God's answer. The words which stood out were in verse five: *'For you are not sent to a people of unfamiliar speech and of hard language ... whose words you cannot understand ...'*. So although they did not dismiss the idea for ever, they both felt that they should put thoughts of the mission field out of their minds for the time being.

Some of Mary's happiest times were spent with the choir, which often received invitations to sing around the area. Most of the members were choral scholars, and several were ordinands training for the ministry, so most Sundays they would travel to churches within a radius of about fifty miles to take services. They would sing evangelistic anthems and one of the ordinands would preach, then they would usually be invited back to the vicarage for coffee before piling back into the cars for home.

Soon Mary had picked up her life again, and was back enjoying the busy whirl with the other choir members. One of these was undoubtedly happy to know that Mary no longer sustained a serious attachment. They were thrown together more closely because both were soloists for the group. Mary with her fine soprano voice, and Gordon[1] with his rich tenor.

All through the following year Mary and Gordon went out together and it soon became clear that their romance could be heading towards marriage. In those days it was

---

1. not his real name

customary to first ask a girl's father for permission to marry his daughter, and this Gordon dutifully did. Then he formally asked Mary, and they planned to become officially engaged on her twenty-first birthday.

It was, therefore, rather disappointing that Gordon's parents felt it would be better to wait until Gordon had finished his two years at Ridley college before announcing their engagement. However, Mary considered that two more years in their lifetime would be a small price to pay, and accepted the decision stoically.

Since her future seemed to be developing satisfactorily, Mary and her parents decided that she could make an alteration to her course.

She had already majored in Divinity, but it would be advantageous if she could spend a year at a Bible College to achieve graduate status and so be able to teach Divinity up to sixth form standard. Finances were a little more stable now, as Mary's father had work, and she had also been able to have a full grant for her course, so she did not need to help to support the family at the moment. She could therefore take advantage of a place at an Anglican Bible College - a choice which would help her in her future life as the wife of an Anglican minister.

Mary took on a course which was a combination of three fields of study - missionary, Scripture and a special course for clergy wives.

She began enthusiastically, and worked willingly with her future as a teacher and a clergyman's wife in view, and the added possibility that God might, at some point send her - and her husband - out on to the mission field.

Half way through the year, however, Mary was hit by a second bomb-shell. One weekend, Gordon came over to see her, but he was not his usual cheerful self. With rising dread, she listened as he explained as kindly as he could that he felt that they were not right together after all, and that he must call off their marriage. He quickly added that no other person was involved, but he needed more time to think about it.

Once more, Mary was shattered. Not only was her future wrecked again, but now she had an additional spiritual problem. How could she now ever know the Lord's will for her life? Twice she had been convinced of his leading, and twice it had all come to nothing. She had read Psalm 37 many times: *'Commit your way to the Lord, Trust also in Him, and He shall bring it to pass'* it said. She had done this all along the way, and yet it all seemed to go wrong. Where should she go from here?

Her fellow students were lost to provide adequate words of help, and she found herself struggling alone with her broken dreams.

She returned to Psalm 37 and read on: 'Rest *in the Lord, and wait patiently for him ...'*.

4. Unexpected Opportunities

Mary had been warned that two or three years at one's first teaching post should be sufficient, and then one should move on to advance a career. If she had not been advised in this way, she would have remained a lot longer at the Charles Dickens School in Broadstairs.

She began her teaching career in 1956, just after the school opened, and relished the enthusiasm which a new building, new equipment and a new staff engenders. She would have settled down to remain happy there for years if it had not been for that nagging advice. She recognised that there was sense in the suggestion, since those who remained in the same teaching post for years - especially their first years - were bound to become set in the ways of the one school and would find it difficult to change or even get another job should the need arise. So at the end of her second year at the Charles Dickens School, she began to pray that God would show her where she should go next.

There were frequent teaching events and meetings to attend throughout the terms, in which in-service training might be given or interesting new ideas discussed. These were times too, when staffs from different schools enjoyed meeting one another and swopping ideas.

It was through such meetings that Mary got to know the Headmaster and some of the staff from what was at that time The Frank Hooker School, in Canterbury. She also learned that a vacancy existed for a Religious Instruction teacher, and she was encouraged to apply. And there began six of the happiest years of her teaching career.

She found a forward looking school which fulfilled all her expectations of a Secondary Modern for non-selected children. She approved of the discipline which encouraged well-behaved and secure children, and of a caring staff whose main aims were to give their pupils all possible opportunities.

This school banished Mary's thoughts about career moves. It succeeded in meeting her own needs and hopes in that it encouraged her ambitions for her pupils, and she gave no thought to moving on.

She also made many friends amongst the staff, several of whom were Christians. A topic of conversation often centred around the Africa Inland Mission, which was of particular interest to some staff members. Mary enjoyed these chats since she had always been fascinated by Africa and the possibility of perhaps serving the Lord there one day. Eventually her enthusiasm was fired to the point where she actually applied for further details of missionary work with the organisation.

Their encouraging reply gave Mary something else to work for. They said that they would like her to teach for five years first, then they would be able to use her in a teacher training college somewhere in Africa. Mary was happy with this response, and set to working hard and learning all she could in preparation.

She was four years into her five year target for the Africa Inland Mission, when her life took a tragic turn. Mary was enjoying her first holiday in Switzerland with a friend, when news came that her mother had been rushed into hospital with a massive stroke.

On her rapid return, Mary found her mother unconscious with her life hanging in the balance. When consciousness did eventually return, she could not speak or move, and remained for the whole of the following year in hospital. Mary's father was devastated, and before the year was out, he too collapsed and became unable ever to work again.

On her mother's eventual discharge from hospital,

Mary and her father were distressed to discover that she was permanently paralysed down her right side, and remained unable to say much more than 'yes' or 'no' for the next seventeen years.

Now Mary's life changed radically. She had to take on the mantle of breadwinner for the family, with responsibility for all the finances, including outstanding mortgage payments.

The burden of keeping the home and family together meant that Mary could do little more than keep up her teaching post, and care for her parents. All her outside activities were curtailed. She had to give up serving in beach missions for the Children's Special Service Mission (CSSM) and Inter-School Fellowship camps and her pioneering mixed camps; her work running the Young People's Fellowship at her church had to go, and she was obliged to reduce church attendance to only once each Sunday. Her life became a round of work and caring, in spite of the devotion of her father, who did all he could to help.

About five-and-a-half years after she began teaching at The Frank Hooker School, Mary received a letter from an acquaintance whom she had met several times over the years. Her friend was the Head Teacher of a girls' school in Sittingbourne, and she explained that she had a vacancy for a deputy head - but she was particularly anxious to appoint a Christian for the post. She suggested that Mary should apply.

Mary's immediate reaction was to throw the letter into the waste paper bin. In the first place she continued to be very happy in the post she already occupied, and had no ambitions concerning promotion. In the second place, a teaching post in Sittingbourne would mean lengthy travelling each day when her time and social life were at a premium; and in the third place it was a school for girls, and Mary preferred a co-educational school. There seemed no sense in creating more difficulties - even though the extra pay would be useful as she supported her parents through their ill-health. So Mary placed the letter to one side and attempted to forget it.

This did not prove so easily done, however. The letter continued to remain on her mind, especially when she came to her daily prayer time. It dominated her thoughts to the extent that she mentioned it to one or two friends who advised that there could not be any harm in applying for the job. The general opinion was that she would be unlikely to get it anyway - at thirty years old she was much too young for such a post.

When she was called for interview, her colleagues vented their further opinion on the subject. 'Why on earth should you want to bury yourself in such a 'nunnery'?' they asked. 'You have little enough social life as it is. It can't be much advantage to you to go all that way to Sittingbourne.'

'Don't worry,' assured Mary. 'There are four or five others applying for the job who are already on the staff - and I gather I am the youngest applicant - so there is no chance of me getting the job, anyway!'

To Mary's utter amazement she was, indeed, appointed to the post, and since it was such an unlikely happening, she accepted it as God's leading for her life, and settled down to travelling the forty miles each day to and from Westland Girls' School in Sittingbourne.

For two years Mary worked very amicably with her Head Teacher colleague, whose first words to Mary had been: 'Right. Now I'm going to train you to be a Head - you have great potential!'

'But I have no ambition to be a Head Teacher!' exclaimed Mary, reminding her ruefully that she had not even had ambitions to become a Deputy Head. 'I have enough on my plate already with my parents to look after,' she went on, 'and I really enjoy being in the classroom - I have no wish to give it all up for a Head's study.'

But God had other ideas, and Mary found her carefully organised routine disturbed once more.

One morning the Head Teacher took Mary to one side to impart some serious news. There was to be a major shift of policy for the school, resulting in a change from girls' only, to becoming a co-educational establishment. But that was not all. Her Head Teacher colleague had never before worked in a co-ed school and since she felt disinclined to the task, she had decided to move on. She would therefore be looking for another post, and in the meantime, the school Governors had requested that Mary should take over the task of Acting Head until the post could be formally advertised and appointed, when they would be pleased to receive her application.

Once again, Mary considered her situation. She was now thirty-three years old, and it seemed to her that this was another milestone in her life, as it had been for the Lord himself. She felt as though he was leading her gently along as she tentatively went on from one step to the next. It would not be easy for her to take on the Headship - it would be something of a sacrifice in her position - but she recognised that it would prove convenient for the school, and so gave in gracefully.

Surprisingly, she found she enjoyed the job enormously. There were timetables to prepare, parents to meet, and discussions to be held with staff. She kept her hand in by teaching for a quarter of the week, and found her time passing with more fulfilment than she had expected. She gave up fighting the prospect, and was eventually appointed to the permanent post of Head Teacher, and fell to preparing for the forthcoming changes at the school.

As the time approached for the amalgamation of the

two schools, a pattern began to emerge. The Head of the boys' school was about to retire, and his Deputy Head was to take over. Then Mary found she had three vacancies coming up at her school - one for Science, one for Maths and one for History.

After getting together for discussions, the two heads and deputies decided that with the amalgamation looming, it would be an advantage for Mary to appoint men to the posts if possible.

So three bachelors came to be appointed to Westlands Girls' School. They were all in their mid-thirties, but the man appointed for Science had been a mature student who was now applying for his first teaching post. He was just one year older than Mary herself.

****

Michael had not been long at Westlands Girl's School before he began to find himself at the centre of what amounted to a conspiracy. At first he did not notice the innuendos and hints which came his way.

'Miss Bogg is a very fine woman, don't you think?' he was asked by a female colleague.

Then another would say, 'What a pity she isn't married - it seems a shame doesn't it?' Michael had not noticed, apart from the fact that he had to agree that she was indeed a fine woman, and that he respected her professionalism.

As the hints began to take effect, he became irritable. He had absolutely no intention of pinning himself down with a wife, and that's all there was to it. They could hint all they liked, but he had dedicated his life to the Lord, and that could not include the inconvenience of having to consider a wife and her needs. One should serve God completely and not be hampered by another's interests. Marriage would not be for him - he needed to be free for the Lord's work.

The hints did not abate, however, and a colleague tried a frontal attack. 'You really ought to take Miss Bogg out, you know,' she insisted, 'she is a very nice person.'

Michael's temper snapped. 'Don't you realise that when you tell me like that it makes it all the more impossible?' he steamed. 'It's time you understood that I am the kind of person who won't do what people tell me I ought to do!'

But he was sensitive enough to pray about the subject. Some time before he had asked the Lord to send him a girlfriend, and God had answered the prayer, so he knew that God could direct in this way.

The trouble was that when you asked God for things, he was likely to respond positively, and that could mean that you got what *you* wanted, and not what God wanted. Sometimes God taught lessons in this way - he would give you what you asked for, but it might mean that you would miss the best he had for you instead. One had to learn to pray for God's will and not one's own.

So as the subject of himself and Mary Bogg kept rearing its head, he would certainly pray about it, but he had no intention of stepping foolishly into something without God's full approval first - no matter what the rest of the staff might think.

He did not ask Miss Bogg out, but it was strange how they seemed obliged to meet. The forthcoming amalgamation with the boys' school meant that there were all sorts of details to be worked out, and so little time in school hours to do it.

'Look, I can't talk now,' one would say to the other, 'I've got to be in Canterbury directly after school. Why don't we meet there for a few minutes and discuss it then?'

Or perhaps something would come up which had to be sorted out immediately, and they would have to meet somewhere before the next morning. All the meetings they had at first were purely concerning professional matters, but they did seem to be happening fairly frequently. Michael liked the way she worked. She was efficient and had a sincere desire to do things well. He could appreciate that at least.

He could not avoid the times when they worked at out-of-school activities, either. Their mutual commitment to God led them frequently into sharing the gospel with others - often in the evenings with the young people whom they taught daily on a more formal basis. In spite of his protestations about avoiding a close relationship, Michael found his friendship with Mary becoming deeper.

For Mary's part, she found herself looking forward to her times with Michael, but she too was reticent about becoming emotionally involved. She did not want a third repeat of those two previous occasions which had promised so much, and yet ended in tears.

She was, however, pleased to receive an invitation from Michael to come to an after church fellowship at his flat. There was to be a missionary speaker at his church that day, and a get-together was planned after the service.

Mary agreed to come, and arranged to be at his flat as soon after the start of the eight o'clock meeting as her journey from Tankerton would allow.

Michael was very impressed with the missionary speaker. He listened intently, oblivious, like everyone else at the service, to the fact that the usual finishing time for the service had long gone.

Mary left her own church service in Tankerton, and made her way to Sittingbourne. She arrived there at about 8.15 pm to find the house in darkness. She knocked at the door, but was met with silence. Puzzled, she knocked again, but there was still no reply. What could have happened?

She began to feel embarrassed. Here she was, the Head

Teacher of the local school, knocking on the door of the home of one of her male staff members on a Sunday night. She looked around her anxiously. What would the girls or their parents think if they saw her?

Suddenly, and entirely unbidden, words came clearly into her mind. '*Now is a crossroads of decision. This man is my servant. I will always be first in his life. Any relationship with him will not be a cosy, comfortable, mutual self-indulgence, but a life of sacrifice and service. Choose now to stay or to walk away.*' In wonder, Mary stayed, and fifteen minutes later Michael arrived with the group from church. She was never to forget those silent words, however, and they were to return to her mind often in the difficult times which lay ahead.

The forthcoming speaker at the Assemblies of God in Sittingbourne sounded interesting. He was a Jordanian from Bethlehem called Bajet Bartarseh, and had become a Christian through Roy and Dora Whitman who were missionaries in Jordan, sent out by Mary's home church in Tankerton.

Michael was very enthusiastic when he heard him speak. Here was a man who preached a living Christ and not just religious platitudes. He longed to meet him personally, and was sure that Mary would be interested too. As soon as possible he arranged an evening get-together, and they all three met for a cup of tea at Michael's flat.

The evening proved so successful that Mary invited their visitor to her school to talk to the girls. It was suggested that he should take a lesson and talk about how people lived in Bethlehem, then at break time he could preach the gospel for any girls who wished to hear.

The girls were fascinated, and during the ten minute break, seven girls committed their lives to Christ. The interest was so great that Mary gave them a further invitation to meet Bajet Bartarseh that evening in Sitting-bourne. With written permission from the girls' parents, the meeting went ahead with thirty-five girls attending, and after an uplifting time of challenge, praise and worship, twenty of them had become Christians.

What rejoicing there was that these young people had been won for God! But when the euphoria abated, the practicalities of getting all the girls home had to be faced, in addition to returning Bajet to his lodgings.

It was by now getting quite late, and Mary at least, had a considerable distance to travel. It was decided, therefore, that Michael would make sure all the girls got home safely, and that Mary would take Bajet on her way back to her home in Tankerton, near Whitstable.

Mary noted anxiously that the weather was deteriorating into a foggy mist which threatened to make driving difficult. This would mean that she would not only have to travel alone across country as she made her way home, but the weather looked bad into the bargain. Bajet noticed her nervousness, and before she set off again after leaving him at his lodgings, he told her that he had received a word of prophecy from the Lord. His first words had nothing to do with her anxiety.

'The Lord says that he has work for you to do in a Moslem land,' said Bajet. 'But you will not go there alone. Michael will be with you - as your husband.'

Mary was amazed, but Bajet had not quite finished.

'The immediate proof of this word from the Lord is that you will drive back home in record time, without any difficulty whatsoever.'

When Mary arrived home easily under very difficult conditions - exactly as prophesied, she considered what she had been told. Could it really be true? She determined to keep her council until God revealed more.

The school Christian Union grew very large, and

Michael rejoiced. God was working and he felt strongly that there was joy in heaven over each repenting sinner. As he drove to school he would praise the Lord all the way, sometimes in tongues - until by the time he got there, he was in high spirits. It was a good time, even though some of his colleagues could not accept his overt enthusiasm. Michael considered their attitudes mundane and predictable, and received criticism for his radical 'What are you going to do today, Lord?' kind of outlook.

He did not tell them, therefore, about his experiences with his diary.

He had become aware that every so often he felt compelled to mark a particular day in his diary to be kept free for something the Lord had for him to do. His diary did tend to be chock full, so it seemed that God was making sure that he found the time to fit in specific events. Gladly Michael would mark the day, and then wait to see what happened. There was always something interesting.

It all came to mind again when September 1st 1969 seemed to be impressed upon him. He thought and prayed for a moment to make sure, and then as the feeling increased, he marked the day clearly in his diary. He spotted it easily. The first to the sixth of September were the only days he had free that summer! Michael had already committed himself to helping with no less than three Christian summer camps and a Science course, and the last few days of the long holiday were all that remained free. No wonder God had warned him in advance! It was unlikely that those days would remain free much longer! He mused about what might happen on the first of September. It could even be the day he went to Heaven, he thought joyfully. He would be ready for that too!

Before the amalgamation of the boys' and girls' schools, Michael found himself with an assistant whose parents were missionaries in Pakistan. His colleague was a lapsed

Christian, but his background proved interesting to Michael and they talked often.

Strangely, another link with Pakistan came to light when they discovered that a large intake of girls at the school came from the Milton area of Sittingbourne where there was a Pakistani vicar who had been married to a Hindu woman. Tragically she had been killed in the horrific Quetta earthquake a few years previously, and this had been the turning point of his own conversion. He was now married to an Indian Christian woman.

Michael and Mary eventually became acquainted with the couple, and spent some happy occasions sharing tea with them, and learning about Quetta, near the Iranian border in South West Pakistan. It all seemed somehow significant to Michael, and he began to experience a strange unsettling feeling.

5. Radical Changes

It had been a wonderful Whitsun weekend. Michael had frequently attended some meetings that were being held in South Chard, Somerset, and he had looked forward to this next visit. The Christians there had a new way of treating problems of life - they would simply pray earnestly about them and watch God repairing and renewing lives. It was a whole new dimension to their Christian faith and practice. It had been an inspiring time. Michael left enthused and rejoicing for his next appointment in Cleveden, Bristol where, in August, he was to be the best man at his friend's wedding. He made his way there now to help with the preparations.

Back at her home in Tankerton, Mary was praying. She felt a compulsion to pray earnestly for those things which were on her mind. Firstly, she craved a new and deeper infilling of the Holy Spirit. She was now convinced that she could experience more, and she prayed that God would lead her to a greater fulfilment with Him.

Secondly, she felt sure that when Michael returned from his weekend away, he would know with certainty whether they were to become definitely attached or whether they were to part. In her own heart, she now knew she loved him, but although it would be painful to part, she recoiled from a third broken engagement, and entreated the Lord to make everything clear before that stage was reached. So she told the Lord that she was willing for Him to make the decision through Michael, and she was sure that Michael would know by the end of the weekend.

It was a good journey to Cleveden. As he travelled, singing and praising God all the way, Michael thought back over the last few years.

His friend, Richard, had been the young man whom he had met on his first night at college and who had been doubtful about God. He had come running across the campus in the middle of that night to tell Michael that he had seen Jesus in his room. That experience had changed Richard's life, and he and Michael had remained friends ever since.

It had been arranged that he would stay with his friend in a room at the top of a house next door to where the bride and her family lived, their flats being situated above the premises of a bank. The two men had a good evening reminiscing about the old days, and it was inevitable that his friend should remark: 'Well, Mike, I never thought I would be getting married, but here I am ...'.

It was indeed strange how life worked out, thought Michael, and he went to sleep that night musing over the turn things had taken. Fancy his confirmed bachelor friend taking this step at last! Michael had never expected it - his friend had declared that he would never marry.

'Still,' he thought, 'that's up to him. It must be the Lord's will. There's no point in criticising a brother in the Lord for his change of heart - but there is no way that I will be changing my resolves in that direction.'

Michael turned over and prided himself on his strength of mind. He thought things out, and stuck to them. There would be no turning back where he was concerned.

It was the middle of the night when Michael awoke. He looked at the clock and wondered what had woken him. Instantly, a thought came to his mind. He knew without any doubts at all that he was in love with Mary Bogg. But as he pondered over the unbidden revelation, he knew more. He was absolutely convinced that it was God's will that he should marry her.

Without any hesitation, he woke up Richard and bombarded him with the news. 'Richard,' he exclaimed,

'I believe the Lord wants me to get married.'

'Nonsense,' retorted his friend, 'it's just in your mind because of our wedding. Go to sleep.'

'No,' insisted Michael. 'I realise that's possible, but it really isn't that. This is real. I'm certain I must ask her at least. She could refuse me, and she probably will, but I'm certain I have to ask. I need to ask her *now*.'

'But it's three o'clock in the morning!' exclaimed the incredulous Richard.

'I know,' said Michael, 'but there's an urgency about this. I really must ask her right now.'

'You're ridiculous!' retorted Richard, and they continued to argue the point for the next hour. By that time, Richard was weakening. 'Look,' he attempted. 'You can't ring her now anyway - you'd disturb all the family.'

But Michael's mind was made up. He was convinced that God was speaking to him, and his determination was in full force.

'Well,' gave in Richard, 'I'll tell you what we could do. I know where they keep the key to the bank vaults in the basement. We can turn off the alarm, and use the telephone there. You won't disturb the family that way.'

So in pitch darkness the two fumbled their way down through the house to the vaults. After shooing Richard outside to wait for him, Michael dialled Mary's number. By this time it was about half-past-four in the morning, but she picked up the phone immediately.

Mary had been praying all night. With a lurch of her heart she snatched up the receiver.

'Hello,' she said, as she picked up the phone.

'Mary - it's me,' said the excited Michael, and then without more ado, he added, 'I believe the Lord wants me to marry you, how do you feel about that?'

'It's - it's wonderful!' said Mary.

'Well, I know I must ask you properly,' Michael

continued, hardly able to contain his excitement, 'but I want you to think and pray about it until I return.'

'Yes, I will,' said the bemused Mary, 'Yes! It would be wonderful!'

With that, Michael replaced the receiver and yelled out to his friend, 'Richard! She said 'yes'!'

The two men embraced each other and returned to their beds in a haze of euphoria. Later he rang Mary again, with a little more restraint this time, and impressed upon her that he had meant what he said.

They arranged to speak to each of their parents in the formal manner, so that appropriate agreement could be given, and later, when the formalities were over, Michael romantically asked for Mary's hand in marriage on the lawn of his parent's home.

Mary's parents were overjoyed for her, although it meant that new arrangements had to be made for their support and for the care of Mary's mother, but they had no intentions of standing in the way of her new life, and gave their blessing readily.

And so, on September 1st, 1969, just three months after his proposal and on the only day remaining free in Michael's diary, they were married.

The staff at school had known it all along. Most felt it had only been a matter of time, and although they were pleased for the two of them, they were not surprised.

But there was one outstanding problem to overcome. In those days, a Head Teacher was not normally expected to marry a member of her staff and remain as the Head Teacher, and with the schools amalgamating, Mary had been offered the Headship of the joint schools.

After some careful consideration, therefore, Mary decided to refuse the new Headship. It would not have been fair to accept the job under the circumstances, especially with the double possibility that being in their thirties, they would not want to wait long before starting a family, and there was also the other part of the prophecy of Bajet Bartarseh to consider ....

So it was that Mary became Deputy Head of the new school, and Michael the Head of Biology, and they began their life together rejoicing in the Lord, and living in their own flat in Sittingbourne.

****

It was to be only six months after their marriage, that Mary gave up her teaching post to prepare for the birth of their daughter, Ruth. They were rather surprised that she should arrive just nine months after they were married, but they were none-the-less overjoyed with the new arrival. Her delicate wisps of ginger hair promised to mirror her father's looks, and by the determined way she made her presence known, she was likely to mirror his character too!

During most of his school holidays, Michael had become involved with teams of helpers, leading outward-bound activities in Christian camps all over the country as a mountaineering or walking officer.

After their marriage Mary began to accompany him on these trips, and now little Ruth came along too, together with all the equipment necessary for a young baby, living in a tent for the duration of the sessions of several weeks - winter or summer. But before the actual start of any camp holiday, Michael would need to reconnoitre the area in preparation, so would spend a week or so at the site.

It was in the February of 1971, just before one of these pre-camp visits, when Ruth was just ten months old, that Mary discovered she was expecting their second baby.

Their stay in Wales would be over Easter in March, and they set off happily. The journey to the campsite was not uneventful, however. On the way they had stopped at some road works, but the driver of the car behind had presumably lost concentration for a moment and he ran into the back of them. They were a little shaken, but there did not seem to be too much damage - simply a broken rear light. They resumed the journey, but before long Mary began to feel backache.

It was cold and wet. Mary remained in the tent with Ruth as Michael went off to prepare his mountain routes for the boys, but she was rather anxious. The backache had not abated, but instead seemed to be getting worse. A day or so later - the evening before Easter Sunday - it was clear that Mary was miscarrying. Michael rushed to telephone for the doctor, but for some reason the doctor was reluctant to come out. He suggested that the trouble was probably not anything so dramatic as a miscarriage, and that she should take some pain killers until things settled down.

Since they were miles from the nearest hospital, there did not seem much more that Michael could do except wait and see what happened. At four o'clock on Easter Sunday morning, Mary lay in great pain in her sleeping bag, knowing that she was losing her baby. As she lay there thoughts of the resurrection of Jesus came into her mind. She seemed to see the Lord in the Garden of Gethsemane and she heard him call her name.

'*Mary,*' said the gentle voice - just as he had called that other Mary so long ago. '*Mary,*' he continued, '*I know what is happening, it is all in my hands.*'

Then into Mary's mind came the story of the death of King David's son. He grieved for the child, but eventually accepted that God had taken him. '*I shall go to him, he shall not return to me*', he admitted (2 Samuel 12: 23). In some inexplicable way Mary found comfort in these words, and rested in the fact that God had confirmed His control over the situation.

By the dawn, it was over. Michael drove Mary in to the town to see the doctor, and he agreed that it had been a miscarriage and that the baby would have been a boy. But he found Mary in surprisingly good spirits.

'It's all right,' she told him, 'the Lord has chosen to take this baby, but one day I will see him in Heaven.'

The doctor had not come across this kind of attitude, and he could not understand it. Mary had undergone a severe trauma, yet her strong faith supported her at this difficult time. Instead of admitting her to the nearest hospital, however, the doctor suggested that since they were leaving for home the next day, Mary should go to her own local hospital. So with very little medical care, they set off for the long journey home.

She was to suffer some time later with a degree of depression, but on those days the assurance given to her by God on that fateful night returned to her, and helped to relieve the worst of the symptoms. She would never forget hearing the voice of Jesus calling her own name, and she knew that one day she would be calling the name of their little boy, and that no sadness would then cloud the moment.

6. Prepared to go Anywhere

As Michael gave himself completely to the leading of the Holy Spirit, he never ceased to be amazed at how willingly and surprisingly the Lord would lead. Once again he felt drawn to note a particular day in his diary, and, as before, the first week in September sprang to his attention. The third was the day, but this time the year was 1971 and he had no idea what could be happening on that day.

In the November of 1970 he had occasion to go to a meeting at the Leprosy Mission in London, and on the way there, he found a strange 'word' buzzing around in his mind. It sounded like '*peshoweranswot*'. He mulled it over as he drove, and curled it round his tongue several times, but could make nothing of it. All he knew was that not much came into his mind which was completely meaningless, and he prayerfully committed the sounds to the Lord. When he returned home, he told Mary all about it, and also the growing conviction that the sound had something to do with September 3rd.

As the days passed, another conviction began to impress itself into Michael's mind. He began to believe that God intended Mary and himself to undergo some kind of journey. He wondered if it was simply the interest generated by the visit of Bajet Bartarseh, or the input concerning the Pakistani vicar in nearby Milton, but whatever it was, Michael had the feeling that God was leading him into something more and he should be ready for it.

Some time later, a young friend whom they met at the Chard fellowship came to stay with them for a day or two. They enjoyed her company, and she appreciated Mary and Michael's radical Christian living. One evening as she helped by ironing a few of little Ruth's clothes, a discussion went on about being always ready to do anything or go anywhere for God. When the conversation reached a lull, Mary and Michael went out to the kitchen to wash up.

'Look here,' said Michael as he wielded the tea towel. 'It's no good telling God that you're prepared to go anywhere for him if you are not actually *ready* to go. We need passports in case God says "go tomorrow".'

Mary agreed, although she mused that a journey with a young baby would need considerable organisation - wherever it should lead them. They returned to the sitting room, but their friend had something to say.

'I've been thinking and praying while I've been doing the ironing,' she began. 'I haven't got a lot of money, but I believe the Lord is telling me to give you forty pounds.' Mary and Michael did not know what to say. Forty pounds was a considerable sum - perhaps a month's average wage. The young woman went on.

'That's not all. He also told me that it is for your journey.' She looked at them with a puzzled frown. 'Are you going on a journey somewhere?'

Mary grinned. 'We're about to, I think,' she said, 'but we have no idea where!'

It was not until some time later that they discovered their young friend to be the daughter of missionaries in Pakistan - but by that time they had ceased to be surprised by that kind of coincidence!

The time had definitely come to make a conscious effort to discover what God had in store for them. They thought carefully about all the fragments of information and the experiences they had had so far. Somehow there was a pattern which would soon come to light. Gradually they began to feel that the strange word *peshoweranswot* might hold the key to the puzzle.

Michael decided to ring the Worldwide Evangelisation Crusade headquarters and see if they could throw any light on the problem. 'Tell me,' he inquired, 'does the word *peshoweranswot* mean anything to you?'

'Yes,' came back the immediate response. Peshawar is the capital of the North West Frontier of Pakistan, and Swat is a state there.'

In surprise, Michael realised that the sound had been not one word, but two. Now he understood. Suddenly he remembered the map God had shown him in a vision one night when he was in college. That was the area of the map! He had not visualised the strange spellings with the sound he had heard, but now it all came back.

Then another memory came to mind. Several months before when they had been visiting Mary's parents, her father had asked Michael to reach for a book high on a bookshelf for him. As he took the book down, a wad of booklets and papers fell out from behind it.

'What's all this?' asked Michael.

'Those are my prayer notes,' replied Mary's father. 'They are information and prayer requests for the North West Frontier of Pakistan. I have been receiving them and praying for the area for nineteen years.'

Mary and Michael looked at each other in surprise. Mary had no idea her father was praying for Pakistan - especially for nineteen years! And yet here it was again - Pakistan. Mentions of it seemed to be cropping up everywhere.

But not only that. Mary remembered that wherever they went, sermons or talks were often about Abraham and Sarah: Abraham, who just went off - he knew not where - at the Lord's command, and Sarah who was willing to go too, in submission and obedience. It seemed as though the Lord was saying, 'You've always known about them - now *you* do it!'

As the conviction grew that God intended them to go to Pakistan, Michael began to think of doing something positive. Wherever they went, they would need an income of some kind, and they both decided that if God was calling them to become missionaries, then to begin with they would not apply for support from any missionary society. They felt that any initial journey should be an exploratory one, to test whether it was a genuine call from God or not. They would therefore go as 'tentmakers' - they would support themselves as Paul the tentmaker did on his missionary journeys - only in their case, the 'trade' would be teaching.

In his discussions with the various folk who had been connected with Pakistan, Michael had learned that English teachers were sometimes needed in Commonwealth countries, and Pakistan was one of these. He decided, therefore, to write to the British Council and ask if there were any vacancies in the near future.

Unfortunately, by the time Michael's letter reached its destination, a war had begun to brew up between India and Pakistan, causing some ill-feeling between the two countries over Britain's alleged favouring of India, and Michael received a negative reply to his application. Nothing daunted, however, he continued to feel that God was leading him in this direction, and that He would open up something else in due time.

Several busy months went by and Mary and Michael had an increasing urgency regarding their possible journey. Michael began to plan a route. He pored over maps and worked out distances, and made notes about things they would need. It would be a huge undertaking. There would be hostile territory to cross and difficult terrain to cover, and as Ruth was just over a year old, he could not imagine the equipment that would be needed for her and where they would put it.

Then Mary's parents had to be considered. They both prayed about this problem in particular with much heart-searching, wondering if Mary's father would be able to manage to look after his ailing wife. He seemed to be coping fairly well, but would need additional support.

They believed that they should commit them to the care of the Lord, in the hope that members of the church would help sometimes, but they also agreed that they would immediately return home if they should be needed at any time.

Then they mentioned the direction in which they believed God was taking them to the four church fellowships with whom they were involved: Mary's home church in Tankerton, the Hempstead Fellowship, and two Brethren Assemblies where Michael had received his fundamental Christian teaching. There was some hesitation that they should be taking on such a project, firstly, with a young baby, and secondly, with no guaranteed financial backing. But they did give a positive, if hesitant, response, praising God for the willingness of Mary and Michael to serve, and praying for the success of the venture.

It was now time to prepare in earnest, and to try to accumulate a little money. One sum came from a friend to whom Michael sold some tyres from his old van, and with the money he bought a tent which he found going cheaply in a sale. Soon they had £100, plus their car, and began to think they had enough to get started. They knew it would probably not be enough for an extended journey, but they reckoned God would provide whatever they needed, when it was needed.

Mary collected together the equipment she would need for Ruth. Nappies were a problem. The journey alone could be a month long, and there would be no washing machine, nor even a handy launderette for most of the time. So a bucket and soap was included, although Ruth was now almost potty trained, and Mary hoped she wouldn't have to wash nappies too often. The minimum of necessary equipment was carefully packed. Just three plates, cups, knives, forks, spoons, and one small washing up bowl; a few pots and pans to prepare food, together with a small oil stove to cook on.

They could not afford to stay in hotels, so they would have to take sleeping bags of course, and Mary made one for Ruth out of an adult sleeping bag doubled over, sewing reins into the inside so that the toddling baby could not crawl away in the night.

Michael collected together the boxes of Christian literature and tracts which he had acquired from the Scripture Gift Mission and the Pocket Testament League, and stacked them in the car. Some of the literature was to be delivered to addresses in Yugoslavia and Bulgaria where Christian literature was banned. The tracts were for handing out to interested persons along the way.

Michael was perfectly aware of the penalties of being found carrying Christian literature into communist countries, but he was firmly convinced that God had told him to take it all, so he packed it confidently. He also stuck a text on the front and back windows of the car. 'How else will people know we are Christians?' he said candidly. All was packed systematically and neatly into the car boot and a small trailer which, in spite of the economy of possessions, were bursting at the seams by the time everything had been made ready.

They had to admit, however, that when one looked at the sagging Saab with its bulging little trailer, and then at the amount of essential equipment which they were obliged to leave behind, then the whole project did seem a trifle 'eccentric' - if not actually mad, as some less diplomatic folk had commented. But no matter what anyone said, the Holy Spirit had made it plain to them that they must go, and go they must.

After all, they thought, as they checked their equipment lists for the final time, Abraham and Sarah probably felt the same way when they were told to '*get out of your country, from your kindred and from your father's house, to a land that I will show you ...*' (Genesis 12:1*).

It had seemed crazy to other people then, too, but Abraham and Sarah knew, as Michael and Mary knew now, that if God tells someone to do something, and they do it, then he will honour their obedience - even if they make mistakes in the implementation of the order.

'God doesn't require people to be perfect,' reminded Michael as they settled their last minute nerves, 'but He does require them to live by faith.'

'It doesn't matter if you make mistakes,' he continued firmly, 'but some people are so afraid of making mistakes that they never do anything at all!'

They turned and went back into the house. This would be their last night in the comfort of their own beds. From tomorrow, nothing was certain. They knew the route they intended to take, but that was all. The rest was up to God.

'We'll adopt one rule as we travel,' said Michael. 'We will do all our driving from Monday to Friday. On Saturdays we will stop to do the necessary chores - like washing the clothes, shopping, or tidying up - that sort of thing, and Sundays we will keep as a holy day as usual. We will try to find a place of worship, but if that is not possible, we will spend time with God together. In that way we will honour God in our travelling and be rested in body and soul.'

'Right,' agreed Mary. 'An excellent plan.'

And so it came about that on the warm evening of September 3rd, 1971, Mary, Michael and their little daughter set off on a journey which would traverse nine countries over a period of twenty-five days.

The RAC had already informed Michael that there were no ferry sailings available for that day. He should have booked a long time before. But it made no difference

- Michael was convinced that September 3rd was the day to begin, and off they went.

It was nearly midnight when they reached the ferry terminal, and Michael simply drove straight on board. They parked the car and the trailer, and an official directed them to where they should go.

'What about the ticket?' asked Michael.

The man looked puzzled. 'I don't take your ticket,' he frowned. 'Someone should have already taken it.'

'I haven't got one,' went on Michael blithely, 'they told us there weren't any available.'

The man's eyebrows raised. 'You shouldn't have come on board if you haven't got a ticket,' he countered. 'Still, there is plenty of room, so go and get one now.'

As Mary took Ruth up to the sitting area, Michael went for their ferry ticket which he got easily, and then settled down for the journey, wondering what else God had in store for them.

The next stage of the journey was unclear. They alighted at Ostende, and Michael decided to head for Kraainem where he had a contact - a young man he had met at a camp years before lived there, although they had not seen each other for a long time. He studied the address. It simply said, 'Kraainem, Kraainem, Brussels.'

What kind of an address was that? Now that he came to think about it, it gave no clue as to how one could find the place. There was no house number or road given, and did not seem to make sense.

Michael drove around for a while, searching for he knew not what.

After a few minutes they came to a hillock with some trees ahead of them. They drove towards it, and suddenly Michael called out, 'Look! There's a gate post with "Kraainem" printed on it.'

As Mary strained to look, she saw two palatial gateposts at the beginning of a wide avenue. They drove straight through and on up to a further set of gates, this time in wrought iron, where police stood on guard. The small, packed, white Saab with its loaded trailer passed unchallenged, and Michael drove on until another set of gates opened onto an immaculate lawn the size of a village green, set elegantly with classical statues. Around the lawn were five very similar mansions.

In his inimitable fashion, Michael made for the most imposing front door, and rang the bell. A butler appeared, took Michael's offered card, and invited the little family in.

Then began a luxurious evening in the welcoming, congenial company of a Belgian Cabinet Minister and his wife. Michael's young acquaintance was not at home, but it did not seem to matter. His parents were delighted to meet a friend of their son's, and made Mary, Michael and little Ruth very welcome.

It was insisted that they remain for dinner, which was to be together with about five other ministers of state in the exquisite dining room, and attended by a company of servants. Afterwards the company listened, fascinated, as Michael told them how their trip came about. Eyes were raised in incredulity to hear that such a journey should be undertaken with what they considered to be inadequate equipment and arrangements, and with the encumbrance of a toddling baby! This was British eccentricity at its peak!

At the end of the evening, Michael and Mary were shown to sumptuous bedrooms, where they spent a luxurious night in comfort for the last time in many weeks to come.

The next morning they were waved off with smiles and good wishes, and made their way on the next leg of their journey to Frankfurt. Here they stayed with the Sisters of Mary who were entertaining a group of Christians from the NATO mission in Brussels.

When Michael and Mary mentioned whom they had stayed with in Kraainem, eyes lit up, and the evening's conversation was ensured. God was, indeed, leading them to the right places at the right times.

The journey continued on through Germany and into Austria. Here they stayed with a missionary who was working into Bulgaria, Hungary and Czechoslovakia. Also staying here were Robert and Elizabeth Sherrill the well-known writers, who were working on the autobiography of Nicky Cruz, a young gang leader reached by David Wilkerson through 'Teen Challenge,' and saved by God from his life of crime.

They were worried when they learned that Michael and Mary had packed large quantities of religious tracts into the car for distribution along the way. In their experience it was dangerous to carry overt literature like this - it could lead to all kinds of problems.

'The Lord has told us to take them,' explained Michael simply. 'So who are we to remove them? Besides, if we are stopped, then that's all part of the adventure. The worst that can happen is that we could be killed and if that should happen, we go to be with the Lord anyway.'

Their friends were not so sure. 'It may well be far worse to be in prison in these Eastern countries,' they warned darkly.

'We must go through with the tracts if the Lord has told us to,' insisted the indomitable Michael. He secretly felt a twinge of unease for his wife and daughter, but feared more to disobey his Lord.

As they said goodbye to the friends who had accommodated them, the journey began to lose its 'holiday' feel and become more of an adventure. Austria was the last free European country through which they would pass. From here on things could get difficult.

They kept to their travelling rule of driving for five

days of the week and stopping on Saturdays to deal with the necessary chores, then worshipping on Sundays, but watching out all the time for people with whom they could share the gospel.

And so they approached the border of communist controlled Yugoslavia. Michael was still resolute regarding the tracts they carried, but equally determined not to remove the Bible texts which were emblazoned one on the front and one on the rear window of the car.

They crossed the border without incident, and proceeded to an address where some of their cargo needed to be delivered. This was accomplished easily too, and they moved on into Bulgaria. This time they knew they were being followed. Michael had no trouble spotting the small police buggy with the two dour-faced, plain-clothed security men inside, and they became quite used to the familiar 'tail' wherever they went.

Stopping eventually for a meal in a restaurant, Michael was amused to notice that his followers took the welcome opportunity of a meal, too - at the next table. This was too much for Michael, and he went up to them boldly, greeting them cheerfully as though to old friends.

In some consternation, the two men stammered that they did not speak English. With a grin Michael left them, but he noticed that for two people who could not understand English, they were taking a remarkably close interest in his conversation with Mary throughout the meal!

Having eaten, their next port of call should have been to visit some Pentecostal brothers. However, bearing in mind their persistent 'shadows', they felt that it would be very unwise to put these Christians at risk. They had heard many horror stories of the treatment meted out to 'dissidents', so it was decided, regretfully, to miss out the visit.

By the time they approached the border between Bulgaria and Turkey, Mary was getting anxious. Ruth had been very good, but she had certain needs to be attended to. It was high time she was 'pottied'.

'We must stop,' appealed Mary, 'I can't let her go on any longer.'

So Michael drew up at the first available spot beside the road, and gave Mary a few minutes to see to Ruth in an adjacent cornfield. As he waited, a car drew up behind him. An elderly man got out, came up to their car and pointed to the text on the back window. With a lurch of his stomach, Michael prepared for trouble.

The man approached. He grinned broadly, and in German told Michael that he was a Christian too, and how good it was to see words from the Bible on the car! With great relief, Michael shook his hand, and they wished each other God's blessing. They were glad to leave Bulgaria. It seemed a dead and dreary country, and yet a spark for the Lord still glowed in small corners.

Turkey was a different matter. The atmosphere lifted, and the smiling people appeared to be genuinely happy. They drove on up onto a hillside, where they found a peaceful spot to put up the tent for the night.

They had not been there long before a young man rode up on a horse. He indicated that they must not remain there, but move on.

'We're camping for the night,' Michael told him.

'Dangerous, dangerous,' responded the man, and then he went off, returning a few minutes later with reinforcements consisting of two more men on horseback.

'Dangerous people here,' they said, unable to understand why Michael was not rapidly packing up his belongings and moving his family on. They eventually gave up the task, and Mary and Michael remained. The next morning, the first man was there again as soon as it was light, and allowed a smiling Michael to take his name and address.

It appeared that the young man was the son of a local chieftain, and that he operated as a kind of brigand. Michael was of the opinion that the only danger in the area consisted of the young man and his fellow brigands!

Some considerable time later, he would be surprised to receive copies of the Gospels from the determined camper!

The long drive across Turkey to the border of Iran left the family tired, scruffy and dusty - and a little unnerved.

Having looked for some time for a safe place to camp, they eventually set up the tent in a field. It was clear that there were jackals in the vicinity - their calls could be heard across the darkening night, and they posed a threat for the unwary, but a greater danger might arise from some men hovering around who might well be brigands.

Michael set the tent in the centre of the field to avoid the worst of the creepy-crawlies which lurked in the hedges, and settled Ruth down to sleep. They had taught her to sleep in reins, and she did not seem to mind where she was laid - on the floor, with the reins secured to a chair leg, or on a high bed with the reins tucked in.

After an uneventful night, although rather fitful sleep, they set off again and arrived tired and dirty at a border town near Mount Ararat, not far from the Iranian border.

Here, they could find nowhere to set up the tent, so they were obliged to spend the night on benches by the border post. But Michael had standards to keep up, and in the morning he decided that they must find somewhere to have a much needed wash and brush up. They also needed a meal, so they decided to eat in a nearby restaurant, and gratefully took the opportunity of using the facilities to have a wash while they were there.

Then, dressed neatly in his typically English blazer and flannels with a clean white shirt setting off his moderate tie, Michael made his way to the checkpoint with their passports. He cut an imposing figure with his wiry frame and tall build topped by a shock of ginger hair and elegant beard. It was time to assert a little British authority. He presented himself at the checkpoint desk.

'Good morning,' he began clearly and impressively. 'Here is my passport, and I wonder if you would do your very best to see that it's cleared as soon as possible - SIR!'

The man at the desk was taken aback. It was not often one came across a true British eccentric these days in this part of the world. But something seemed to click into place, and he looked more closely.

'Just a moment,' he said, 'Aren't you the scruffy individual I saw in the restaurant on the Turkish side of the border last night?'

'I beg your pardon?' answered Michael, equally taken aback now.

'Yes, I'm sure it was you,' went on the young man more confidently, and then he added, 'but why are you looking so smart now?'

This was easy. Michael drew himself up to his full height, stroked his red beard, set his feet firmly and told the man, 'I've just entered a new country. If someone comes to my house for the first time I expect them to be well dressed. It is simply the way I honour Iran.'

'Thank you sir,' smiled the man, and signed the passport, clearing it immediately. Michael left gratefully, conscious that he had not really worked out this plan of action, but that God seemed to have given him the wisdom to act in the appropriate manner for the moment. But he stored the incident in his mind for future use. It was only good manners to behave politely in new countries and situations.

And so Michael, Mary and baby Ruth crossed the border and launched out into the unknown of the Middle East, their hopes high, their trust in God firm, but their purse becoming dangerously low in funds.

7. Journey to - Nowhere?

The journey across Northern Iran involved using the 'Asian Highway', an ancient route first built by the Romans and used ever since. This busy road to the East was now under reconstruction, which meant that parts of it were non-existent, the surface dropping perhaps two feet where it had been worn away or stripped for resurfacing.

Mary and Michael pressed on through the dusty desert, the temperature unbearably hot in the day time, but surprisingly cold at night, and often the 'road' became indistinct and unrecognisable from the surrounding desert.

Michael drove on as best he could in temperatures upwards of one hundred and twenty degrees Fahrenheit, often through clouds of impenetrable dry dust. In the stifling heat the dirty menace crept in through the windows and under the floor until it gritted their eyes, dusted their hair and filled their noses and mouths. Mary placed a cover over Ruth's carry cot, but she could not protect her from the heat. The little girl became uncomfortable and fractious. Anxiously Michael pushed ahead, hoping to get clear of the pervading dust.

He could pick out no landmarks in the dust 'fog'. There was only the stony, uneven surface of the road leading them on, and Michael kept travelling hopefully straight ahead, praying that he would come across something which would provide orientation. After some time he had to admit that road and surrounding area had merged, and that he had no idea where he was - or even if he was still on the road. He stopped to consider what could be done.

Suddenly he remembered the compass. As a good sailor, Michael had considered a compass to be vital navigational equipment for such a journey and had included it in their meagre supplies. He retrieved it from where it had been carefully packed, and put it to good use. Now they could move on. Dust or no, Michael could easily ascertain their direction, and he drove off more confidently.

The compass led them on steadily eastward, and a tunnel ahead gave a good indication that they were at least still on the road. Confidently Michael drove through it. It emerged at a bridge, and intrepidly, he pressed forward.

Suddenly they were airborne. A split second later, the car smashed onto the road with a bang. They stopped to assess the damage. The road had disappeared at the bridge. This was one of the places where it was undergoing renovation, and the surface had been removed. The car had jumped the space of several metres, falling heavily onto the next available strip of road, causing all three of its occupants to hit their heads on the roof of the car. Ruth's frightened screams brought Mary and Michael rushing to her aid with hearts lurching. Terrified, they saw the blood on her head, and forgetting their own heads which were also bleeding, they anxiously dealt with her wound.

Thankfully they soon saw that the cut was small and that she suffered from fear rather than injury, then Ruth comforted, they dealt with their own cuts.

Michael's next fear was that the car had been damaged beyond repair. The fall had been heavy, and there was no knowing what damage could have been done. He envisaged being stranded in this inhospitable desert with his wife and baby and few supplies. Nervously, he checked the car over as much as he could, but amazingly, could find no obvious damage. Praying continually, he started up the engine again, and moved forward. The car responded as well as ever, and Michael praised God. Settling themselves once more, they pressed onward towards the town of Mashhad near the Afghanistan border.

Just as they thought they were doing well, one of the tyres punctured. But there was no handy garage here to put the tyre to rights while they sat in the shade with a cool drink. Michael was obliged to remove the tyre and mend the puncture himself, struggling alone in the oppressive glare of the sun.

It took some time to lever off the tyre and patch the inner tube. By the time he had finished, he was severely overheated and dehydrated. He drove on, fighting the effects of the heat.

As they neared Mashhad, and the relief of shade and rest beckoned, another tyre punctured. Once more, in the searing heat Michael had to get out, remove the wheel and the tyre, mend the inner tube, replace it all again, and pump up the tyre again. Now he was undoubtedly suffering from heatstoke, and had difficulty in going on.

The remainder of the journey to Mashhad was a nightmare for them both. By the time they reached the town, Michael was incoherent and feverish, but in addition to the heatstroke he had developed painful gastroenteritis.

Somehow they managed to erect the tent on the sparse camp site, but Michael was to get little sleep that night. When daylight eventually crept over the hillside, he lay still for a few moments, thinking over his dreadful night, and then he realised that he felt better. His head did not ache, his temperature had gone down, and although he was still very weak, it was clear that the fever had abated.

During Michael's ensuing weakness, Mary was in some difficulty. Here in these Eastern countries, women were not allowed to go out alone. In fact, even when they did go out, a married woman was required to walk behind her husband, and let him do any necessary talking to strangers - even the shopping.

What was she to do? They needed food, but Michael

was in no fit state to wander around the bazaar, and she could not go alone. She did not wear what was considered to be the right dress, for a start, and stones were thrown at Westerners who behaved 'inappropriately'.

She tended Michael as best she could, but having no medicines or even nourishing food with which to tempt him, she could only make him as comfortable as possible and wait for him to recover.

Sooner or later, however, she would have to go to the bazaar and buy food. Her solution to the problem was to look around the disreputable campsite, select a hippy who did not look as drug-crazed as the rest, and ask him if he would accompany her to the bazaar! The young man agreed, possibly out of sheer surprise, and Mary was able to buy something to eat.

For a while they were obliged to remain where they were so that Michael could regain his strength. However, the 'hippy' campsite was not the most congenial place to recuperate, and Michael had no intention of delaying their important journey longer than absolutely necessary. He therefore willed himself to a degree of recovery.

The next stop would be the Iranian-Afghanistan border, but here Michael was to discover that the determination, resolve and good manners which held him in good stead on the Turkish-Iranian border could not always win over ignorance and inexperience. They drove into the checkpoint along with a Hindu couple in a tiny car. They were all to discover their vulnerability.

The delay was interminable. Papers were checked and rechecked, questions were asked and asked again, and obstacles were erected where there were none to start with. The border guards played a sinister game. Slowly Michael became aware that he was being manipulated. He was questioned about what he was carrying in the car, and what currency he had. Whatever it was, it proved the wrong kind or illegal, so that he had to reveal more of his assets in order to fulfil the conditions and be allowed to pass. They refused travellers cheques, the better to ascertain how much money the traveller carried on him, and at the end of the debacle, a further chunk of their diminishing financial resources had changed hands, and Michael was infinitely more exasperated. On later trips he learned to play the guards at their own game, and reduce the manipulation to a minimum, but on this occasion he was innocent and vulnerable.

Michael and Mary noticed that the Hindu couple were even less able to withstand the onslaught from the guards than they could themselves, and viewed their distress with pity.

When the delay could be extended no longer, however, and Michael and Mary were finally given clearance, they decided that they would have a meal before starting off again. It was a wise decision, because some time later they came across the Hindu couple again. They were desperately hungry, but even worse, a little way down the road they had been forced to abandon their car. It had apparently had paper stuffed into the exhaust and had overheated. Now they feared being robbed.

Michael too, had his fears. They had been an interminable time at the border, and night was now approaching fast, but to make matters worse, a sandstorm had arisen. It was soon a whirling menace, obscuring everything in view and even the road itself.

As they came out of the cafe, they noticed that oil drums had been placed across the road, and a man with a rifle now stood on guard near one of the frequent road toll booths which were set at intervals along the border.

Michael drove the car up to him, and was informed that there was a tax to pay. Getting out of the car, he wondered what his next move should be, but was left in no doubt when the man indicated by gesturing with the rifle, and led him away from the vehicle towards the tollbooth about fifty yards away on the hillside, where other guards waited.

Having drawn him away from the security of his car, and to a point where he could see neither it nor Mary, the guard then demanded an extortionate toll tax which Michael flatly refused to pay. At this the guards sat down and began to argue.

In the meantime, Mary had wound up the windows in order to avoid the stinging clouds of sand, but was by now being accosted by other guards. She saw Michael lured away to the tollbooth and he was soon out of sight and sound. Her fear was heightened by the fact that darkness had fallen by now, and she had no idea what was happening to Michael. Suddenly she felt very vulnerable. Then the soldier on guard duty started rocking the car and trying to get in it.

Mary started to pray, at first in English for the Lord's strength and deliverance, and then as she realised she was the focus of a definite Satanic and murderous intention, she found herself praying in tongues. She committed whatever was about to happen to the Lord, knowing she could not even sound the car horn without being shot.

Suddenly the headlights of a car loomed in the darkness. Even more miraculously Michael was released and he rejoined Mary. A man in a heavily braided uniform got out of the arriving car, and Michael could see that he was a senior officer of the Afghan police.

In beautiful English he asked, 'Are you all right, sir?'

The guards responded in their own language, and Michael noticed that the gun had mysteriously disappeared. The policeman turned to Michael.

'He says you are quite all right and that they are trying to help you,' he translated. 'But are you really all right?'

'No,' retorted Michael, 'they were pointing a gun at

my wife, and extorting money from me.' A few moments later the guards left chastened, and Mary and Michael travelling together with the police car in convoy until they reached safety.

Some time later they came across the Hindus again. They had been robbed of everything.

It was clearly unsafe to camp now, and Mary and Michael, still shaken, spent the night in a cheap, downtown hotel in the town of Herat, but they were to discover that the presence of evil throughout Afghanistan was so great that it was almost tangible. Even in the hotel they came across a lapsed Salvation Army man who was now a drugs trafficker. Hearing their English voices the man had been drawn to them, and seemed pleased to chat. On hearing the story, Mary and Michael pleaded and prayed with the man, but were never to know if he would have a change of heart.

Some time later, Mary found that her treasured wedding Bible was missing. She knew that the last place she had seen it was in the hotel in Herat, and since it would be no use to anyone who could not speak English, they transferred their sadness into prayer, asking that the Lord would use it to help whoever had stolen it.

At Qandahar they fared much better. The hundred pounds with which they started the journey was almost gone and Michael was embarrassed. They needed a place to rest before going on into Pakistan, but they did not have sufficient funds to pay for accommodation. Michael was also suffering a recurrence of the gastroenteritis and did not feel at all well.

However, a word or two of explanation at another downtown hotel brought kindness and help. Here, they found a people who took hospitality to strangers very seriously.

The kindly manager directed them to a place where

they could put up the tent, insisted on giving them food but refused to take any further payment. It was to be the start of a friendship which lasted through the years, to include the time when Michael happened to be in Qandahar on the day the Russians drove in and destroyed the whole area. He was there to share in the devastation and suffering with his friend.

After a restful night sampling Afghan hospitality, the little family prepared for the last stages of their arduous journey. The gastroenteritis continued to recur as they made their way towards the border of Pakistan. At Jalalabad Michael was forced to stop and rest while the infection took its course, and they booked once more into a cheap hotel. Now, as Michael lay on the bed, his body racked with pain and discomfort, he worried.

They had travelled thousands of miles overland at the prompting of nothing more than Michael's inner conviction that God wanted them to work with the Pathan people of Pakistan. But it was not only his own life which had been disrupted, he had dragged his wife along with him - and at a totally inappropriate time when they had the baby to consider as well. He had not considered the dangers sufficiently - they had been almost murdered back at the Afghan border. The truth of how close they had come to death only struck home when they learned that just one week before, two Western missionary ladies were stopped at a nearby spot and they had been found shot dead.

He lay back, weak and depressed. The whole venture had been madness. They had not even had enough money to fund a trip of this kind in the first place - let alone get them home again! Oh, yes, he had uttered brave words about God providing ... but here they were, forty miles from Pakistan, and they had just six rupees left. God had not provided any more cash, and they would need more food yet, apart from the cost of accommodation when -

and if - they reached their destination.

What was he to do? He could not even stand up, let alone provide for his family. The whole enterprise had been a disaster - a figment of his imagination - and it only went to prove that God was not real after all.

His mind churned over their situation. He had been thoroughly wilful in bringing all this on his wife of only a couple of years, and their young baby .... Had he been right in the first place? .... Perhaps he should not have got married .... He was an escapist who could not cope with reality .... Maybe he was trying to escape from something in his past ....They would all perish before ever reaching Pakistan and it would be all his fault.

Mary tried to ease his fears and attend as best she could to his discomfort, but Michael was too weak to rally, and she was forced to wait for the infection to die down. As she waited, she prayed. They were, indeed, at their lowest point, but as she thought back over the way God had led them, did it not seem significant that the closer they drew to their destination, the worse their situation became? Could it be that the devil was trying to thwart the work God had for them to do in Pakistan? This would account for the deterioration in their condition.

She picked up her Bible and turned to 1 John 4:4: ' *The one who is in you is greater than the one who is in the world.*' Yes! God's Spirit which indwells the believer is infinitely greater than the devil who rules the world. There was no need to doubt this wonderful God.

The battle had already been won! God was in control no matter what the circumstances might be. They had relied on his provision thus far, and he would provide to the end. She would hope and pray for them both until Michael got better and they could resume the last stage of the journey. Then they would see what God had in store for them there.

It was Michael's birthday as they approached the border of Pakistan. He was still weak, but had recovered his strength enough to press on the last forty miles.

They drove up to the 'Dak' bungalow - one of a string of postal points situated in every town across the country, where mail could be collected and where overlanders could find temporary accommodation.

It was not an attractive proposition. These resting places of the 'Post-horses' had become rallying points for hippies, drug addicts, criminals and displaced persons, and could be very dangerous. There was no choice, however, Michael would have to set up camp here.

As he pitched the tent, Mary used their last six rupees to buy a bottle of 'Seven-Up' with fresh lime. Then they sat by the tent, savoured the refreshing drink, and celebrated Michael's birthday.

They now had no money left at all. There was nothing more to be done but to remain where they were and wait for further leading from God. But Michael was no longer convinced of God's existence. He was inclined to think that their adventures had been due entirely to his own foolhardiness. He began to despair and blame himself for their impossible situation. He had dragged his wife and baby thousands of miles across hostile territory, and now all they could show for it was a battered tent on a dangerous site where they could be robbed or murdered at any moment. And if that wasn't enough, there were scorpions, snakes and stinging ants *three centimetres long* to avoid!

They had only been at the Dak bungalow for two hours when a man in Western clothes approached them.

'Excuse me,' he began. 'Are you English?' Receiving a puzzled but affirmative answer, he went on excitedly. 'Are you a blood donor by any chance? I need your blood. There's a woman dying at the hospital and she needs a blood transfusion. Would you be willing to help?'

The surprised Michael agreed to be collected and taken to the hospital as soon as it could be arranged, and the man left.

Fifteen minutes later two Pakistani gentlemen came in. It was obvious from their dress and demeanour that they were well-educated and probably held very high profile jobs. They looked admiringly at Michael's Saab.

'Look at that,' said one to the other, 'we don't see cars like that in Pakistan,' and they went on to discuss the merits of Swedish made cars. But then they looked closer.

'I recognise that badge,' said one man, pointing to the front bumper. 'This man is a member of the Institute of Advanced Motorists. It looks as though his name is M. Cawthorne. That's strange, I had an 'M. Cawthorne' apply for a teaching post a few months ago when I was Director of Education in Karachi. He was the only man who had a really interesting biodata - it was fascinating.'

Michael could hardly believe his ears. He turned to the men and said, 'I am Michael Cawthorne, and it was I who applied for the teaching post - I'm still looking for one.'

'Really?' responded the incredulous Pakistani. 'Where are you living now?'

'Here,' said Michael, pointing to the tent.

'Oh, dear, we can't have that,' said the man with a frown.

'I realise we can't stay long,' agreed Michael, 'but we will have to stay here tonight.'

'Well,' the man went on, 'I am the Principal of University Public School in Peshawar. Come and see me tomorrow and I'll see what I can do.' He gave Michael his card and they left amiably.

A few minutes later, Michael was collected and taken to the hospital by the Englishman who introduced himself as Michael Close, a Professor of English at the University of Peshawar.

He had been a major in the Indian Army, but now in addition to his work he had become something of a philanthropist, trying to organise blood donors into giving their blood instead of extorting large sums of money for the service as was the custom in Pakistan. He explained that the woman needing the transfusion was a Pakistani, and that she would die if blood could not be found for her.

They had already ascertained that Michael's blood group was compatible with the woman's, and the task began. Rather more than a pint of blood was taken, but as he recovered, Michael was treated royally.

He gratefully accepted the offer of a cup of tea, but was quite unprepared when a servant was ordered to bring in a tray of pastries, cakes and the Pakistani snack of samosas, all of which were piled high on the plate. The hungry Michael, whose last meal had been half a bottle of 'Seven-Up', tucked in with a will.

Having made good inroads into the plateful of delicacies, he was alarmed when the servant returned, this time bringing in the *proper* meal! He set before Michael lamb and rice enough for six people. A short time later, the husband of the sick woman sat down to question this strange visitor.

'The woman you have given blood for is my wife. What you have done was dangerous. Why did you give your blood for her?'

'But I am a blood donor back at home. Why shouldn't I help in this way?'

The Pakistani could not grasp the concept. 'I don't know why you should put your life at risk for a woman you don't know. She is a good woman, and I appreciate what you have done, but if she dies, I can get another wife. Why do you risk your life for her?'

Suddenly Michael's eyes were opened. 'Do you realise that Jesus Christ gave his blood for you, me and the whole world to cleanse us from our sin?' he said. In an instant, he realised that God had used the incident of the blood transfusion to remind him that in spite of his wavering faith, Jesus had still died to reconcile people to God.

Michael's spirits soared. He felt an overwhelming gratefulness to God that he had been able to give a little of his blood to save the woman's life, and that it was in a simple way a picture of how Jesus had given His blood for mankind. How wonderful that God had let him share himself in this way! His faith came flooding back, and with it a growing love for the Pathan people of the North West Frontier of Pakistan. He returned to Mary rejoicing.

The offer of a possible teaching post was wonderful, but the problem still remained of finding somewhere to live, and even if he got the job, there would presumably be no pay until the end of the month, so they could not pay for accommodation until then.

But God had shown that He was in control, hadn't He? They would wait patiently.

They did not wait long. The next day, a man came looking for the English couple who were camping at the Dak bungalow. He found Mary and Michael easily, and shook hands with them both, greeting them warmly.

'Look here,' he began with a smile, 'I am the British Council Officer in Peshawar, and I heard that an English couple were camping here. Well, we can't have that - educated people like you staying in this awful place with disreputable people - it's not *on* at all!' He frowned as he looked around him in disgust.

'Now, I have something to suggest.' He turned to Michael and Mary resolutely. 'I have to go up to Dir and Chittral (two states of the North West Frontier) for a couple of weeks, and I do not want to leave my house empty. I would much rather have someone I know living in it. There's a larder and fridge full ...'.

Michael lost no time in pointing out to their generous friend that God had worked another miracle, and they gratefully accepted.

As soon as they moved in, there was a knock at the door. When Mary opened it she found a smiling Pathan man there holding an armful of sweetcorn.

'We heard that new people are coming here,' he began in faltering English, 'so please to accept this gift,' and he held out the sweetcorn.

Mary accepted the welcome gift gratefully, and smilingly returned her thanks. It was to be their introduction to the generous nature of the Pathans, which includes taking a gift to new people in the area, and it increased their regard and love for their adopted neighbours.

8. Step By Step in Faith

It was not going to be easy for the Principal to employ Michael at University Public School with its entirely Muslim Pathan teaching staff and student body, but he was determined to do so. He had wanted to appoint him when he first received Michael's application some time before. No other candidate could offer qualifications which fitted the requirements exactly, and he had not forgotten the photograph of the man with the red hair and beard like the Prophet Mohammed. He would employ him somehow, and fight it out with the authorities as and when they found out.

His school was one of two prestigious schools which aimed to model themselves upon public schools in England. At the moment, he had doubts as to whether his school was number one in the popularity stakes, and this public-school-educated, striking young man with the impressive ginger hair so revered by Moslems, would help to redress the balance.

To begin with, his biology experience could be put to good use by undertaking an analysis of the school diet. He had heard rumours that the other school had better food, so it would be very useful if Michael could prove conclusively that this school was just as good, if not superior.

Michael therefore found himself studying the meagre diet of the well-to-do boys instead of teaching them.

A few days later, when Mary and Michael had begun to settle in to their new temporary home, the telephone rang. 'Can I speak to Mr. West[1]?' a voice said as Michael picked up the receiver.

'I'm sorry, he's not here,' answered Michael.

1. not his real name

'Oh,' said the caller, a little puzzled at the strange voice. 'I wanted to invite him to our Bible Study.'

'Well, I'd like to come to that, if I may,' put in Michael, quickly.

'Er - yes, but who are you?' inquired the voice, even more puzzled.

'My name is Michael Cawthorne, and I have just arrived from England with my family to discover what the Lord wants me to do here.'

'Now just a minute,' went on the voice, 'I remember you. Didn't we meet at WEC (World Evangelisation Crusade) headquarters some time ago when I was there inquiring about the work in Pakistan? I believe you bought my son an ice-cream.'

'Yes, that's right,' grinned Michael. 'How amazing! It's good to hear from you again.'

'Well, come on round and we'll have a good chat,' said the astonished caller, and went on to tell Michael where he lived. It was not long before Michael had found his way to 1, Swati Gate, a sprawling bungalow built many years before by a Pathan Army Officer for his family, and hidden behind a high wall on the edge of a Pathan village. He entered through the high gate, and followed round to the front door set in the centre of a long verandah. The bungalow had once been an elegant residence, but over the years it had lost its former glory, and was now rented out to missionaries, with usually at least two families sharing the divided premises. The two men greeted each other warmly, and Michael was led inside.

The Bible Study proved very interesting, and afterwards, round a cup of tea, the group heard the story of Mary and Michael's call to Pakistan.

'How would you like to come with me on my next trip to one of the out stations, to meet some of the local people?' asked the host, genially.

Michael jumped at the chance, and the trip was arranged. It was to give him his first initiation into preaching in the open air through a translator. He enjoyed the experience immensely, but it also showed him that any prolonged stay in Pakistan must include learning the language so that he could operate independently, and not be a burden to anyone else.

The end of the two weeks in their loaned accommodation approached, and once more they faced camping in the open. Then someone suggested that they go to Abbottabad to visit another missionary who ran a school for Pakistani Christian children. It might be that Michael could obtain work there.

Michael prayed about it, and then, as he still had enough petrol for the 186 mile journey, he decided 'nothing lost - nothing gained', and they set off.

On arrival they found out that the missionary, who was a member of a group from The Evangelical Alliance Mission of USA and Canada (TEAM), had become very ill with cancer and had been flown home. However, these kindly people had arranged that one of the other TEAM missionaries, a Mr. Don DeHart, would offer them accommodation. This was very generous, but Michael was embarrassed. He had no money, and could not buy the customary gift. But the missionary had not finished.

'Er ... I wonder if you could help me?' asked his new-found friend. 'If you come to stay with me, do you think you could do me a favour?'

'Certainly,' said Michael eagerly, 'if I can, I would be glad to.'

'Well, I have some films which need to be taken to the Christian School for the children of missionaries at Murree up in the mountains. I can't go myself. I'd be most grateful if you could do this for me.'

'Of course,' answered Michael immediately, but he

did not mention that his petrol had now almost gone, and that he could not buy more.

'Great!' said Mr. DeHart, 'You'll love it! You will be going through some magnificent scenery - you'll never want to go back to England once you've been to Murree! Oh, and don't worry - I'll give you some money for petrol for the journey.'

Convinced now that this was part of God's plan, Michael and Mary looked forward to it eagerly. First they stayed a few days with the DeHart family, whom Mary and Michael soon realised were ideal missionary role-models. Their expertise was to inspire a profound love and respect from the newcomers.

Soon the preparations were complete, the petrol tank filled up with petrol and they set off expectantly for the 75 mile, whole day's journey. They had learned that the school at Murree was originally built by the British as a garrison church, and it had been adapted and extended over the years. It apparently enjoyed a beautiful location.

As they began to climb into the hills, the temperature began to settle to a comfortable warmth, and they were able to take in the beauty around them.

It was very different from the busy town they had left behind. Now the quiet hills rose in stately grandeur, reaching for the deep blue of the sky above.

Little Ruth sat as usual in her child seat, and Mary pointed to this and that, saying the words for her to copy. The little girl looked interestedly out of the window as they bumped over the stony road, but although she could not fully understand, she seemed to be happily sharing the adventure.

On reaching Murree, Michael and Mary were pounced on joyfully. The staff at the school had already heard that the visitors on their way were teachers from England.

'Teachers!' they cried. 'Wonderful! Will you stay and

teach for us? We have just heard that three American teachers whom we were expecting, have not been granted visas, so we are in desperate need of someone who can help for this next term. We have a house you can rent - how about it?'

It sounded marvellous, but as Mary would not be taking a job while Ruth was young, the salary for Michael would be only eighty percent of the rent required for the house. Michael agreed to pray about the proposition, and to let them know soon.

In the next post, he received a letter which had been sent on to him from Peshawar. It was from a young naval officer with whom he had served in the Navy. The young man had been going aboard his ship in Perth, Australia, when he believed the Lord spoke to him and told him to send his old friend, Michael Cawthorne, a cheque for £50. He duly found out where Michael and Mary could be contacted, and the cheque eventually reached a stunned Michael at a crucial moment.

Taking it as a sign that God would provide whatever finance should be needed for the rent of the house here at Murree, Michael accepted the job, and they moved in.

It was all very interesting. The pupils at the school were the children of American and European missionaries, and they boarded there while their parents were working many miles away in different parts of the country.

Michael enjoyed the work, but one thing bothered him. He believed God had sent him to work with the Pathan people. How could he work with them while he was teaching only Western children? However, he believed the Lord had put him there, so he worked on, watching and praying.

As the term wore on and the weather got colder, Michael began to wonder where God would send them next. His contract would end with the Christmas holidays, and they had heard how cold the Pakistani nights could be in winter. It had already become too cold for Mary and Ruth to walk up to the school each day, and at night the temperature fell below freezing. Michael envisaged them celebrating Christmas in the flimsy tent, struggling to keep warm.

Throughout the term, once each week in the evening, Mary and Michael held an 'open house' for the boys boarding at the school. These had become very popular times which included Bible Studies, question times and singing. A rapport soon developed between Michael and his pupils, who responded to his forthright attitude and willingness to listen to them and understand their problems.

Three of the pupils who enjoyed Michael's teaching were the children of Don DeHart, and they soon realised that their teacher had nowhere to go for Christmas.

They reported this to their parents and begged to be allowed to invite Mr. Cawthorne, his wife and baby to stay with them, adding that as a mountaineer, they might be able to persuade him to take them on a long-wanted climbing trip up a nearby mountain. Their parents readily agreed, and Michael gladly received the invitation to go back to Abbottabad.

The DeHart's were a very special family of Mennonite Christians, with five sons and one daughter, who worshipped God without any formal services or rituals.

Before their visitors arrived they explained that they liked to celebrate Christmas very simply.

They did not keep Christmas Day particularly, although they remembered, of course, that Christ was given by God to a sinful world. They did give presents, but only those which they had made themselves, so that no hint of commercialism or greed could mar the time.

This set Mary and Michael into a frenzy of gift-making, and by the time the end of term came, they had assembled a gift for each member of the DeHart family, for themselves and little Ruth.

As they made their way back down from the hills towards Abbottabad, a verse of Scripture came to Michael's mind. It was from Psalm 50: '... *to him that ordereth his conversation aright I will show the salvation of God*'. It went round and round his mind, and Michael prayed as he drove that this verse might be real to them all.

They stopped for a few moments to take in the view from a hillside looking across into Kashmir. Involuntarily, Michael switched on the radio. It was something he rarely did, but as it was one o'clock he tuned in to the World Service to hear the news.

Suddenly their attention was no longer on the scenery. They listened as the news reader announced that war had been declared between India and Pakistan. Exchanging alarmed glances, they realised that they were parked on a hillside in Pakistan, looking over the border into Indian territory. Indian soldiers could appear over the hill at any moment! Michael started up the engine and drove on quickly to Abbottabad.

The DeHart family made them very welcome, and before long they felt as though they had known each other for years. Christmas came, and Michael and Mary experienced one of the nicest and most memorable times that they had ever had.

The talk inevitably revolved much around the war, since by now a blackout and a curfew had been imposed and restrictions on foreigners were anticipated. But it did not mar the peace brought by the Son of God as a group of His people worshipped Him together.

Eventually, however, they all were obliged to discuss their futures when the British Embassy decreed that all foreigners should go home immediately.

Michael was adamant. He had received no indication

from God that he should go home, and until he received positive leading from the Lord Himself, he would ignore all orders from people, whoever they were, and remain where he was.

Mr. DeHart worked among the Pathans in the Bazaars and at the Bach Mission Hospital in Qalanderabad, and the main effect of the war upon him was that some of the Pakistani medical personnel from the hospital had been sent to serve in the army and they were now seriously short of staff. The issue was decided with the next government decree which restricted all foreigners from moving about the country. Michael and Mary were therefore obliged to remain in Abbottabad instead of returning to Murree or Peshawar.

The DeHarts now offered Mary and Michael their closed-in verandah as temporary accommodation, and as the hospital were desperate for workers, Michael found himself in demand, and was offered work. The hospital authorities heard of his experience as a biologist who could use a microscope, and were only too anxious for him to take the place of the laboratory technician who had joined the army.

It was not easy. He had to start from scratch and read copiously in order to grasp the basics. He could use the microscope, yes, but identifying bacteria was another matter. He was trying to do that for which the professionals had had years of training, and what took them a few minutes, took Michael perhaps four hours! He worked all day, and often through the night to catch up with the backlog.

The war set in, and any foreigners remaining in the country found themselves in an insecure position. At one point the British Embassy warned Michael that the last plane had gone, and that they should get out immediately, but Michael would not budge.'I have no authority to leave,' he said firmly. 'I must remain until God tells me to go.'

'Be it on your own head,' he was told tartly. Michael was unperturbed. He would rather risk the war than step out of God's will.

Living close to the Indian border was not the best place to be, and as foreigners they were bound to be a target for aggression. In addition, they were British, and the British stand with India against Pakistan still rankled acutely.

It was therefore somewhat to be expected that occasionally bricks or stones were hurled angrily at their door by the irate Pakistanis, and sometimes soldiers would knock to find out who these foreigners were, and if anything should be done about them.

Gratefully, the war did not last longer than a few months, and by April it was all over. Not very many bombs had been dropped, but it was only some time later that Michael and Mary learned that the home of a family who had originally asked them to stay over Christmas in Lahore, had been completely destroyed by one of these rare bombs. The family had been on furlough and so were saved, but once again, Michael saw the hand of God at work in their preservation.

But now the war was over, and they could look towards the future.

****

Three times Michael had contacted the Education Authorities for permission to teach in Pakistan. He was still convinced that God wanted him at the school in Peshawar, and that sooner or later permission would be given. It would also provide them with something of a permanent home, too, since a house went with the job.

With the lifting of the ban on the movements of foreigners, he at last decided to return to the school and see what was happening there.

Sadly, he discovered that the house which was to be

theirs had been bombed in the war, and now needed extensive restoration. Added to this, an application to employ a foreign teacher had been delayed through several departments on its journey to the Director of Education, who finally responded just as Michael was about to return to Abbottabad, saying that on no account were any Europeans to be employed on the Frontier. It seemed that all the doors to paid work and a home were closed.

When Don DeHart introduced Michael to Naveed Khan[1], it may have been because he wanted to encourage Michael's flagging spirits. Or perhaps it was because he thought Naveed Khan might be able to open a door for Michael to reach the Pathan people. Whatever it was, it turned out to be the start of a close friendship.

Naveed Khan was one of the rare Pakistani Moslems who had accepted Christ as his Saviour, and who now travelled around the villages preaching to his own people. They were introduced at the hospital where they were both working, and the two men began to get to know each other. It was not long before he had told Michael all about his own village 100 miles away, and sensing Michael's interest, he offered to take him there on a visit. Michael jumped at the opportunity, and the trip was arranged.

There was not much preparation to do - they took no luggage - just a toothbrush wrapped in a cloth, and a few copies of one of the Gospels to hand out along the way. Then, with only the clothes they stood up in, they set off for the ten day, 100 mile trek. Here and there they were able to take a bus for some of the distance, but wherever they stopped, Naveed Khan introduced Michael to many folk he knew and from whom they gratefully accepted hospitality.

At every home where they rested, they mentioned that it was their habit to read and study a portion of the Bible

1. not his real name

each morning, and that their hosts were very welcome to join in. Michael would listen to Naveed Khan intently, trying to attune his ears to the language, and then he would read in English.

Many such trips were later undertaken by Michael with his friend, travelling lightly in the same way for several weeks at a time. This was meeting the Pathan people on their own level, and Michael was fascinated by all he heard and saw.

Occasionally they visited sugar makers who would stop and listen to the gospel as they watched the cane bubbling up in a pan on the fire, and sometimes they would stop in a village and join in as the people met together in a dirty barn for an evening's entertainment.

At these times they might have a sitar player who would bring out the long-necked, lute-like stringed instrument and play the Asian music which had such a strange sound to the Western ear. Or a story might be told - perhaps a legend or historical tale.

Then Michael would ask permission to tell a story from the Christian tradition. Sometimes permission would be granted and he would tell a Bible story, and sometimes the request was refused. At other times he might tell the story, and then someone would take him to one side and remonstrate with him about the veracity of what he had said! Michael did not mind this, because it led to further discussion. These were exciting times, with many people hearing the gospel, some for the first time.

Throughout the trips, Michael recognised the hand of God in their protection, remembering that he and Naveed Khan were never harmed, although preaching Christ in a Moslem country could be a dangerous business. A Moslem converted to Christ could expect to find himself at least cut off from his family and home, or at worst, killed.

Naveed Khan had been in danger of his life when he

renounced Islam and embraced Christianity. He had been forced to leave home and only returned, tentatively, much later. It was a measure of the love his father had for him that the rift was eventually healed. Naveed Khan was not surprised, therefore, when occasionally he and Michael were threatened, or not allowed into a village. But they were never harmed, and the Lord always provided a place for them to stay and food for them to eat every night.

They only knew that it cost Naveed Khan's family much inconvenience to open their home to the two itinerate evangelists.

It consisted of one room of about fifteen square feet, built of hardened mud, and in it Naveed Khan's parents had brought up seven children.

During the day the mother would cook all the food for her brood of children on a little stove resembling not much more than a two-litre paint tin, and they would eat inside or outside the room. There was no furniture apart from two large tin boxes which held all the family clothes, and the *charpai's* - single-sized beds made of wooden frames strung with thick coloured cords which doubled as seats until set out for sleep at night.

Michael noticed that there was a structure to the sleeping arrangements. Naveed Khan's mother and eldest sister shared the first bed at the back of the room. The next bed set at right angles to them held two more sisters. Beside this two more brothers shared another charpai, and then there was the father's bed beside the door. Sometimes the youngest son was allowed to share it, otherwise he would have a mat on the floor, but Naveed Khan, as the eldest son, had his charpai set up against the door, and he also held the gun which was the family's protection.

All these beds were squashed together into one half of the room, however, and soon Michael found out why. Before Naveed Khan could set up his charpai, the family cattle were brought inside. The four or five cows and their calves would be shunted into the right-hand side of the room, then Naveed Khan would push his charpai up against the door. The cattle did not all belong to Naveed Khan's family. Some were owned by other people who paid a small amount to have them raised by someone else. The additional income that this brought to Naveed Khan's father, helped to supplement the small wage he received for the work he did at the huge Tarbela Dam not far away.

On the nights that Michael stayed, he would be allotted another charpai, which was hauled in and squashed in the most favoured position between the father's head, and Naveed Khan's feet, with the cattle on one side. This ensured that he would be safe and warm - that is, in normal circumstances. However, one night, something went wrong.

Naveed Khan's mother seemed to have completely 'house-trained' the cattle. Unable to sleep soundly in the crowded room, Michael could not fail to notice that at about three-thirty every morning she would get up and, taking a piece of wood she would tap each animal on the back. At this signal, each cow would perform its natural functions, the mother would collect the results and remove it for disposal!

Unfortunately, one night all did not go according to plan, and Michael was rudely awakened by a foul smelling shower which covered him from head to foot!

The poor woman was distraught, but unable to offer any explanation as to why it should have happened. She could only apologise and insist on washing Michael's clothes. This she did as best she could, but not having any washing powder, the results were not quite what Michael would have hoped.

When he eventually returned home after several days walking, he happened to meet a missionary friend whom he embraced warmly. But the friend behaved most strangely, pushing away in horror! Quite used to the pungent odour by that time, Michael could not understand what he had done to offend his friend!

In spite of the disadvantages, Michael knew that at last he was doing what God had sent him to do - he was reaching the Pathan people. But he still had one major deficiency to overcome. He must learn the language.

Michael and Mary had heard that a language school was held each summer up in Murree. It would be just what they needed to help them in their work, and they thought that they might have just saved enough money to be able to afford to go.

They decided that Michael would learn Pashtu, the language of the Pathan people, and that Mary would learn Urdu, the national language. Between them they could then cover most eventualities. However, they discovered that only Urdu was taught at the school, together with one or two tribal languages, but Pashtu was not among them. This was a problem, because Michael felt he had been called to the Pathans, and Pashtu was the language he needed to learn most. But they remained convinced that God still wanted them to attend the school, so they proposed to press on and leave the details to Him.

Now they prepared to bid 'goodbye' to the DeHarts, whom they had grown to love and who had sacrificed so much to provide the wandering English family with shelter. Michael and Mary would look back many years later, and remember the good advice and understanding tuition which they lovingly received from this unassuming Christian couple, who taught them everything they needed to know about becoming good missionaries.

And so, thanking the DeHarts warmly for their kindness and friendship, they made their way back to Murree.

The problem of lessons in the Pashtu language was solved when they were introduced to a young, educated

Pathan living on the hillside nearby, who was persuaded to give Michael the required tuition, and they all quickly fell into a routine.

In the mornings Mary would go to her classes to learn Urdu while Michael looked after little Ruth. Then in the afternoons and evenings, Michael studied at home with the young Pathan, while Mary took over the chores and the caring.

And so began a time of intensive study for both Michael and Mary, as they balanced their language studies with the care of baby Ruth.

But although they had now been in Pakistan for nearly a year, they had not become entirely immune to local diseases. The water supply was far from being pure, and although one did all one could to prevent sickness, it was not altogether surprising when Europeans, used to Western plumbing, succumbed to infection.

Michael seemed to have incurred his share of illness during their long journey to Pakistan, and now it was Mary's turn. It soon became evident that she was suffering from amoebic dysentery, an intestinal disease causing chronic pain and acute discomfort.

But this did not prove to be the full extent of her problems. Added to the dysentery, or maybe because of it, she suffered an early miscarriage.

She became very ill for some time, but not wishing to miss any of the vital language studies, as soon as she could drag herself from her bed, she struggled the seemingly unending distance up the mountainside and through to the other side of the town each day to the school and back.

Michael and Mary had hoped that by the time the language course had ended, the promised teaching post at the public school would have materialised together with somewhere to live. It was with some sadness, then, that as the last day approached and they had heard nothing, they came to the conclusion that their first sojourn into Pakistan had ended. It seemed to be the right time to return to England and report back to the churches who had watched their progress with interest.

They had no doubts that God would open up the way for them to return, but next time it would perhaps be different. They felt they had now proved their calling from God to those who may have feared the recklessness of the first journey, and they now hoped that they could reasonably expect official financial support.

So returning to Peshawar, they spent their last two weeks in Pakistan lodging with their missionary friends at Swati Gate as they prepared for the long journey home. It was here that a possible opportunity of accommodation in the future opened up.

Their friends explained that they too, had decided to return to England in the Spring of the next year. They would not be gone for a short furlough, however. They would be remaining in England for two years, for the sake of their children's education.

The problem was that they needed responsible people to look after their house while they were gone. Mary and Michael could immediately see the possibilities, but their friends were not so sure. They held the view that a couple with a young child taking off on a journey to Pakistan with no finances or backing from a missionary society could be sheer folly, and not the Lord's leading.

Now, since the Lord had not yet revealed any definite work for Michael, they put forward the theory that perhaps God was showing them that missionary work was not part of His plan for them. Michael was incensed. Hadn't God clearly led them and cared for them all this past year - even without a regular job? They had had examples of God's leading all the time. There could be no doubt at all of their calling.

'I am so sure that God wants us to return,' said the determined Michael, 'that I am going home to order a brand new Land Rover. We really need a good vehicle in this terrain so that I can get around the villages more easily.'

'Oh,' said the surprised missionary. 'I didn't realise that you had the resources to buy a Land Rover.'

'I haven't,' said Michael, 'I have just ten pounds in our car fund, but with that, God is going to provide us with the vehicle we need.'

'But you need a full deposit at least, before you can order such a vehicle,' the missionary was aghast.

'We'll see,' said Michael, his eyes twinkling.

'Well, I tell you what,' said the missionary, prepared to join in a test of a venture of faith, 'if you can order a Land Rover with just ten pounds, and the Lord provides you with one before May next year, then you can stay in this house.'

'Right,' agreed Michael, 'we'll see you in May!'

There was just one more thing Michael wanted to do before leaving for home, and that was to have the Saab overhauled in preparation for the month-long journey. The cost proved far too great, however, for their limited resources.

Then, as if to rub salt into the wound, a careless lorry driver backed into it causing extensive damage. The depot address which Michael extracted from him proved to be wrong, so all hope of recovering the cost of repairs disappeared.

Nothing daunted, Michael set to prayer, and waited. As he had hoped, in the post at just the right moment came a letter from one of their stalwart supporters in England. It contained a cheque for an amount which was to cover the full cost of the Saab's repairs and overhaul.

Rejoicing, they saw to it that the work was completed, then packed the car and trailer, and set off for home.

9. Returning to Advance

Their spirits were high as they motored steadily Westward. They did not have the same apprehension about the journey as they had had when they came out a year ago. For a start they knew the route, and what to expect. They would not make the kind of mistakes they made last time when going through unfamiliar countries with strange customs.

Michael was in his element. He loved travelling and meeting new people, and finding those with whom he could share the gospel. He had a pleasant confidence in situations like these where he could perhaps be the first in a chain which might lead someone to the Lord. This was his forte - front line evangelism - and he watched for any opportunity to use his gift.

He was not so good at follow-up work. He always started with the best of intentions, but was often away on another project after a few weeks or months. This left Mary to faithfully maintain the weekly Bible study and prayer meeting, handing back to Michael when he happened to be at home.

But a long overland journey like this with its opportunities for evangelism had Michael's adrenaline flowing, and he looked forward to it eagerly.

Mary looked forward to the trip because she would be seeing her parents again. She had kept in close contact by writing to them every week, and they had written back weekly, too, but it would be good to see them and reassure herself of their wellbeing.

It would also be good to report back to the churches who had supported them in prayer and with a little financial help. Mary and Michael hoped that their year-long experience would perhaps encourage them to commit themselves further when the time came to go back to Pakistan.

Little Ruth was now over two years old, and although a lively toddler, she loved travelling. Her eyes took in all the new sights and sounds, and she laughed and chattered happily. It did not seem to matter how long the journeys were, she always seemed to be quite enthralled by them, and settled down in her car seat eagerly.

It was not far to the Khyber Pass between Pakistan and Afghanistan, and soon they were viewing its lonely, rugged beauty as they wound their way down through the mountains. The first day's travelling took them as far as Kabul where they were to make their first stop.

They were welcomed by the staff of a hostel which functioned as a rescue centre to help young people in trouble. The hostel, called 'Dil Aram' - 'Heart's Rest', had been started by the American, Floyd McClung, through his organisation, 'Youth With a Mission' (YWAM). It had a staff of dedicated Christians who had become used to dealing with all kinds of traumas, most of which were caused by drug abuse.

Mary and Michael checked into a small hotel. Mary would remain here with Ruth, keeping a low profile as the hotel was full of Moslem men, while Michael visited the YWAM hostel. Mary would not be able to leave their room unless Michael was with her.

As he rested from their journey, Michael was saddened to hear the stories of young people whose lives had been wrecked by the drugs they had found so cheaply in the Eastern countries. The staff at the hostel did what they could to rehabilitate the youngsters, and there were success stories of those who had been released from addiction by the power of God, and who went on to become fine Christians - some of them remaining to help in the hostel.

More often, however, the stories were tragic. Drug abuse often led to brain damage, terminal illness and sometimes suicide. Often the staff would rescue a young man or woman from prison or hospital and take them to the hostel where they would be cared for as far as possible; and frequently it would be found that the youngsters had contracted hepatitis through using infected hypodermic needles.

The devil's power was very evident, and so often the young addicts could not bring themselves to respond to the power of Jesus Christ which would be their salvation.

As they left, Mary and Michael gladly added their prayers to those of the staff for the success of the centre, and promised to continue to pray for them all.

After crossing the border into Iran, they stopped next at the campsite in Mashhad. When they had stopped there on the outward journey, the campsite had been brand new. The Shah, who at that time was still king, had wanted to encourage tourism. He had therefore set up new campsites with reasonable facilities for the convenience of travellers. Unfortunately, as Mary and Michael had discovered, they attracted a disreputable element which angered the local people and caused incidents.

Crossing Northern Iran, they stopped in Teheran at one of two houses belonging to 'Operation Mobilisation'. This organisation trained young people to spread the gospel, and sent them out into other countries for a limited time. Preaching could not be practised overtly, but the love of God could be shown to needy people, and they did this by helping in any way they could.

Mary and Michael stayed in the house for young men (the other was for the women), and they soon made many friends. They were to become further acquainted with the young people after the Afghanistan war some time later, when the group had to move to Peshawar.

111

Their journey continued across Iran to a campsite in Tabriz, near the border with Turkey. It was a good site by Eastern standards, even though the piped water was cold only. Mary took the opportunity of washing out a few clothes, knowing they would dry quickly in the hot Iranian sun.

While she worked, Michael enjoyed a talk with an Iranian Air Force officer who could speak English. The officer told Michael all about his country and the Shah, and listened politely to the gospel from Michael.

Mary was glad to meet a young English woman in the washroom. They chatted for a short time, and in conversation, the young woman mentioned that she wanted to go to the bazaar.

'We're going there,' said Mary, 'would you like to come with us?'

The young woman agreed gratefully, and before long she was seated in the back seat of the car, next to Ruth. Ruth was very happy to be in her car seat again, even though she had spent much of the last few days in it. She began to sing light-heartedly.

'*Jesus loves me, this I know ...*' she sang as she surveyed the scenery. '*Yes, Jesus loves Me .... the Bible tells me so,*' she went on, skipping the dull bits and getting straight to the important parts. Then she turned to the visitor beside her and looking into her eyes, said, 'I love Jesus. Do you love Jesus too?'

She did not receive a reply, but a moment later the young woman burst into tears. Mary and Michael stopped the car and spent a few minutes with the tearful passenger, while the puzzled Ruth looked on. It transpired that the young woman had been brought up in a Christian home, and knew the gospel. She had once professed conversion, but now she had drifted away and was travelling with a young man who was not her husband. The disgrace of this behaviour was great at that time, even outside Christian circles, and Ruth's simple words had touched the young woman deeply.

The visit to the bazaar went on, and eventually they all returned to the campsite. The next morning they said goodbye and went their separate ways, but for some time Mary and Michael added the convicted young woman to their prayers in the hope that she would be reached for God once more.

They pressed on eagerly. Back they travelled through dirty, happy Turkey, crossing the Bosphorus spanned by the brand-new, twenty-nine kilometre suspension bridge at Istanbul. Then on through oppressive Bulgaria and Yugoslavia, keeping their spirits up with the thoughts of seeing home, friends and family once again.

At last they entered Austria, and the atmosphere lifted. Here Michael came across a Saab garage and decided to get the car serviced while he had the opportunity. Strangely, as they approached the garage it stopped and refused to move.

They pushed it into the garage and the mechanic took a look. He discovered that both front springs were broken, and that they had settled down one complete notch.

'It must have been some accident to leave the car in this state,' said the mechanic. 'You were lucky to get it this far.'

'But we haven't had an accident,' said the mystified Michael. For a moment or two they were both puzzled, then Michael remembered.

'We did have a nasty bump when we jumped a huge hole in a road,' he said slowly.

'That's it,' the mechanic nodded. 'The front suspension has dropped an inch-and-a-half lower.'

'But that happened over a year ago,' said Michael.

'You don't mean you have driven it all that time like this?' the mechanic was incredulous.

Michael nodded. 'Yes, and not on neat, tarmacked roads, but across rivers, over plains and through mountains.'

'But that's impossible!' responded the amazed mechanic.

'I assure you it's true,' Michael grinned. 'It's the Lord's doing, Look at the number plate - SKM 196H - that's "*S*aviour, *K*ing and *M*aster", Psalm 19: 6: "*Its rising is from one end of heaven, and its circuit to the other end*"... - "*H*allelujah!' - I know the verse is talking about the sun, but to me it's a promise of the Lord's presence wherever we go.'

The mechanic had a lot to think about as he put the Saab to rights.

Now home seemed to beckon tantalisingly, and the remainder of the journey seemed to flash by. Soon they found themselves at Ostende, and their excitement mounted. Michael held Ruth in his arms as they stood on the ferry, looking out over the water. She laughed in delight. She did not seem in the least affected by the month-long journey. Each new stage seemed to attract her attention anew, and she responded happily.

Now was the time to let Mary's parents know they were nearly home. There had been no point in contacting them during the journey, since they never knew how long it would take them to travel each stage of the four thousand five hundred mile or so trek - especially when it could take a whole day to cover just seventy miles of the difficult terrains in lesser developed countries. They had agreed to telephone from Dover, where they would be one-and-a-half to two hours from home.

Their meeting was exciting for them all. Little Ruth had grown so much in the year-long absence, and she shyly hugged the grandparents she had been too young to know when the adventure had begun. Although Mary's mother was paralysed and could hardly speak, the delight showed in her eyes as she eagerly greeted her daughter.

Michael's first task was to contact the Land Rover retailers and order his vehicle. The salesman was at first delighted to explain the specifications of the vehicle which he knew would be just what his customer wanted. But his face fell when he discovered that Michael had no more than £10 for the deposit! In astonishment he listened to the resolute Michael's explanation of how the Lord would provide not only the deposit, but the full cost of the Land Rover so that they could take it back to Pakistan with them in six month's time. All Michael required was for the salesman to get the order in *immediately*, so that the car would be ready.

The bemused salesman protested that he would have to speak to his superiors, but, fearing further delay, Michael persisted until the man tentatively put the order through. He later discovered that the 'superiors' had agreed, rather reluctantly, that their audacious customer, whose employment was described dubiously as 'missionary work', did, indeed have a good record with regard to payments. However, they were more convinced when he returned with another £40 which had been raised in one week! Then, in spite of the fact that they had not yet received the full usual deposit, they gave in and let the order go ahead!

Now began a time of visiting the churches and people who had been concerned for them while they had been away, and reporting all that God had done throughout the past year. Mary and Michael could now give their account of how the Lord had provided work when it was necessary, or sent money from totally unexpected sources just when it was needed. They explained the work they had done so far, in preparation for what they hoped would be their future work in earnest. They also told the people that to get about into the Pathan villages, a vehicle was very necessary, and that a Land Rover had been ordered in preparation for their return. They explained that they were now looking to God to cover the cost of its purchase.

It was wonderful to Mary and Michael to hear Eric Williams, the minister of Tankerton church which had originally been Mary's home church, telling his people graciously that there could now be no doubt that God had sent these two people to work for Him in Pakistan. God's provision and leading could be clearly seen, and he expected that the church would now be willing to support Mary and Michael's future efforts officially, to the best of their ability.

A similar response came from the other three interested churches, and these four were to become the mainstay of Michael and Mary's prayer backing, and to some extent financial support over the next twelve years.

By March of the next year, 1973, the total cost of the Land Rover had been collected. It came through donations from all kinds of people in large and small amounts, and Mary and Michael praised God for the provision of this essential piece of equipment.

Now they could begin to prepare for a return to Pakistan in earnest, with a stay of at least three years. It would be hard leaving their friends and family again, but they knew that if God was sending them so far away, then He would take care of those they loved at home.

They intended to begin the outward journey again in the middle of March so as to be in Peshawar for a while before their friends would be coming home and their house became vacant.

Then in February, just before they left, Mary learned that she was expecting another baby.

In view of the fact that Mary had by now had two miscarriages, there could be no possibility of her travelling with Michael overland back to Pakistan. She would have to go by air, and Ruth would naturally go with her.

On the 24th of March, therefore, Michael left for the long drive back to Pakistan, leaving Mary and Ruth to fly out as far as Kabul, where they would meet up again on Mary's birthday, April 3rd. He was to try to complete the journey in eleven days, by a constant round the clock push of eight hours driving and eight hours sleeping.

Mary and Ruth arrived in Kabul in plenty of time, staying with Christians there until Michael's arrival, but by April 3rd he had still not appeared. Mary began to worry. It was most unlike him to be late. He always planned his journeys meticulously, and knew almost to the minute how long they would take. Something must be wrong.

The American family with whom Mary was staying had to go out that day, but Mary assured them that she would be all right alone. Michael would soon be there. The morning passed, and the afternoon wore on. Mary imagined all kinds of disasters which could have overtaken him.

Finally at nine o'clock in the evening, Michael arrived, totally exhausted by the punishing journey, having given lifts to all kinds of hippies along the way and sharing the gospel with them. After a meal he fell into bed. Mary's birthday celebrations would have to wait for some other time!

When Michael had recovered sufficiently, they finished the last leg of the journey together, arriving at their intended accommodation complete with the promised brand new Land Rover. Their missionary friends could offer no further objections to their call to Pakistan, and gratefully left their home in Mary and Michael's care for the next two years.

Mary was now five months pregnant, and once again the summer was upon them. She could hardly move in the stifling heat, and with the lively three-year-old Ruth to amuse, she wondered if she would ever have the strength to get down once again to her language studies. Michael needed language study too, but he found that he could to some degree converse in a mixture of Pashtu and English since many of the older men had known the days of the British Raj, and the younger, better educated men had been taught English at school.

Mary's pregnancy posed many problems in a country without the benefits of Western medical care. To begin with, her blood group was Rhesus Negative and this cancelled any thoughts of giving birth at home. But the local mission hospital had no maternity ward and could not cope with any emergency which a Rhesus Negative blood group might entail.

The only solution was that Mary would have to be booked into the American Mission Hospital in Abbottabad, seventy miles away over the mountains. This meant that she would be admitted one week before the date of her confinement, since the journey there took a whole day.

The regulations of the hospital posed further problems because inadequate staff meant that there could be no round the clock care for maternity cases. Each mother was therefore required to provide herself with her own nurse who would do everything for her except the delivery. However, should it be discovered that Mary's baby needed an exchange blood transfusion - as was possible in cases where the mother was Rhesus Negative - then there could be nothing more for it, but to fly Mary back to England. There just was no suitable equipment in the Bach American Hospital - or indeed anywhere else in Pakistan at that time - for such procedures.

But that was not the end to the difficulties. In order that there could be a warning of a possible exchange transfusion, Mary needed to have a blood test every month and the only place where this could be done was at the Armed Forces Blood Transfusion Service in Rawalpindi, a day's journey away.

Every month, therefore, Mary went off to the Khyber Medical Hospital in Peshawar to have a blood sample taken. This was then processed ready for checking, and packed in ice in a vacuum flask. Michael would then have to rush it the long, dusty distance to Rawalpindi for the essential testing, then stay overnight and travel back the next day.

They were both relieved when a week before the baby was due, the time came to travel to Abbottabad. A Pakistani nurse friend came with them to look after Mary, but she also had two little boys who were obliged to come too.

Michael and the boys stayed in accommodation nearby, but their stay could not be for much longer than a week since the two boys had to return to Peshawar to start school. They all hoped that the baby would arrive on time.

The week came and went. The nurse began to get anxious. She was needed back at home now, and her boys must return to school.

As there was still no sign of the arrival of Mary's baby, Michael offered to help. He would take the boys back to Peshawar, if the nurse could stay a bit longer. This was agreed, albeit rather reluctantly, and the nurse said goodbye to her sons.

The hospital authorities promised to ring Michael as soon as Mary went into labour so that he could travel back to be present at the birth, but with a day's journey to cover, he realised it was doubtful whether he could arrive in time.

It was to be two weeks after her due date that Mary finally went into labour, but any hope of contacting Michael disappeared when it was discovered that all the telephone lines were down. In addition, the nurse caring for Mary was not a midwife, and could not supervise the delivery, so Mary had to be taken from the guest house where foreigners were accommodated, across to the operating theatre - the only sterile area of the hospital. This had to be accomplished by wheelchair, but by the time it arrived, Mary was in an advanced stage of labour and could hardly be lifted into it - let alone suffer the ordeal of being pushed across a bumpy orchard to the hospital!

Baby Sarah was born just half-an-hour later.

Back in Peshawar, Michael had begun to worry. It was now more than two weeks after the due date of the baby's arrival, and he still had had no word from the hospital. He knew, too, that the nurse would be desperate to return home by now. He would have to telephone them and find out if anything was wrong. To his amazement, he discovered the reason why he had not been contacted, and heard the news that he had a four-day-old daughter!

There could be no hope of further time for Mary to recover. The nurse had to return home immediately, so the next day found them all setting off in Michael's Land Rover for the journey back to Peshawar. It was not a pleasant journey. The weather was oppressively hot and the road dusty, and all the windows of the Land Rover had to be opened to avoid suffocation. Unfortunately, they were therefore at the mercy of the mosquitos, and were all bitten liberally.

It was not surprising, therefore, that as soon as they arrived home, Michael collapsed with malaria.

This led to further problems, since they could not contact the Pakistani servant to whom they gave much needed employment. As soon as Michael heard that the baby had arrived, he had given the servant a ten-day holiday, which would be the usual duration of a stay in hospital after a birth. There was now no way of contacting him to say that Mary had returned early, apart from driving to the man's home, and that was impossible with

Michael prostrate with malaria. In addition, Mary could not go out in the heat of the day after giving birth, and even if she could, ladies simply did not drive in Pakistan! She would have to cope alone until the end of the ten days.

Then to make matters worse, Michael was soon very ill and delirious. Mary's work load now included looking after Michael, as well as the baby and the rest of the house. Before long, she too succumbed to illness when her stitches ruptured and she developed septicaemia.

The next month was a blur for them both as they battled with pain, illness and the ubiquitous 120 degree heat, struggling to look after the new baby and the lively little three-year-old Ruth at the same time.

Some relief came when their servant returned, but Mary still had to attend the hospital in Peshawar daily for treatment.

Slowly they recovered, and the new, red-haired baby whom they called Sarah, thrived. Michael got back to his language study and visiting in the villages.

10. Goodbye to the West

The Christians from YWAM whom they had met in Kabul on their journeys to and from England, had a regular three-monthly problem. The authorities, anxious to discourage the disreputable hippy travellers who stopped in Afghanistan to obtain cheap drugs, had decreed that all foreigners must renew their visas on a regular basis. It was therefore necessary for both the staff of the rescue centre, and their young guests, to leave Afghanistan every three months to renew their visas before being allowed back again. This would mean a three or four day stay over the border in Pakistan in the home of the missionaries at Swati Gate.

It was now Mary and Michael who were the hosts, and since telephones were a luxury which often did not work, every so often a group of perhaps twelve lively young people would arrive without warning on their doorstep.

These were no considerate, thoughtful house-guests, however. They were mainly drug-crazed hippies whose minds had often been damaged beyond hope, and the few staff members with them were hard put to control their irrational charges. All nationalities were represented. Norwegians, Germans, French - all in need of urgent help and sometimes impossible to contain.

One such young Frenchman had been rescued after having taken LSD for some time. His mind had been almost destroyed by drug abuse, leaving him completely incontinent and also liable to wander off. He would need permanent care for the rest of his life, so the French Embassy had tried to contact his family. Eventually they found his mother, who wrote to him. The young man would not show the letter to anyone, and no-one knew if he had even understood it or not. The YWAM folk and

Michael took it in turns to watch him around the clock.

His stay with Mary and Michael included a Sunday, and the young man was taken with the others to church. During the service someone suddenly realised that the Frenchman was missing. In spite of extensive searching, he was never seen again. No-one ever found out what had happened to him, but they guessed that in his crazed state he may have offended someone, and possibly been shot. The letter from his mother was found back at the house, and in it they read that she never wanted to see him again.

But there were also other young people who proved to be a real joy to their carers. Through the ministry of Floyd McClung and his willing staff, many lives were transformed as they responded to the saving power of Jesus Christ, and went on into useful and successful service for Him - some of them as carers themselves within the refuge.

Although Mary and Michael were very willing to give hospitality to the folk from Afghanistan, their frequent visits posed a problem which they would not dream of making obvious to their visitors.

It all boiled down, as so often happened, to money. Although they all relied on God to supply their needs, there were times when He seemed to leave the provision to the last moment! With no regular income, both the folk at the Afghan refuge, and Mary and Michael, were often hard put to make ends meet. God had never let them down, of course, but they sometimes found themselves wondering if His provision would ever arrive! In Mary and Michael's case, the frequent influx of twelve or so extra mouths to feed posed an oppressive burden on their meagre finances.

It had not been quite so difficult for the missionaries who had let their bungalow to Mary and Michael. They received a regular salary from a missionary society, and this gave them a little security to fall back upon. Mary and Michael had no regular support at all, living only on what Michael could earn in occasional work, and from gifts sent randomly from prayer partners back in England. These generous and vital gifts had been their lifeline, but the folk at home had no idea how the rate of inflation had been rising, and the gifts were now worth far less than they had been in the beginning.

Eventually, Mary and Michael had to admit that their resources were drying up, and that they could no longer go on without an infusion of cash.

It had been part of Michael's principle never to ask anyone for money. He had decided before coming to Pakistan that whenever they had a need, they would pray and rely on God to supply. Up until now, that principle had worked satisfactorily. Often sums of money had appeared at just the right moments.

Now, however, something seemed to be wrong. They probably could have managed if they had not had to provide for the young people from Afghanistan, but the help they had willingly given had drained their resources entirely. They had almost nothing left.

Michael now had to face a crisis. He had been totally convinced that God had been with them when they returned to Pakistan, and he had prayed constantly for God to supply their desperate need. So far, there had been little response. What should he do next? They could not remain in Pakistan without money, and he had vowed never to ask anyone for donations. Should he now set aside that vow and make some kind of appeal? Or did God now want them to give up all they had so far achieved and return home?

After much heart-searching and fervent prayer, Michael decided to write to the churches at home and inform them of the dilemma. He explained that their finances were drying up, and that if God did not indicate to the contrary, they would have to return home.

The response was immediate. The good folk from the four churches in England who had recognised God's call to evangelism in Mary and Michael, now recognised in themselves God's call to further support his people. They responded willingly, and the crisis passed.

****

During the war between Pakistan and India, all English personnel working for the British council had been sent home. Up until that time workers were often employed on a voluntary basis to teach English in Pakistani Public schools, but since the volunteers had all left, English had not been taught, and the quality of spoken English had begun to deteriorate.

Then Michael came home one day to tell Mary some exciting news. The Pakistani British Council Officer had had a wonderful idea. He knew there must be wives of missionaries in the area who were teachers and who would be available to fill the gap in the children's education. Perhaps they would be willing to volunteer for the job if their transport costs were covered.

He discovered that there were two ladies in this category, one was the Scottish wife of the Medical Superintendent at the hospital, and the other was Mary Cawthorne, who, in spite of there never having been women teachers in the schools before, might be persuaded to help if a Principal could be persuaded to accept them.

Michael saw it as significant that the same school Principal who had wanted to employ him before they ever came to Pakistan was only too anxious to take up this new idea and put it into practice. It was the Lord's leading.

There would not be a salary, of course, and naturally

Mary would not be able to preach to the children in any way, but he was sure that such a position would lead to other opportunities. The culture in Pakistan was such that the gregarious people would invite into their homes anyone who showed them genuine friendship. Michael could see that if Mary got to know her young students, then sooner or later she would be invited to meet their families, who would then ask why she lived and worked in Pakistan, and that would lead to her explaining the gospel.

There was no need to give out literature, or press people to convert - by human standards that would be almost impossible in a Moslem country. The only way to evangelise was simply to answer questions when you were asked and leave the rest to the Holy Spirit. Prayer and obedience would do far more than any human effort.

You had to be prepared to listen to their side of the story too, of course, but Michael and Mary never minded that if it meant they could tell someone about the Lord Jesus Christ and what He had done for all people - not just the Christians.

Mary was not quite as enthusiastic as Michael had hoped. She was still breast-feeding Sarah who at seven months old had a long way to go yet before she could be weaned. Dried milk was not easily available, and even if it could be obtained, the water was not good enough to mix with it, boiled or not. Breast-feeding was therefore the only option to a mother, and it continued sometimes until the child reached eighteen months or even two years of age.

Ruth was not such a problem, she now went to the Pakistani Air Force School. It had not been easy for her at first - she had been the only Western child there, and at four years of age she had to learn Urdu very fast to be able to get on with the other children. She had been confused and lonely at first, but it did not take the bright little girl long to get into her stride, and it seemed no time at all before she could converse comfortably with all her new friends. They soon regarded her as their ringleader because she was full of ideas for new play and games.

Pakistani culture did not at that time encourage children to think for themselves - they simply did as they were told and learned everything by rote, so when Ruth arrived with her independent spirit and bold attitude, they willingly followed her lead. Suddenly games in the yard were full of interest and fun, and Ruth loved every minute too. In later years she became completely bilingual, speaking Urdu without a trace of foreign accent. Ruth, therefore, was catered for. Sarah was another matter.

It was agreed finally that Mary should teach English for just three hours each morning, and for five instead of the usual six days each week. During this time Michael would look after Sarah between her feeds until Mary got back.

The presence of the two new English teachers was not welcomed by all, however. The radical idea of women teachers in all-male public schools - and Christians at that - caused outrage amongst some of the staff. Their view was that the two ladies were a threat to Islam, and they threatened to resign if the situation continued.

The Principal was quick to point out that the ladies did not preach, and that the children's English had improved in leaps and bounds since their new teachers' arrival. Two months later, the same masters were queuing outside the Principal's office asking if their own sons could be transferred to the ladies' classes because the other boys were learning so much!

When Mary had been teaching for a few months and they had been at Swati Gate for nearly two years, the Pakistani owner of the house informed them that he had arranged a wedding for his son, and that Mary and Michael would have to find alternative accommodation.

For some time Michael had been feeling that if one wanted to reach the people of any country with the gospel, then one should live amongst them. Swati Gate was situated at the end of a Pathan village and therefore set Mary and Michael somewhat apart from the villagers. Perhaps God was now saying that the time had come for them to find a more central house.

The simple concept was a surprisingly radical step, and other missionaries in the area were extremely doubtful about the wisdom of such a move. It was bad enough that Swati Gate was *near* the village. Missionaries should really live on a proper mission station. Their culture was vastly different from that of the Asians, and they believed the two could not mix. A move right into the village could be disastrous.

'This is no pretty English village,' they reminded the headstrong Michael. 'It is dangerous territory. You know how hostile some Moslems can be about any compromising of their faith by Christians. They would kill even a family member if they thought they were influenced by Christianity. There would be no qualms at all about killing you or your family if they considered you a threat.'

'And then there's the culture,' warned another. 'Can you, a Westerner, live in the standard two roomed, mud brick house with no gas, electricity or water? And with two small children too?' The idea was preposterous.

'I know all that,' Michael responded a little irritably. 'But if God has directed me to live in the village, then I have to obey. My family is in His hands. He will look after us.'

'And what about your wife?' they continued. 'It is difficult enough for Western women to have to learn to cover their heads and wear national dress to be able to get around here *at all*, but if you lived in the village she would have to remain in *purdah*.'

Michael thought about this. So did Mary.

Purdah was the state of seclusion in which Moslem women were required to live. They were not allowed out of the house without a male relative, and even within the house they were more or less confined to the small, private family room. Male visitors would only come to see the husband, and they would be entertained in the outer room. The wife could not be allowed to be seen by any other man.

They would be required to employ a servant, but not as the Western concept of a servant would be. He would be an otherwise destitute man who would be given a very small, but life-saving salary to do all that the wife was not allowed to do. Most of his time would be taken up in shopping for local food in the bazaar, and then preparing and cooking it for the family. The wife could not, of course, be seen out alone in the bazaar. She would be effectively confined more or less to the family room for most of her life.

If they moved into the village, Mary would have to live in purdah most of the time, looking after the children and her home, and forget her 'right' to any other kind of existence, and there was also the danger of Ruth and Sarah's safety.

The cook that Mary and Michael employed at Swati Gate was anxious for them too. He had heard that if they moved into a house in the village, some men had vowed that they would climb over the wall and shoot them. This was no idle threat. Mary had heard it said often in her comings and goings.

Michael was adamant. He had known he was right as soon as he had learned that the village was called 'Swati Village'.

He had often recalled the vision he had received at college when the map appeared on his bedroom wall, and the strange word *peshoweranswot* buzzed through his head. The map had proved to be of Pakistan, and he found out that Peshawar (pronounced Pe*shower)* was a town, and that Swat (pronounced Swot) was a state. But when he heard that Swati village was so called because its people had originated from the state of Swat, he just knew that was where God wanted them to be.

The time had now come to move into the village and they must obey. He located a vacant house, and negotiated to rent it.

Mary spent the whole night before they were due to move in prayer. Her life was about to change radically, and although she was willing to obey the Lord's will in anything, she wanted to be personally certain that they were doing the right thing.

As she prayed she read Psalm 27. '*He shall hide me in His pavilion,*' she read, '*In the secret place of His tabernacle .... And now my head shall be lifted up above my enemies all around me ...*'.

The next morning, the day they were due to move, the young man who was teaching Michael the Pathan language called. He was an expert in Pashtu and a highly respected Islamic scholar who had been influenced by Christianity. He had become good friends with Mary and Michael, but had no idea they were moving. When Mary had related her fears concerning their safety, the young man took charge. 'Don't do anything until I have talked with the village elders,' he ordered, and he went off immediately.

A little while later he returned to report his findings. The elders had no objection to Mary going into the village because they had noticed that she wore modest Pakistani clothes and she didn't shout or make a noise around the village. She also walked behind her husband and didn't speak unless she was spoken to. They did not therefore consider her a threat to the normal way of life in the village.

But they did not want them to move into the particular house they had chosen. It was near to a well where the women came to draw water, and they were anxious about all the hippies from Kabul that stayed with Michael and Mary regularly. Their behaviour could not be guaranteed at all. They would rather they moved to a different house in the village, and that they did not have all these foreigners who did not dress or behave appropriately.

Of course, Mary and Michael assured their young friend that there would be no room to accommodate the hippies, and they would not dream of bringing them into the village anyway. The other missionary would soon be back from furlough and he would take over the hospitality as he had done previously.

The elders were therefore satisfied, and indicated an alternative house in which they would be happy for Mary and Michael to live. This one was the last in a block of three newly built houses, and had not yet been occupied by anyone. It was not near the main well and would suit nicely.

And so in October 1974, Mary and Michael moved into the little straw-roofed, mud brick house in Khyber Quarters in Swati Village, and began a very different lifestyle - particularly for the formerly independent Mary.

The village consisted of one compacted gravel street with narrow alleys going off to the left and right of it. Each alley had about four houses on each side, and each house had the usual two rooms which were about two-and-a-half metres wide by three-and-a-half or maybe four metres long, with a small courtyard surrounded by a high wall.

There was no piped water and no electricity, and gas had not even been discovered at that time in Pakistan. There were not usually any toilet facilities other than a hole in the ground or in a bare concrete floor. Outside in the street and alleys were open sewers, and these were freely used as toilets.

Rubbish would be piled into a concrete bunker and left until some 'Christian' sweeper could be found to empty it, or until the contents had decayed down. Water was obtained by most villagers from the village well, but this would be contaminated by the insanitary conditions, and caused much illness.

In the centre of the village was the mosque, and from here five times daily, starting at five-thirty in the morning, the *mullah* (Moslem priest) would sing out - with the help of a loud microphone - his mournful, insistent call to prayer, and all the male members of the village would respond by gathering around, placing their prayer mats in the dust of the street and kneeling to perform their ritual prayers.

Mary and Michael's new house offered one or two refinements over the traditional accommodation. For a start they had three rooms. The outer room from the alley was the guest room. Here, Michael greeted and entertained his male guests while Mary remained in seclusion with her children in the two small family rooms behind, or in the courtyard.

They also had a kitchen - a small concrete room with a table for the oil stove and a plastic bowl. An additional luxury was a bathroom and *two* toilets - *room* being about the extent of the description! The 'bathroom' consisted of a bare concrete space with absolutely no fittings apart from one tap set in a wall. There was a tap in the kitchen too, but since no water had been piped to them, they were both quite useless.

The toilets provided some attempt at sanitation and Mary and Michael were grateful for them. One was simply a ceramic surround set in a hole in the floor with two depressions where the feet would go as one crouched over it, and the other should have been flushable, but of course this could not be utilised properly without running water.

It was not long before the resourceful Michael found a way to make use of the two futile taps. From the time they moved into the house, all their water was obtained from a carrier from whom they bought eight gallon kerosene cans daily, thus relieving Mary of the burden of going to the well with the other village women each day.

Having discovered therefore, after a little investigation, that some pipe work was attached to the taps, Michael acquired an old oil drum, cleaned it and painted it white inside and set it on the roof. Then with a little additional piping he linked the oil drum to the taps; filled it up with water bought from the carrier, and lo and behold! - they had water on tap! True, it was heated by the sun in summer and therefore always warm, and bitterly cold all the time in the winter, but at least it was more convenient!

The water could not be wasted, however. It became a very precious commodity which they learned to recycle at every opportunity. By the time a bowlful had been used to flush the non-flushable toilet, it would have been already used for washing, washing up, and perhaps household cleaning!

However, although Michael had done all he could to provide healthy living conditions for his family, they had been just six months in the village when one afternoon he was brought home in a state of collapse. His bright yellow colouring announced that he had contracted hepatitis, and Mary's heart sank. In these primitive conditions it would be difficult to stop the rest of the family catching it too, and it could be very dangerous for their girls.

So Mary set up a *charpai* for Michael in the outer guest

room, where he could remain apart from the children, and a male nurse friend came to stay for a couple of days to monitor the constant drip medication Michael was required to receive. Meanwhile, Mary determined to see that every utensil was well disinfected, and that her nose and mouth were covered by a cotton mask whenever she went into the room.

It was an anxious and difficult time for them all, but gradually Michael recovered, and they were relieved when it became apparent that the rest of the family were going to be clear of the disease.

When he had fully recovered his strength, Michael determined to provide the luxury of a little more space for Mary and the children.

Their house was the third and last of the line in their alley. Next to them was an empty plot. Understanding how restricting the life-style was for Mary in particular, he asked the landlord if they could rent the empty plot.

Soon, with a little help from some of the villagers, they had built a wall all around the plot, and also a three-walled, lean-to room which would act as an extension to Mary's living space, and a play area for the children. In the extended courtyard they installed a kennel for their dog who was a constant playmate for the little girls, and later several puppies added to their delight.

It was here that the girls played happily without any of the sophisticated toys of the Western world. They had experienced no other kind of life, and so grew up without the pressures to which Western children might be subjected.

There was no television with all its temptations to attract their attention, and toys were simple. They played together or with the children of Pakistani friends who lived opposite, and created their own play. Sometimes Mary would read to them, and gradually they learned to read for themselves, and as they did, so the Narnia stories of C. S. Lewis became particularly special.

As time went by, the vivid, unimpaired imaginations of the two little girls created a Land of Narnia in the secluded 'garden' courtyard, and many a happy hour was spent acting out adventures of which C. S. Lewis had never dreamed.

Although Mary was now effectively in *purdah,* for a while her routine was lightened by excursions to the University Public School to teach English. Her life, therefore, seemed to consist of two extremes.

Each morning she would climb into the *tonga* - a kind of horse-drawn taxi specially hired for her by the Principal, and make the forty-five minute, nine-mile journey to the school together with her colleague, the wife of the Medical Superintendent. As a former British Head Teacher, Mary was not expected to use the overcrowded public transport. Certainly not. The Principal could not have that. The *tonga* would be sent for her and her colleague, and it would deliver them back home afterwards. It was the least they could do in the absence of a proper salary.

So each morning Mary became a VIP, spending three hours teaching the sons of chieftains, princes and the well-to-do, before returning home to her little house in the village where women wore no shoes, and the little girls went out collecting buffalo dung to be patted into cakes and put out to dry for fuel.

There was, however, another family in the alley which by Pakistani standards did not altogether belong there.

In this Pathan village, the language spoken was Pashtu. Mary therefore was even more effectively alone since she had learned Urdu. There lived across the alley, however, a family of which the wife's natural tongue happened to be Urdu. It was because her husband was Punjabi that they had been settled in this less central part of the village, and the wife herself had been brought up in Lahore, the home of the Urdu language. Her husband, an engineer with Pakistan International Airlines (PIA), had been to England for six months taking a course in engineering and had enjoyed himself so much, and been so well treated, that he had become something of an 'Anglophile' ever since.

The wife was therefore pleased to get to know Mary, and Mary enjoyed the company of another woman with whom she could converse.

Before long, the whole family became firm friends. Michael, as usual, at first visited the husband while Mary visited the wife, and their children played together. But later Michael became accepted as a 'brother' and the strict purdah rules were relaxed, allowing the families to mix together.

They were not to know then that this was to be the start of a friendship which still exists twenty years later, even though most of the family eventually emigrated to America.

Mary was grateful to have a friend when she returned from her three hours at school beyond the walls of her secluded life, but she was even more grateful after two years when the time came to give up the job and strict purdah beckoned without the daily relief of school.

11. East Meets West

About a year after they began teaching English at the school, Mary's colleague, the Scottish lady, decided to give it up. Once more there was a vacancy and Mary quickly suggested that Michael could fill it, and at the same time he applied once again for the oft-refused work permit, since the war with India and Pakistan was by now well over.

At last the long-awaited permit arrived, and Michael could accept the offered teaching vacancy. However, now that he had a work permit he could accept a salary, and although it would be at the much smaller Pakistani rate, the Principal agreed to employ him on that basis. For the first time since they arrived, they had a regular, if very small sum of money coming in, and their continued presence in Pakistan was more assured.

With both of them working, care of Sarah became a carefully planned responsibility, Michael looking after her while Mary was at school, and Mary taking over when she returned home and Michael went off to school. The arrangement worked very well, and Mary was enabled to continue her few hours away each day.

But now she travelled alone in the *tonga* every morning, discreetly veiled, as was the required custom, lest she should be seen by any man.

One day, on the way home from school in the heat of the summer sun, she saw two ladies waiting at a bus stop. The younger woman appeared to be concerned for her older companion who seemed frail and troubled by the excessive heat.

Mary felt sorry for the two women who would not be so comfortable on the bus as she was even on the bumpy, dusty tonga. She felt a pang of anger at the injustice of a system which decreed that women and children had to be squashed into a few - often broken - back seats of a bus, while the rest of the seats were reserved for the men.

Suddenly, the younger woman waved her hand at the tonga driver. She obviously thought that it was for public hire, and that it would be a better ride for her elderly companion than the bus.

The tonga driver took no notice. He had been hired to carry this foreign lady *only*, and he did not dare stop for anyone else. But Mary could order him to stop if she wished. Quickly, she indicated this to him, and he reined in the horse, puzzled. The two ladies clambered gratefully into the tonga, the older woman sitting with the driver, and the younger with Mary in the back.

In surprise, Mary discovered that the young woman could speak English, and was therefore very well educated, and before long they were chatting happily.

She told Mary that she had been taking her aunt to see a doctor at the University hospital, and that they were so grateful for the lift. She was also pleased to meet an English lady. She added that her whole family loved the English and they wished they could make Mary and Michael's further acquaintance, but sadly they only lived in a village where there was no piped water, or even electricity, and could therefore not expect them to visit in such a place.

Mary gladly told her that she too lived in a similar village and that there would be no barrier to them meeting again. At this, the lady said that she was sure her father would love to meet Michael, and that it would be arranged. She went on to tell Mary something of her background.

Mary's eyes opened wide when she heard that the family's mother tongue was actually Persian; the lady's father being descended from a prince of one of the provinces of the USSR. His family had to flee early in the nineteenth century when there had been persecution of Moslems, and they had gone to the northern province of Chittral in Pakistan. Here, they became friendly with the Prince of Chittral, and eventually married into the royal family. Her mother was, therefore, descended from the former prince, and she was also the daughter of the Prime Minister of the state of Chittral.

She mentioned that her father should, by right, be the ruler of the Russian province which now formed part of the USSR, but with no likelihood of any change in the communist domination of the province, he assumed he would never be called to take up the crown and so contented himself with his business as a sugar cane farmer in a village fifteen miles from Peshawar. (Twenty years later the situation was to change dramatically, and the possibility of a return to his unexpected position as ruler not quite so unlikely.) Before she said goodbye, the lady assured Mary that her father would be pleased to call on Michael and invite him to their home.

Once again, this eventually proved to be the start of a life-long friendship, with Michael accepted as a 'brother' and the purdah rules relaxed so that their families could mix freely. Mary and Michael's visits became a regular Sunday afternoon treat, with the result that Ruth and Sarah were accepted almost as 'second family' to the wife, along with her own six children.

This additional friendship became very dear to Mary, especially later on when her work at the school came to an end. Living in purdah was a great sacrifice to the career woman who had recognised a challenge from God from the moment she decided to remain outside Michael's front door some years ago.

'This man is my servant,' she remembered God saying. 'I will always be first in his life. Choose now whether to go or stay ...'. She had stayed, but she knew that she would have to make sacrifices, and living in purdah was one of the most taxing.

She smiled to herself as she remembered how Michael had been adamant that he would not get married. He thought he could not commit himself fully to God's service if he had a wife. As it happened, Michael could not work at all with these people if he had not been married! Single men were regarded with great suspicion in Asian countries and could not be invited into homes where there were womenfolk. To have access to the people's homes, Michael needed to be a respectable married man!

The Lord in His wisdom had ordained that Michael should be married and have a family because that was the acceptable life-style in a Moslem country. Mary's willing contribution to the furtherance of the gospel was that she took a 'back seat' so that Michael could continue his work contacting the men of the village.

Although his work was very important to him, Michael sympathised with Mary concerning the lifestyle she was required to take on. He had done his best to ease her situation, firstly by making their house more acceptable, and secondly by fitting in as far as he could with her chance to get out of the house and teach.

But it had now been three years since Mary had seen her elderly father and paralysed mother. Getting to and from England was a costly business which they rarely could afford, so Mary usually had to be content with weekly letters to and from her father. Three years was a long time to be away, however, especially where the children were concerned. Ruth had only seen her grand-parents once since the age of fifteen months, and Sarah, at not quite two, had never seen them at all. The time had come to redress the situation, although Michael was worried about the cost of such a journey.

After a time of thought and prayer, it was decided that

they could just manage to scrape together enough for the air fares, but although a good time to leave would be June - to avoid the worst of the summer heat, Michael would have to continue at school until the end of term in late July. They decided, therefore, that Mary and the children would leave in June, so that they could receive the maximum respite from the rigours of the heat and primitive life, and that Michael would follow for just one month's holiday from August to September.

Thus Grandpa and Grandma would get their longed-for opportunity to see their little grandchildren.

The arrangements were made, and in great excitement the children set off to England. Part of the arrangements were that they would be met at the airport by the Pastor and an elder of the Hempstead Christian Fellowship who would give them hospitality overnight.

It was lovely to see friends again and sample the dramatic culture change of life in the West. Mary had often written and told of their way of life in Pakistan, but she was to illustrate unsuspectingly the difference as she walked to the door of the elder's home.

As a woman in Pakistan she had had to learn that men always go first in everything. So she automatically stepped back now to allow the elder to enter the house first. But her friend stepped back to allow her, the lady, to enter first. For a moment there was confusion, but then Mary realised what had happened, and laughingly explained. The incident taught her English friends more graphically of the changes with which she had had to cope than a dozen letters could have done!

The stay in England was a revelation to Ruth. Apart from the holiday when she was two which she did not remember very well, she had known no other life than that of Pakistan, but now she was old enough to notice the enormous differences.

For a start, back in their home in Asia they wore Pakistani dress of *shilvar-camise*. This consisted of baggy trousers (the *shilvar*) covered to below the knees by a kind of loose tabard with slits at the side (the *camise*). On their heads they must always wear a *dopatta* - a veil which should wrap around and cover the mouth most of the time. For a woman not to have her mouth covered could be construed to mean that she was immoral, so the girls had to learn the appropriate manner of dress at an early age.

Suddenly, here in this colourful, glittering country they wore clothes which echoed Ruth's school uniform - only they were prettier - and people had such *huge* houses! Even Grandpa's house had *five* rooms - not counting the kitchen and the bathroom! And how wonderful even these were!

The kitchen had lots of cupboards - all of them full to the brim with lots more things than just Grandpa and Grandma needed to use. Ruth wondered why they had so many cups and saucers, plates and dishes when there were just the two of them living in the house.

And there was something else which Mummy told her was a washing machine. You put the dirty clothes in it, and they came out clean! She thought how often she had seen Mummy scrubbing the washing at home in Pakistan with a little cold water and a bar of hard soap in their small bowl.

But upstairs there was a bathroom with a great bath to get into when you washed! *And* it had hot water coming out of the tap! She turned it on and held her hand in the stream of water until it got too hot to remain there. No-one shouted at you not to waste the water either. She wondered how it got into the tank in the roof. No-one seemed to ever fill it up like Daddy had to do every few days at home.

And then there were the streets outside. There weren't just a few black surfaced roads - they were all like that!

You could walk anywhere without getting dust on your shoes. But all the cars! They looked as though they were all nearly new, and although there were a lot of them, there still didn't seem to be as much noise as there was in the streets back home.

She thought about the horses and carts, the tongas, the buffalo carts, the motor rickshaws, the bicycles and the cars which seemed all old and battered - except for a few like Daddy's Land Rover - but the noise they made! They all tooted their horns all the time! Here in England you hardly ever heard the tooting of a car horn, and there weren't any horses - not pulling carts, anyway - or buffaloes either.

And the shops! The shops were so beautiful! And they were so big. Some were so big you could walk around them for ages and still never see everything - and the shops where you bought food! Well, Ruth had never seen so many tins, packets and racks crammed with so much food in her life! She held tightly to her mother's hand as they walked around the food shop though. It was full of ladies in short skirts and bare heads. There were not very many men with shopping bags at all. It was all very different and very strange.

Mary relished the chance to see her mother who did not seem to be too well. She was glad that she had been able to come home this year, and she also basked in the freedom of being able to move around without restrictions. She had almost forgotten what it was like to be a woman in a Western country.

Michael gave her reminders of the life she had left temporarily behind in the letters he occasionally sent. One of those letters gave such a graphic description of the difference between East and West that it was reproduced for the Tankerton church magazine.

While Mary had been away Michael had been invited

to a wedding in the village where they lived. By now he had gained a high level of respect from the community because of his willingness to come alongside them and to accept without objection anything which living among them involved. The only thing at which he drew the line was in doing anything dishonest. The people knew that he was a man of integrity and that they could rely on his word.

It stood out in stark contrast to the underlying tone of their village which happened to be on a recognised smuggling route into Afghanistan. Through here one could pass over the mountains without passing any custom's posts, and over the years the village had been almost 'custom-built' for smugglers.

The houses had been formed into a maze of escape routes through which those who knew the way could steal from one to another in times of danger.

The police, therefore, hardly ever challenged anyone - they knew they had no chance. They might be perfectly aware that half the population of the village were smugglers, but there would be no way they could do anything about it. Anyone they attempted to approach could disappear without trace any time he liked. They had tried once, sending in a bus load of police, but the episode ended in the bus being set on fire and the police running away as fast as they could! The smugglers, of course, escaped!

It was to these needy people that Michael had set himself to bring the gospel, and his uncompromising reliability and truthfulness had won their esteem in spite of themselves.

The chief's invitation to his son's wedding represented a further example of Michael's acceptance among the villagers, and he attended gladly.

The living accommodation of this wealthy chief was made up of several houses, each with its own courtyard with access to all the others. Moslem tradition allowed a man to have up to four wives, and each wife would have a room of her own where she would bring up her family.

Each son, when he married, brought his wife to live in the family home, the daughters, of course, going to their husband's home and taking their own furniture which would form part of their dowry. The room allocated to each wife would then become the new family's living space where they would bring up their children, sharing a communal room with the rest of the extended family.

By the time Michael arrived for the celebrations, he knew that the actual wedding ceremony would be over. It would have taken place the day before in the bride's home, when the *mullah* would have asked the bride, groom and their respective parents if they were willing for the marriage to take place. Then, this agreed, the groom would take his bride off to her new home with his family.

The next day the *valima* would take place - when the groom's family and friends are invited to meet the new bride. For this, the bride's family invite their guests, and since there is no restriction as to numbers, the groom's family never know how many people they must cater for - there might be anything from two to five hundred people.

As Michael stood in one of the courtyards with all the male members of the family and their male guests, he looked around him at the huge numbers of guests still arriving. How could they possibly know how much food to order? The bride's family could invite whom they pleased - the problem must be colossal! His mind inevitably went to the account in the Bible of the first miracle Jesus ever performed at Cana in Galilee (John 2:1-12).

As an Eastern wedding it would have had similar customs except that in Israel wine was allowed. No wonder it had run out! It would not have been lack of forethought by the groom's family, but simply that an untold number of guests had arrived.

In the middle of the wedding, when the food was served and Michael was trying to enjoy eating blancmange on a saucer with his fingers - knives and forks were never used - he suddenly heard a commotion. Shouting and scuffling had broken out among the guests, and several gun shots were heard.

It soon became clear that one of the guests was a *khan* (chieftain) who had the reputation of being a triple murderer, and that one of the other guests was his sworn enemy. Sides had been taken and guns were being waved around with shots fired alarmingly into the air.

It was no surprise that guns were in evidence. Every male Pathan carried arms - rifles, revolvers, daggers, Kalashnikovs - and it was anomalous to them that Michael refused to do likewise. They had heard his comment: 'The only weapon I carry is a sword, *the sword of the Spirit which is the word of God'* (Ephesians 6:17), but they had difficulty in seeing the relevance of the remark.

It soon became apparent that if something was not done, then someone - maybe many - would be killed or injured. The guests scattered in fear, and the host saw his celebration ending in disaster. He could see only one ray of hope. Michael.

Quickly he found him and suggested a plan. The warring groups could be rounded up and pushed into one of the rooms. The door on one side next to the guests would be locked, but the opposite door opening onto the road would be left open, with Michael's Land Rover waiting outside. Then Michael could drive the warring khan and his cohorts back to their village some miles away, thus avoiding a terrible incident.

It was a simple plan, and although Michael appreciated the faith the host khan had in his ability, he was not at all sure about the part which would leave him completely at the mercy of a gang of armed desperados. But with the proceedings deteriorating into mayhem, there seemed to be no choice and the plan went ahead.

Suddenly, Michael found himself locked in the vacant room along with the hostile group, and he realised that he had been left defenceless while the rest of the company waited with bated breath on the other side of the door in safety. Before he could gather his thoughts, the outside door opened, and the group filed out, still arguing loudly and threatening dire retaliations.

Now Michael took charge. He could not allow the state of affairs to go on any longer. Raising himself to his full height and with his red hair vivid in the bright sunshine, he told the crowd that he had no intention of taking them back to their own village in his vehicle while they were brandishing firearms. Firmly he informed the wild bunch that if he was to act as taxi-driver, then all weapons must be laid on the floor of the Land Rover for the duration of the journey.

Showing no outward fear, but inwardly quaking, he awaited the outcome of his orders. The gang looked at each other and at Michael, and then briefly at the closed door which indicated the end of the festivities for them. Then they meekly climbed into the Land Rover, placing all the weapons in a pile at their feet, and squashed into the limited space.

Michael was by no means sure that he wanted to drive with a car full of angry men and loaded guns behind him - any one of them could have decided to shoot him and abscond with the prized vehicle at any moment, but he posed a fearless front and kept going.

'You will never solve anything with guns,' he shouted to them as the Land Rover bumped over the dusty road. He followed that with: '*All who take the sword will perish by the sword*'(Matthew 26:52). And then as there seemed to be no adverse action from the back he went on, 'God commands us to love our enemies. He even sent His only Son to die for us while we were still His enemies.'

The khan was impressed. This Englishman showed remarkable similarities to the Prophet: the red hair, the commanding personality which seemed to invoke obedience, the religious fervour.

By the end of the journey, he had invited Michael to have tea with him one day. (Michael even took Ruth with him on one of his subsequent visits, and Ruth forever after boasted to her friends that she had tea with a murderer!)

A few years later the khan was killed in another violent incident, but he had heard the gospel message, and Michael could only hope that God had used his witness.

The graphic detail of the wedding fracas left the folk of Michael's and Mary's home churches wide eyed. Cushioned at home in England from violence like this, they could not imagine what life in Pakistan was like. It went a long way to a better understanding of the problems faced on the mission field.

As Mary went around reporting their experiences to the churches, she began to be aware that she was talking about 'our village' and 'our people'.

'You have to live among them and know that God has sent you there,' she explained, '.. to realise that you really love the people with all their strange ways, and that you are willing to overcome all the difficulties involved.' It had once all been so alien, and yet now they were a part of it all. They even missed the simple life they led in the village without all the pressures which a Western society posed. There were so many choices to make here - so much to tempt and lead astray. Perhaps a simpler life-style left more time for God.

The last month of the furlough was spent with Michael. He had driven to Teheran where there was a garage which could see to necessary repairs to the Land Rover. Then he flew on to England while they got on with the job.

He spent two of his holiday weeks as a mountain instructor for West Runton Camps; one week on holiday with Mary and the children in Wales, and the last week they all stayed with Grandpa and Grandma in Tankerton. It seemed as though no sooner had he been on his way home than the time came for him to fly back to Teheran together with Mary and the children, from where they would collect the newly serviced Land Rover and finish the last leg of the journey by road.

12. The Served and the Servants

Mary was a little worried about Sarah. At two years old she was a lively toddler who, at a critical stage of her development, needed to have her mother with her most of the time. Mary wished she could remain at home until her little daughter reached school age.

So although Mary looked forward to her daily respite from the confines of purdah as she taught English at the University Public School, she suggested an idea to Michael. 'Why don't you ask the Principal if you can do my job as well as yours,' she offered, 'so that it would be one full-time job instead of two half-time ones? It may be that you could get full-time pay too.'

A little extra money would help enormously, and Michael liked the idea. He gladly approached the Principal who readily agreed, thus beginning a very helpful arrangement for both Michael, Mary, Sarah and indeed, himself.

They now had a regular income of just enough money to live on, so the contributions coming from England provided a little more security. One of the home churches - a Brethren Assembly at Oxted, Surrey, which had nurtured Mike as a very new Christian - covered the regular National Insurance stamp payment which secured their future pensions and their entitlement to health care during furloughs. Without this vital contribution, Mary and Michael knew they would possibly have faced a bleak future.

Teaching then gave Michael additional opportunities to preach the gospel - in the homes of wealthy Pakistanis whose boys he taught at the school. The gregarious Pakistanis loved to give hospitality to new people, and enjoyed hearing about their lives and work. Michael willingly listened to their views and aspirations, not only because he knew that they would in turn listen to his, and thus learn the good news of the love of God, but because he genuinely loved the people.

Mary devoted her time to Sarah, and to Ruth when she came home from school, and although she was happy to do this, she now had to contend with a more or less permanent seclusion, broken only by weekly services on Sundays at their church fellowship where she could meet with other Pakistani Christians. She still had her friend, the wife of the PIA engineer to talk to, however, and the two ladies and their children built up a firm friendship. Then there were the occasional visits to the '*Chittralis*' - the family of the lady she had met in the tonga.

But apart from these, there would always be at least one other person in their household to whom Mary could talk - their 'cook'. It was customary to provide employment in such a position for a local man, and although some of them knew little about cooking, she was obliged to employ a man to perform the tasks which she herself was prohibited from doing in the Moslem society. Mary, therefore, spent a lot of her time in the company of the various 'cooks' who passed through their employ, sharing the gospel with them, and learning something of their backgrounds.

It did not take Mary long to discover the extreme kindness of the nature of William Pervez, a young man who came to them from the other side of Peshawar, where he lived with his wife in primitive accommodation set aside for Christian Pakistanis. Although William's home was slightly better than most, having two rooms and a small courtyard, other Christians did not fare so well.

Pakistanis who did not embrace Islam were treated at best with disregard by the Moslem population, and if they had homes at all, they would usually be in one or other of the rows of mud-brick or concrete huts called *Bhastis* which could be found at various points around the town.

These were no more than rooms of about eight feet square in which would live an entire family, no matter how many children or dependent relatives there were to accommodate. There was no running water and no toilets, although there might be electricity - for some of the time.

A drain ran the length of the *Bhasti* with the rooms on one side and 'kitchens' on the other.

'Kitchens' consisted of a tiny shed with just enough room for one person to stand, and in it would be a shelf. Nothing more. Cooking was done in the alleyway over the drain on a tiny fire or oil stove, in a container the size of a litre paint tin. The children living in the *Bhasti* would play in this area, skipping over the fires and chasing each other in the confined space.

There were not even any front doors to the rooms in the *Bhastis*, the entrances were simply covered by a dirty, ragged curtain which would let in the severe winter cold at nights.

Kindness was not a particularly prominent characteristic of Moslems on the whole, but as a Roman Catholic, William, like other Christians, had a somewhat gentler nature. Even this, however, could not account fully for the sacrificial kindness he showed to a young Catholic girl whose parents had shown her little love.

When one had a daughter of marriageable age, the custom in Moslem countries was for the parents to arrange her marriage to whomever they thought suitable, and the daughter had little or no choice. Sometimes she would not even see her intended husband until the wedding, although if the family owned property, the marriage might be arranged between cousins to secure the inheritance within the families.

The bride's parents were obliged to provide a dowry which could include a cash payment, plus all the furniture for the one room their daughter and her husband would occupy in the bridegroom's house. The bridegroom's parents had to provide some kind of payment to the bride's parents, plus golden jewellery for their daughter-in-law. Poorer families could be in debt for life through struggling to provide the appropriate jewellery.

In most cases, the parents would choose someone with whom their daughter could have a fair chance of happiness, but occasionally - especially in poor families - the parents might be tempted to arrange a marriage to someone who could pay well for a bride. An older man, for instance, wanting a pretty, young woman, could often persuade parents to part with their daughter if enough money was forthcoming, regardless of the wishes of the girl concerned.

Violet was a young woman from a Catholic community, but she unfortunately had unscrupulous parents who were trying to persuade her to marry a very unpleasant old man. For most of her life Violet had suffered beatings and neglect from her uncaring parents, who now could not resist the temptation to marry her to someone who would pay handsomely to have a young girl bride.

Although Violet had remained subject to her parents until now, the dreadful prospect of marriage to the awful old man proved so terrible that she took the rare step of running away from home. She could not go far unprotected, however, so she went to the place where she thought she would be kindly treated - the home of William Pervez.

William's parents, although poor, took the distraught girl in, but then they faced a problem. They had three daughters of their own (who would all need dowries found for them if they were to marry), but only one son, William, a talented chef with a good job in a Chinese restaurant, who might make a reasonably good marriage one day.

Unfortunately, although Violet was of age, and within her rights to leave home - albeit scandalously in the eyes of the community - she could not be accommodated indefinitely in a household with an unmarried son. There was only one thing that could be done if she was to remain with them and not be turned out onto the street to fend for herself. She could marry their son, if he would agree.

Violet was not a hopeful prospect. She did not possess beauty, or any kind of accomplishments; she had never learned to sew or cook or keep house, and there would not even be a dowry to encourage a prospective husband.

In spite of all this, William and his parents were convinced that if she were to be sent back to marry the old man, she would carry out her threat to kill herself, and they could not risk such a thing.

William, therefore, agreed to save her reputation and her future, by marrying her himself. No dowry or gifts came his way, he just graciously sacrificed himself to help the young woman in distress. Before long, they were married, and Violet took up her place gratefully in the household.

But she was a woman, and she would at least provide that valuable commodity - children. It was the obligation of every wife to present her husband with children - especially boys who would grow up to be an asset to the family both in work and in good marriages. A barren wife was seen as a great disgrace, not only to her husband, but to her in-law family also.

But Violet had been traumatised over the years through her treatment at home and in the threatened disastrous marriage, and it soon became apparent that being unable to conceive children was likely to be the ironic outcome of all her troubles.

By this time William had joined Mary and Michael's

household as their cook, and as the days passed Mary discovered the full extent of his problems brought about by his willingness to help the young woman.

During their daily Bible readings, they read together the story of Isaac and Rebekah, and William's eyes widened as he heard how Isaac prayed for his wife because she was barren, and that soon afterwards she conceived and gave birth to twins. Mary assured William that if he prayed and truly believed, she was sure that God would help them, too.

For some time, therefore, Michael and Mary added their prayers to those of William and Violet. Then to their great joy, as the daily Bible studies continued, William and Violet's faith gradually deepened, until eventually they both came to a personal realisation of Christ as their Saviour.

And some time later, the longed-for baby did appear. In fact, the Lord honoured William's act of kindness in taking on the destitute Violet, by cementing their happiness with the gift of several children.

Mary and Michael remained friends with William and Violet for many years, even though they gave their blessing to William's taking a better paid job with an American. They kept in touch and were pleased to hear that he later became a much sought after chef to the Embassies in Islamabad, excelling himself coping with dinner parties for hundreds of honoured guests.

A man who could cook well was a treasure indeed. But one who could cope with the finer points of Western cooking in addition to Pakistani menus - and all produced on a small oil stove - was nearly miraculous!

Ghulam Mohammed was one such accomplished cook. He was an elderly, retired man who liked to keep busy by catering for the one family, and Mary and Michael grew to love him dearly.

Most Moslems were fervent about Islam, and did their

best to comply with the insistent calls to prayer which resounded around the villages five times each day, but Ghulam Mohammed was more fervent than the average Moslem. It did not matter if the rice burned in the pan, or if the custard got lumpy in the saucepan, he would leave it all to go and pray when the *mullah*'s voice rang out from the mosque.

But although Mary had a few nervous moments over lunchtimes, she could sometimes hardly believe the recipes which Ghulam Mohammed produced from the small, single burner oil stove. Not for him was the traditional curry made once a day and used for breakfast, lunch and supper. No. He would be far more likely to serve his admiring employers with a beautifully cooked Wiener Schnitzel followed by a perfect caramel cream! Although quite delicious, Mary thought how incongruous it all looked in their little mud-brick house!

But Ghulam Mohammed also had a story to tell. It was brief and tragic. He had been living in India at the time of partition in 1947 when Moslems and Hindus were at war with each other.

He had been forced to watch while thirty of his extended family members were killed before his eyes, including his wife and all but two of his children. Ghulam Mohammed managed to retain his life, but lost the sight of one eye, and escaped into Pakistan with his remaining son and daughter.

His devout faith in the 'will of Allah' left him sad but not embittered, and he remained a kindly, delightful old man who lightened Mary's days in purdah with his interesting company.

One day at the end of term Michael came home accompanied by one of his pupils. He told Mary that the lad had requested a lift home as his father's Land Rover was in need of repair.

'My father does not like me travelling on public transport,' he had said, looking at Michael hopefully. 'Would you mind taking me in your Land Rover?'

'Well,' said Michael rather doubtfully, 'my wife is preparing lunch, so I would have to let her know first. I suggest that you have some lunch with us, then I will take you home afterwards.'

Mary quickly prepared a little more and they sat down to eat a meal of cold roast buffalo, potatoes and salad. When their servant was not around, and Mary prepared the food, she liked to avoid using the oil stove as far as possible. She still remembered the fine electric cooker at home in England which would have handled the long, slow cooking of the buffalo meat with ease. The small oil stove was an entirely different matter. There would be no curry today. She hoped their visitor would not find it too strange.

The boy of course, ate with his fingers. Every Pakistani used the right hand for eating; the left hand being reserved for cleaning and toilet purposes. Knives and forks were strange implements which were rarely used by Pathans in tribal areas.

'Where do you live?' asked Michael, expecting that the journey would probably take about an hour if the boy lived in one of the outlying villages. He could be there and back before nightfall.

'My father is a Khan in the state of Swat,' answered the boy, 'he will be very pleased to give you hospitality.'

Michael gulped. Swat! This was not nearby. It was a full day's journey away over the mountains! Even then, one could not simply turn around and come home. A visit like this would require a stay of two or three days at least! Anything less was considered an insult to the host. He would have to rethink his plans for the next week.

This did not turn out to be the only surprise sprung by

the unassuming lad. As they made their way steadily across country, Michael asked him a few questions which revealed that the boy was no ordinary Pakistani. His grandfather had apparently been a 'kingmaker' when the state of Swat had been a kingdom in its own right, and his father now ruled and owned an area almost half the size of the principality, with the present 'king' ruling the other half.

The system that had developed was that as members of parliament they were automatically elected for their area, and since these khans were the only rulers the state had, they had to switch loyalties to whichever party held the majority, thus permanently remaining in office!

As they drove nearer to the boy's home, he began to point out the orchards, fields and lands which belonged to his father, and Michael soon became aware of the wealth and power held by this important man. He could also see why the boy was not allowed to use public transport!

The Khan's house was huge. Michael never ever saw the female members of the household because they were accommodated in their own quarters and remained in purdah. The male guests also had their own quarters complete with separate eating area where the company was waited upon by servants.

In all, at this house the Khan employed twelve male and twenty female servants, but in addition he also owned a fortress-like accommodation half way up a mountain which could only be reached by driving a circuitous route round and round a mountainside.

The Khan was most courteous and welcomed Michael warmly. He had been educated in England and therefore spoke perfect English. He arranged fishing and hunting trips for his honoured guest, and Michael was able to share the gospel with him discreetly as he explained his work in Pakistan.

As they got to know one another, they talked about the summer and Michael was forced to mention that he had no idea yet where his wife and family were to stay during the hot season.

Moving out of Peshawar for the summer was highly desirable since the heat, combined with poor sanitation and drainage, led to enormous outbreaks of disease. Cholera, dysentery, hepatitis and typhoid were rife, and since Mary had already contracted amoebic dysentery, she would be even more at risk. Michael had been mulling this problem over for some time, but had come to no conclusions.

Immediately, the Khan offered the guest accommodation of his fortress in the hills. He had apparently not used it himself for the last eight years since he had had air conditioning added to his regular home, but he kept a battery of servants there to keep it in good order. Michael would be very welcome to take his wife and family with their servant and stay there for the summer if they wished.

In all this, Michael could see God's wonderful provision and care for them, and accepted gratefully. He returned home to tell Mary of the good news, and later, as the summer began to take hold, they gathered their necessary belongings together and made the journey up to the pleasant hill fortress.

When they arrived they were rather puzzled to begin with. The Khan had told them that the servants, who had their own simple accommodation, were retained there to keep the lawns cut, the house in order and the large irrigation pool clean so that it could be used for swimming whenever the Khan chose to visit. Unfortunately, since the Khan had not visited in eight years, things had got somewhat out of hand.

Buffalo and goats belonging to the servants roamed and grazed all over the formerly pristine lawns, the servants themselves had long abandoned their own shacks and moved into the main house, and they had not cleaned anything for a long time!

Michael and Mary moved into the guest accommodation, but watched the proceedings with interest.

Then one day mayhem broke out. It started with a shout reverberating up the mountainside from the valley below, 'The Khan is coming!'

In Pakistani tradition, the Khan was on his way unannounced. He had decided that he and his family could take the opportunity of improving their English, and would therefore spend time with their guests up at the fortress. Soon he set out with his procession of servants, donkeys laden with provisions, and the tractor carrying the members of his family, all of which could be seen for miles.

In panic the terrified servants rushed about trying to put off the moment of inevitable retribution. The buffalo and goats were shooed off the lawns, and attempts were made to remove the dust and dirt of years.

It was of course, to no avail. The Khan's extensive train wound its way around the mountain paths, closer and closer, but the neglect of years could not be erased in an hour or so.

The Khan was horrified. Such was the condition of his house that he had to be seated on the guest house lawn for the confrontation with his recalcitrant employees who stood frightened and desperate, waiting for the impending judgment.

Michael watched with interest from his honoured position in an armchair next to the Khan's. Mary, and the children, however, had to stay behind closed curtains when the Khan arrived with his retinue of male retainers. Only later would they meet all the ladies of the family with their complement of female servants.

As he watched the proceedings, Michael's mind jumped

immediately to the parable Jesus told of the wicked, unconscientious servant: '... *the master of that servant will come on a day when he is not looking for him and at an hour that he is not aware of* ...' it said in Matthew 24:50.

The parable told that retribution awaited anyone who did not look for the coming of the Lord and prepare for it in advance. '*There shall be weeping and gnashing of teeth,*' it concluded.

Michael could see that there was to be 'weeping and gnashing of teeth' here too! The servants quaked before the face of their master, their fears well-founded. The Khan was actually a very kind man who took great care of his people. He took his responsibilities very seriously, even to arranging marriages and providing dowries for the brides, but now his kindness had been betrayed.

He poured forth a tirade of anger, confronting them with their guilt and promising retribution. The servants sloped away to begin setting things to rights.

The Khan turned his attention to Michael and asked him how he was getting on in his temporary surroundings. He was assured that the family were very happy to be away from the worst of the summer heat. As they continued to chat, Michael happened to pass a comment about the beautiful stone wall surrounding the guest quarters. He noted the excellence of the stonework, but remarked that it was a pity one side had been added in a completely incongruous red brick at some time in the past.

Without a moment's hesitation the Khan gave orders for the rogue wall to be demolished, and a new matching stone one to be built to replace it. Immediately, in the full 120 degree heat of midday, the servants had to set about pulling down the wall, and trailing up and down the mountainside with large quantities of the appropriate heavy stones for the rebuilding!

It was not to be the last innocent remark from Michael

which would cause grief to the servants.

The pool, which was essentially for the irrigation of the orchards, could double as a good substitute for a swimming pool if properly cleaned, and the Khan had a fancy for Mary to teach his daughters to swim. A contingent of servants were therefore ordered to empty it, and scrub it by hand with crude brushes and bars of soap.

In an unguarded moment, Michael remarked idly how nice it would be if there were seats around the irrigation pool for spectators. There were several stone seats concreted into the ground in other inappropriate places, and it seemed to Michael a shame that they had not been put around the pool in the first place.

'Good idea!' said the Khan, and straightaway ordered the seats to be excavated from their positions and replaced around the pool. The servants were therefore obliged to dig out the seats, break up the concrete and relocate them - all in the merciless heat of the day!

Some exhausting time later, when the gleaming pool had been refilled, Mary began her task of teaching the Khan's daughters to swim, together with most of the female servants.

It was not easy considering the fact that they all had to be fully clothed at all times! She smiled a little, too, at the row of male servants who had been allocated to protect them, but who were obliged to stand at a distance with their backs to the pool so that they and no-one else caught a view of the ladies!

An additional difficulty was the absence of any shallow end to the pool. It was a universal five feet deep all over! Mary was glad that she had included Ruth and Sarah's inflatable armbands in their luggage - they proved invaluable to the new pupils.

By the time the summer ended, the fortress had been put to rights, and Mary and Michael wondered how long it would stay that way before the servants became complacent about their master's absence and neglected their duties once more.

When the summer sun released its hold, and began to give way to refreshing cooler air, the time came to thank the Khan for his hospitality, and for the grateful family to return to Peshawar.

Once more they fell into the familiar routine of school for Ruth, teaching for Michael and purdah at home for Mary.

Michael, however, had another crusade which he doggedly refused to relinquish. He knew the fight would be long, but he was determined to conquer the system.

Their village had been promised an electricity supply, and he was adamant that a supply would be connected, come what may.

13. Coping With Culture

The village electricity connection was long overdue, and Michael contemplated the difference it would make to the quality of life of the villagers, but nothing - apart from the promise - had ever been done about it. Michael kept on asking and bringing it to the attention of the authorities, yet still the supply remained a wishful dream.

Eventually he was told that they would connect a supply to Michael's house first. This, of course, was unacceptable to Michael. He knew that once his own supply was connected, the rest would be forgotten, so he therefore refused their offer unless the whole village was connected at the same time.

So began a year-long crusade which involved Michael in a weekly argument with bureaucracy in which he seemed to be getting nowhere. He would not give up, however. Week after week he would appear at the appropriate desk and pester the officials, until they knew what he was going to say whenever they saw him approaching. They offered excuses, reasons, and variations of the truth, but avoided the real issue time and time again. Michael was perfectly aware of the routine. They were waiting for a bribe.

Not very much could happen in Pakistan without the obligatory bribes, but Michael refused to succumb to the system. It involved him in a lot of gruelling disputes, but he persisted until the officials grasped the idea that there was to be no bribe and, perhaps more infuriatingly, no peace until the job was done. Eventually they gave in, and the long-awaited electricity supply arrived in Swati Village.

It all brought to mind another parable as he considered all the months of struggle he had had to achieve results. *'Men always ought to pray and not lose heart,'* said Jesus, and he went on to tell about a widow who keeps on pestering a judge to avenge her adversaries. '*Because this widow troubles me I will avenge her,*' says the judge, '*lest by her continual coming she wearies me*' (Luke 18: 1-8).

Michael determined to remember the episode to recount in the future to anyone who needed a practical, present-day example of what Jesus had meant.

The electricity supply which had been so long-awaited and looked forward to, consisted of a pole erected in Mary and Michael's courtyard (since it was Michael's request in the first place), upon which dangled freely maybe a dozen bare wires blowing in the breeze. From this, other wires were taken and continued throughout all the houses in the village, culminating in holes in the walls where sockets should be. It was up to each householder to fit his own plugs and sockets, but as these cost money, more often than not they were left bare; the unprotected wires at the end of each appliance's flex simply being pushed into the holes to make the connection when required.

Accidents were therefore frequent, and Michael's next task was to educate the inhabitants of the village in the safe usage of their new electricity supply.

At last Mary could enjoy the convenience of an electric kettle, and the luxury of a single bar electric fire in winter - for some of the time, at least. Unfortunately there existed no such thing as the regulation of the current, so there could be surges one minute, and reductions the next. One therefore had to be prepared for appliances to overheat or even to explode!

In addition, there were frequent power cuts. Suddenly the lights would go out and the whole village would be plunged into darkness. This would happen particularly when the army, who occupied the barracks some distance away, needed extra power for some reason. Their needs were always a priority, and the surrounding area would simply be cut off. It was all not quite as convenient as Michael and Mary remembered it to be at home in England.

And then a letter from England brought life there into even sharper focus. Mary's father wrote to say that he was concerned about his wife's state of health. He advised Mary to come home and visit her mother as soon as she could.

It was more easily said than done. Once more they were faced with the colossal expense of air fares, but Michael was determined that Mary should take the necessary trip. He scrimped and saved until by the following summer he had gathered together enough for Mary, Ruth and Sarah to go home for a holiday to see Grandma.

His cheque was sent off to London to secure the reservations, and they waited for the return of the tickets. They had intended that Mary should travel at the end of June, but by the end of May there was still no reply. Having made copious enquiries, Michael discovered that the cheque had never reached the travel firm. The envelope had been intercepted, opened, and his signature forged in order to cash the cheque. All their carefully saved cash had been lost.

They had no alternative but to explain to the folks at home that it was now quite impossible for Mary to come home - there was no way they could save the required several hundred pounds again in a short time.

It did not take long for the churches to leap into action. Very soon Mary and Michael received another letter containing the air tickets they needed. Their good friends at home had collected the amount between them and Mary's mother could see her daughter and grandchildren after all.

It was always exciting for the two little girls to spend a few weeks with their grandparents, although Grandma had been unable to speak more than two or three words for the fifteen years since her stroke. Mary was glad to be able to spend a little time with her mother, but as the end of the visit drew nearer, she was forced to wonder if she would ever see her alive again. It would be two more years before their official furlough and she doubted whether her mother's strength would hold out for so long. She said goodbye with a heavy heart, but was comforted by the knowledge that her mother was in God's hands which were better by far than her own.

It was perhaps a good thing for Mary at a sad time, that on her return to Pakistan an interesting piece of news had begun to filter through from the University Public School.

Following a long tradition in the English manner of accepting only boys from the age of thirteen, it appeared that they were now thinking of widening their scope to include a Junior department and kindergarten. They would therefore need to consider appointing educated Pakistani lady teachers who would, in turn, need to be trained in English teaching methods, and soon Mary received the request to come and supervise the new department and its young teachers.

This was a wonderful opportunity, but she had one small problem in the shape of Sarah who was just three-and-a-half years old. How could she be cared for while Mary was at school?

Most highborn Pakistanis employed an *ayah* to care for their young children. This was the equivalent of the English nanny, but with differences. There were nominally Christian ayahs, but they were full of Hindu superstitions from their previous faith, and Mary well knew that the Moslem ayahs were not averse to slipping opium to their young charges to keep them quiet. One also constantly had to remember the threat of kidnap. There could be no question of leaving Sarah in the charge of anybody.

Mary suggested to the Principal, therefore, that she would be willing to take on the offered position, but she could only do it if she could bring Sarah with her. This was unusual, but then, so was Mary, and the Principal readily agreed to the suggestion. And so it was, that a bright little three-year-old began school in a class of five-year-olds, and, with the help of the school nurse, took over the wellbeing of the helpless little boys!

School began at seven-thirty each morning, and finished at one-thirty because it was too hot to study in the afternoons for nine months of the year. A half-hour-break allowed the boys to eat the packed lunches which most of them brought. The only contribution to a canteen was a kind of tuck shop which sold small snacks, but the school could not cater for meals except in the hostel for boys from tribal districts who were boarders.

Any meals service which existed in other schools might consist of a lone man who set up in the school grounds with a large pan and very small oil stove, and there he would cook the day's menu on the spot! At the end of the session he simply packed his few bits of equipment in the pan, set it on his head, and walked off!

The introduction of lady teachers into University Public School necessitated some special arrangements. To begin with, the ladies could not use the men's staff room. They had to be provided with a staff room of their own. Even at University, they would have been heavily veiled and needed to sit at the back of the class so that the men did not constantly have to look at them. Here, the only male contact allowed was the visit from the Principal to their staff room when he had messages or information to impart.

And so Mary happily set to organising and instructing her teachers, while little Sarah learned fast, and saw to it that any boy with a cut knee or a bumped head received the appropriate attention from the nurse. At one-thirty they went home for their siesta, getting up at about four o'clock for afternoon tea.

This was the time for visiting. In Pakistan, everyone visited everyone else for afternoon tea. There would be no formal invitations, or forewarning - one simply visited someone, and they would willingly receive their guests - although the ladies only sat with other ladies, and the men with the men, of course. This was the kind of hospitality system which lent itself to sharing the gospel, and Mary took every opportunity possible when people came to visit.

A cup of tea - or *chai* - would be accompanied by delicacies made from milk solids and boiled sugar with added flavouring and nuts, but the *chai* itself was an interesting beverage. It was well suited to a country where flies would be found on any open sugar-bowl, and where milk might be diluted with water from any ditch or well. It was prepared by boiling water in a pan first, when a handful of tea-leaves would be liberally thrown in. When this had been brought to the boil again, a suitable amount of milk would be added and the mixture would be brought to the boil once more. A cupful or two of sugar came next, and would be stirred in well. Having again been brought to the boil, the brew would be strained into a tea-pot, and the *chai* was ready to drink.

From the days of the British Raj right through to the present, all classes of people have made their *chai* in this way, and the word has filtered into the English language in the *cup of char* so loved by the London cockneys.

The days passed by, and Mary and Michael became accustomed to life in their little mud-brick house. The stresses and strains of village life which they had experienced at first, began to mellow, and the simple life they now led contrasted more attractively with the Western 'Rat Race' they had formerly known. They began to appreciate the simplicity of a life devoid of consumer pressures and competition; settling rather to enjoy what they had, instead of craving the modern conveniences they had left behind in England.

As summer came around again, they were pleased to receive another invitation from the Khan in Swat for them to go to his house in the mountains.

It was an exceptionally happy time. Michael enjoyed talking to the Khan and his male friends and servants. Mary enjoyed lazy days in the sun or swimming pool - or rather the irrigation tank! - with Ruth and Sarah, who also enjoyed riding the donkeys which roamed around the gardens.

Sometimes during the afternoon siesta, Michael would lie on his *charpai* with Ruth and Sarah beside him on the verandah and read to them from Kipling's *Jungle Book*. They loved the story which needed little imagination as they lay in the shade of a Pakistani summer, hearing about animals well-known in neighbouring India.

But they especially enjoyed it when Daddy added the animal noise sound effects. They would look perhaps a little anxiously at the surrounding mountainside at the snarl of Bagheera the panther, *in case* he should appear around a distant rock, or they might just glance below under the verandah when the hiss of Kaa the snake reminded them of the possibility of real snakes beneath their feet. But they would tremble most, yet grin at the same time when Daddy gave the blood-curdling roar of the terrifying Shere Khan, the tiger. *Could* there be tigers in Pakistan?

Their smiles turned to frowns, however, when Daddy seemed to be roaring when Shere Khan did not seem to be in the story. Why was he roaring at this point?

The little girls looked at their Daddy who had stopped reading. They watched his face and saw that the roaring was going on, yet Daddy's mouth was quite shut.

Michael jumped from his charpai. The roaring was coming from beyond the low wall surrounding the garden.

Mary and the girls crept tentatively behind him to see.

Looking over the wall, they saw the source of the agonised roaring. There, pressed against the wall in fear and distress was a mountain lion, about the size of a large dog, but with big angry fangs. He was thin, hungry, and very dangerous.

However, not wishing to kill the creature, they decided to give it something to eat in the hope that it would soon retreat. So Mary and the girls ran indoors to fetch a bowl of bread and milk. This they lowered on strings down to the creature. He ate voraciously, and the crisis over, they all returned to their charpais.

A moment or two later, there was a horrified shout from the servant's quarters a little way away, followed by another terrifying roar. Then the servants began screaming and shouting in fear. Michael did not possess a gun, so he grabbed a pickaxe and ran off to help. The situation was desperate. The mountain lion had been revived by the bread and milk, and was now attacking one of the servants. His determination and strength would be quite enough to kill a man, and in his hungry state he would not hesitate. Michael had no alternative. He brought the pickaxe down heavily on the creature, and felled him instantly.

This, however, was not a country where one would waste anything which could be utilised. The mountain lion's coat was of an unusual marking. Without more ado, Michael, aided by the servant and the intrepid Ruth, skinned the creature, and later, when the pelt had been cured, the result was a small but beautiful foot-rug which has remained in Ruth's possession until the present day!

At some point during their stay in Swat, Michael needed to go down to Peshawar to check on the house and collect any post that might be important. He came back disturbed and disappointed. There had been trouble in their church fellowship.

Some time earlier, before they went up to the mountains for the summer, a couple from Abbottabad had come on a visit to Peshawar. The lady of this family had become a Christian through Michael's witness when he was working at the hospital in Abbottabad, and she very much wanted Michael to baptise her.

Michael took her to the church he attended, to speak to the Pastor about the matter and ask him to join with him in baptising the lady. The Pastor, however, was away, and so also was the church Elder.

Now Michael did not know what to do. The couple had only come for the weekend, and the lady was insistent that she wanted to be baptised as a believer, but that it was not expedient for her to do so in her own home town.

After some anxious prayer, Michael could do no more than gather a few Christian friends around him and go on with the baptism in the nearby river.

Unfortunately, when the Pastor and elders heard what had happened, a misunderstanding arose. It seemed that someone retelling the event had inadvertently relayed the wrong information, and the church leaders heard only part of the truth.

They believed that Michael had used wording in the ceremony which was against the normal teaching of the fellowship, and they felt obliged to act. The only thing to do in cases such as this was to suspend the offending person's membership of the church, and this they did, cutting Mary and Michael off from the fellowship.

When Michael heard the news on his visit from the mountains to Peshawar, he was stunned. He returned to Mary, shaken. He could understand what had been said that could cause offence, and he had tried to put the matter right, but by this time it was difficult for the Pastor to fully understand the details or for Michael to defend himself adequately. Indeed he was not given a hearing.

They could do no more than accept the inevitable and find somewhere else to worship. It was a sad end to an enjoyable summer, but they returned to Peshawar in the knowledge that the Lord had the whole matter under control, and they determined to trust him for the outcome.

Not long after they had returned, the usual round of visiting began, and Mary and Michael were not really surprised when the first few Christian visitors were those who attended another church. They were from the Church of Pakistan, which was an amalgamation of the old Anglican Church together with Methodists, Presbyterians and Lutherans.

The services were held in the cathedral church of Peshawar, a beautiful building in neo-Gothic style which looked as though it had been lifted straight from the meadows of Victorian England and planted in the dusty plains of the North West Frontier! One could almost see the regiments of the Indian Army dutifully attending divine worship in order to show a good example to the heathen of India!

Nowadays, the vicar was a Pakistani; his congregation mainly the descendants of those nationals who were converted all those years ago, and although the excellent pipe organ was usually played for services for the foreigners, more often music was provided by the Pakistani band with their traditional instruments.

Mary and Michael's friends assured them that the vicar was far more open to the leading of the Holy Spirit than perhaps some of his predecessors had been, and they urged them to join the fellowship. The help of experienced Christians such as Mary and Michael would be more than welcome.

It was to be the start of a long and interesting partnership which was to lead to greater things. God did indeed have everything under control.

14. Bitter Lessons

In the autumn of 1977, Ruth went back to school to join the rest of the seven-year-olds in class two of the P.A.F. Junior School. But she was to find that things were not the same as they had been before the holidays. She could not understand the political situation of the time and how it would affect her school, but radical changes had been underway.

The greatest change had occurred when Pakistan was taken out of the Commonwealth under President Zulfiqar Ali Bhutto. As a member of the then almost communist 'People's Party', he wished to appease the Islamic party of the Government, and although they were generally thought to be rather extreme in their beliefs and actions, he sanctioned several measures pleasing to Moslems, the most drastic of which was to bring back Islamic Law. Apart from brutal punishments for criminal offences such as stoning for adultery and cutting off a hand for theft, it also included changing the educational system.

When Ruth returned to school, she discovered that *all* the text books had been changed to include one third Islamic material or information. Mary and Michael noticed, when they saw them, that now Islamic scientists were credited with all sorts of discoveries, which in fact had their beginnings elsewhere; and that History and Geography seemed to have been rewritten to favour Moslems. All Western stories and biographies had been deleted, and even the reading scheme books had been banned because they contained references to a dog named 'Sultan'. (This being the title of a Persian prince, it was considered offensive.)

More followed. It became necessary for Ruth to drop 'Islamyat' from the syllabus since it was completely inappropriate for a Christian child, with the result that she would receive no marks in the annual examinations. It was not deemed to be excluded from her course work, but rather that she had completely failed the examination.

A subject she enjoyed and did not want to drop, however, was Urdu. Being by now more or less bilingual, she stood to gain excellent marks in the Urdu exam. All went well until one day all the children were asked to stand up and read a passage from the Urdu book. The passage read: 'We are all Moslems, Mohammed is our prophet, the Koran is our Holy Book.'

Ruth, at seven years old, knew exactly what it meant to be a Christian. She saw daily the influence of a living Lord Jesus in the lives of those in her family, and she understood completely that Islam and Christianity were entirely different. She knew that to read the required statement would be a complete lie.

'I'm sorry,' she said boldly to the teacher, 'I cannot read this because I am a Christian.' There were, in fact, other Christian Pakistanis in the class, but they said nothing. The teacher was adamant. Ruth *must* read it, and not only that, she must learn it and recite it for the Urdu examination.

Ruth was equally adamant. 'I *cannot* read it,' she insisted, and added, 'but if you like, I can read in Urdu, "*You* are all Moslems, Mohammed is *your* prophet, the Koran is *your* Holy Book".' This seemed a very reasonable compromise to the determined little girl.

The Headmistress was summoned, and the contretemps explained. This lady was a woman of narrow experience and heavy prejudice. She ordered Ruth to read the passage, and on receiving the same refusal, she hit her.

When the distressed Ruth told her Mummy and Daddy what had happened, they were horrified. They assured her that they were very proud of her for the stand she had taken, and that she had been entirely right.

Then Michael went to the school to discuss the matter. He spoke to the Principal and again suggested that Ruth could replace the original 'We' and 'our' of the passage to 'You' and 'your', but was told that it would not be permissible. If Ruth did not repeat the affirmation as stated, she would receive no marks in the examination. Regardless of whether she achieved maximum marks for everything else on the paper, to change this one passage meant that the whole exam would be counted as nil.

And so it was that instead of being placed her usual second or third in the class, Ruth came twelfth, scoring no marks for Islamyat or Urdu.

In later years Ruth was to find that being a Christian often meant persecution - even in English schools. A firm stand for Christianity, and her efforts on behalf of Christian groups in the schools she later attended, often brought ridicule and exclusion from her peers, yet she succeeded in bringing the gospel to many.

The expatriate community in Peshawar included some interesting people, many of whom were the British wives of Pakistani professors, lawyers and doctors who had been educated in England. In the days of the Commonwealth, they had all been brought together annually when the High Commissioner or the Consul would come from Islamabad and a dinner would be arranged. Everyone enjoyed these gatherings when they could renew friendships and indulge in a little nostalgia, but it also gave the ladies a welcome opportunity to dress in Western clothes - even if they had to be hidden in a car and driven from door to door so as not to be seen by any Pakistani men!

Wearing Western clothes was a rare treat, but that they should also be evening dress was an added luxury. They were all disappointed when Pakistan was taken out of the Commonwealth and the dinners ceased.

However, the friendships continued, and Mary and

Michael discussed Ruth and the school situation with the well-known English professor, Dame Margaret Harbottle, who had lived for many years in Pakistan. She offered an opinion that it had been good for Ruth to grow up with the nationals and learn their culture and language, but that at about eight years old she should be sent to a Christian school. The Islamic education allowed no creativity or initiative, but inculcated only rote learning and obedience.

Mary and Michael therefore decided that after the furlough they were going to have the next year in 1978, Ruth would be transferred to the Christian School in the Murree hills. By that time Sarah would be five-and-a-half, and it might be possible for her to start there too instead of going to the PAF school as Ruth had done.

However, there were six months before the furlough was due, and a great deal of planning had to be done. It was to be an opportunity for Michael to indulge his love of travelling, and for the girls - or the older Ruth at least - to increase their education. Mary had always said that if Michael had lived in the nineteenth century, he would have emulated David Livingstone, or perhaps have accompanied Stanley to search for him!

He was happiest when he had a journey to plan and exotic places to explore, and it would be especially good to have his bright little daughter with him, to whom he would show all the sights and point out new wonders. They would take an overland route home, but instead of the usual northern, more direct route, they would take a southern, far more interesting route.

It would be a comparatively leisurely journey, taking between six to eight weeks, and would include most of the places mentioned in Revelation, and also much of the journeys of Paul.

As usual they would take literature in all the languages of the countries through which they would pass, since opportunities for evangelism while passing through were often greater than those of Christian workers within the countries, and Michael relished the chance to meet and discuss his faith with new people.

Their stay in England was to be for about six months, and bearing in mind the changes which would arise from the girls' change of school, and the fact that they could not afford to retain their house during their absence, it would be necessary to give up their little house in Swati village before leaving.

They were surprised to feel very sad at leaving the village. Their unhurried life with minimal belongings, poor sanitation, and intermittent electricity, suddenly seemed quite attractive compared with the rush and pressures of life in England - in spite of the excitement of the luxury it offered.

So it was with many a tear that they cleared the house, packed the Land Rover and said a temporary farewell to all the friends who had made them so welcome, promising to return in 1979.

They set off on April 9th 1978, armed with names and addresses of many friends and acquaintances in the countries through which they would pass where they might be able to stay a night or two. They would camp for much of the time, of course, but it was not always safe, and they could not afford to stay all the time in hotels, so had to rely on the hospitality of expatriates or national Christians.

They travelled first to Kabul where they stayed with a family of American evangelists. The husband worked mainly in India and Pakistan, travelling for extended periods while his wife remained in Kabul with their eight children. Outreach in Afghanistan was a very low-key matter. The small community of Christians went about their work quietly, worshipping in a little church in Kabul. But even before Mary and Michael had set out, they learned that the peaceful existence of the Christians here had been disrupted.

The Russian ambassador had been making more and more frequent visits to the King of Afghanistan, and he had made it quite clear that the USSR would not look kindly on any associate country which permitted Christianity.

Therefore, persuaded by other pro-communist leaders, the king sent a letter to the Christian leaders saying that they must surrender the keys of the church, whereupon it would be demolished. The Christians sent back a letter saying, 'We will give your Majesty the keys to this building, but we would remind you that it has been dedicated to God and that anyone who destroys it is answerable to God for what he has done.'

The king had always been friendly to the expatriate community and did not really want to destroy the church, but his monarchy was far from secure and he needed to placate the many communists. The building was therefore demolished, and the Christians thereafter met in the home of the Pastor.

Not long afterwards, they learned that the king had been deposed. He had escaped with his life, but two thousand people had been killed by Russian bombs, and the Afghan leaders would now be no more than puppets. The king who feared his Russian overlords more than God had lost everything.

When Mary and Michael met up with their friends in Kabul, all seemed reasonably peaceful on the surface, but there were undercurrents of unrest. However, they had an enjoyable time together catching up on the news.

Mary had brought with her several gifts which she intended to give to the various folk with whom they stayed. In particular she had two beautiful cashmere shawls, one of which was for her mother in England who was confined to a wheelchair and would appreciate the gift for her eightieth birthday, and the other she intended for her American friend here in Kabul. She showed her friend the two shawls, and asked her to choose one.

Uncharacteristically, her friend could not make up her mind. She was so undecided that Mary began to feel that she ought to give her both shawls. Some time later, a decision still had not been made, and Mary took the step of buying another Afghan-type shawl in the bazaar for her mother, so that she could give both shawls to her American friend. It seemed a rather foolish decision, but Mary could not abandon the feeling that she must give away both shawls. This done, they set off again on their journey.

It was to take three days to travel from Kabul to Teheran across a lonely desert, and would necessitate taking adequate supplies of diesel fuel for the Land Rover and supplies for themselves. They traversed Afghanistan via Ghazni, Qandahar and Herat, and crossed the border into Iran, staying for a short time with an eye-surgeon friend and his wife in Mashhad. Little did Mary know that some years later when he had returned to England, it would just so happen that the same eye-surgeon would remove cataracts from her father's eyes.

They eventually arrived in Teheran on the following Saturday night and were welcomed by the 'Operation Mobilisation' workers with whom they had stayed before.

From OM's point of view the visit was timely since their 'cook' was out of action with a poisoned finger, and in return for accommodation, Mary agreed to take over the cooking.

Michael's time was to be taken up with seeing that minor repairs to the Land Rover were carried out successfully. He had learned from experience that although the mechanics in Eastern countries were willing to repair anything, lack of supervision meant that they would be quite likely to replace the original parts with ones they had made themselves from tin! Michael had no intention of allowing this to happen. The answer was to remain with your vehicle for the length of time it took to repair, and supervise the work yourself.

For the next ten days therefore, Mary spent most of her time in the kitchen cooking for fourteen hungry folk, and Michael took himself daily to the Land Rover garage to keep an eye on the repairs.

On the first Sunday morning they got up to attend the eight o'clock prayer meeting with the expatriates, and heard a news bulletin which announced that there had been another coup in Kabul. An Afghan leader had defied the Communists, and the country was plunged once more into conflict.

The coup was discussed later at the home of American Christians who had invited the little family to lunch. They mentioned that the Lord had clearly indicated to them that there would be a coup in Iran too. This did not surprise Michael and Mary. They recounted what they had heard when they had last driven through Iran to Pakistan three years previously. It happened to be the anniversary of the Shah's accession, and everywhere there were huge placards proclaiming that the Shah was *Shah en Shah* - or 'King of Kings'.

Michael and Mary had looked at each other and said that the Lord would not for long permit someone else to assume the glory and usurp the title due to Himself alone. There had been no signs of impending change at the time, and now they ruefully remembered that there had been no real signs of change in Afghanistan either.

Resuming their journey, they turned this time to the southwest towards the town of Hamadan. On the way, Ruth and Sarah were delighted to see huge, untidy nests of storks high up in the treetops and enormous turtles trundling their way across the road!

At Hamadan they saw the tomb of Mordecai and his cousin Esther, the queen who saved the Jewish race from disaster during the reign of King Xerxes. They also saw a large party of Kurdish horsemen racing across the plains. The desert dust rose in clouds as the magnificent horses thundered past, their riders urging them on to even greater speeds. Ruth and Sarah watched the moving picture in awed silence. They had seen many horses, but nothing to match the beauty of these creatures and the excitement of their ride.

Michael and Mary had particularly wanted to visit Sanandaj, the birth place of a famous Kurd, Dr. Saeed of Iran who converted to Christianity, and they had managed to obtain several copies of the book of his life story, written in Persian. Dr. Saeed was a highly respected Iranian whose name announced that he was descended from the prophet Mohammed's family, and his conversion to Christianity provoked much animosity. Mary and Michael spent an evening at the little university of Sanandaj, talking to a group of interested professors to whom they were able to give copies of *Dr. Saeed of Iran*.

Their last day in Iran was spent with American missionaries in the town of Rezaieh where there was a large salt lake. Here, Ruth and Sarah experienced the sensation of floating without sinking! Just like the Dead Sea in Israel, the lake at Rezaieh was dense with salt and one could relax incongruously on the surface of the water while reading a newspaper!

As usual, before they left, their friends prayed with the little family. Amongst the expected prayers of blessing for the journey, came a word of prophecy which stated that the Lord would go before them to prepare the way. It was a kindly, normal enough prayer, but somehow it made an impression upon Mary and Michael.

They set off for the next leg of the journey through

Turkey with just a little apprehension. Their southern route took them along part of the famous E2 Highway which ran all the way from the West to the East.

The name 'Highway' was rather misleading. As it snaked its way through Eastern Europe and Asia it deteriorated until it was only wide enough for two cars to pass with difficulty!

At the corner where Iran, Iraq and Turkey meet, and the 'Highway' petered out to a dusty, pot-holed track, they were amused to see a weather-worn signpost pointing bravely in a westerly direction and declaring that they should turn left for Calais!

They had motored on gingerly for several hours, until with absolutely no warning notices and no diversions or detours offered, the road suddenly came to an abrupt end. The 'Highway' was being reconstructed and the way ahead was obliterated.

Michael assessed the situation. The only available direction in which they could proceed was up a precarious mountain road. This could be dangerous, difficult or impossible, or a combination of all three! He looked around in vain for a more attractive possibility, but there was positively no other alternative. It was the only way free for them to go.

The road wound round the mountainside, rising steadily upwards until the valley below was lost from view. They persisted for about two hours when an ominous sound made them look at each other in alarm. A long, low rumble followed by the clatter of stones ahead of them could mean only one thing - an avalanche.

Instinctively they looked behind to see if they could turn back. It was quite impossible. There was no room at all to turn round, so going back would mean reversing the entire length they had travelled up the mountain. Worse still, dark clouds formed overhead, threatening to engulf them in mist. And ice and snow from above joined the perilous avalanche of rocks.

Uttering earnest prayers, they moved doggedly on, expecting at any moment to be halted by a wall of rock. They passed many heaps of stones which could only be passed with difficulty, but each time they managed to continue. Hour by hour and mile by mile they crept forward, waiting and watching for the moment when the turning point would come and they would be going down instead of up the mountainside.

The only sign of human life amongst the barren peaks was a derelict bulldozer abandoned on the road, and with care they managed to squeeze around it.

It was eight o'clock in the evening and long after dark when they began to feel the change which heralded the downward slope. They pressed on optimistically and to their great relief they found themselves eventually in a small Turkish village situated in the narrow mountain pass.

In seconds the Land Rover was surrounded by soldiers. Several officers came forward and Michael gratefully discovered that they could speak a little German.

'Where have you come from?' they asked warily.

'From Iran, over the mountains,' answered Michael.

'But that is impossible,' said a mystified officer. 'The way is closed - the road has been blocked and there is no way through from Iran at all.'

'The Lord went before us and opened the way,' Michael told him, and went on to explain that they were travelling home from Pakistan to England. It transpired that the derelict bulldozer had been placed there to close off the way. The soldiers could not understand how the Land Rover had managed to get round it!

When it had been established that Michael and Mary were simply bona fide travellers trying to get home, the soldiers were less aggressive. The next problem would be where they were to stay for the night.

Michael pointed down the street to a large pink-washed building labelled 'Hotel'.

'Not possible,' said an officer, shaking his head, and went on to explain that the hotel had been commandeered by the army and now had 200 soldiers resident there.

There followed some discussion as to what was to happen to the family. With a degree of sympathy the officers recognised that the travellers were exhausted from their hazardous journey over the mountains and that the two little children must be settled somewhere for the night. Eventually a solution was reached. The captain offered them the officer's room at the top of the hotel. It was the only possible place for them to stay.

Gratefully, as Michael carried up their sleeping bags, and Mary helped Ruth and Sarah up the stairs, they were led to the officer's room.

It was a dirty, grubby concrete room with two rope beds - nothing more - but at least it would be a place to rest.

Before going to bed, they were also grateful to share the soldiers' meal of black bread and beans washed down with the boiled tea which would ensure safe water. During the meal, Michael was able to explain the gospel in simple English and hand out a few tracts written in Turkish.

Some time later he was amazed and gratified to receive a further inquiry from one of the soldiers who was put in touch with Turkish Christians.

When at last they settled down for the night, Mary shared one bed with Sarah, and Michael shared the other with Ruth, but he pushed his bed across the door for extra security.

15. Joyful Sorrow

Now they began to feel like tourists again. Some of the dangers disappeared as they motored across Turkey toward the Mediterranean Sea.

They had chosen to take the southern route rather than the more direct northern route, so that they could take the girls to visit some of the better known sites mentioned in the Bible. It was now that they were approaching some of the places mentioned in Revelation, and towns where Paul had travelled on his missionary journeys.

The first well-known place through which they passed when they reached the Mediterranean was Tarsus, Paul's home town. As they looked around, history came to life for the alert Ruth as she saw the places she had read about in the Bible, and viewed the spectacular remains left by the Romans.

They motored on, enjoying the Turkish countryside, swimming in the warm, blue water, and setting up camp at weekends, as was their custom, in order to catch up on necessary chores and worship on Sundays. Now and again they allowed themselves the luxury of a stay in a modest hotel so that they could have a wash and brush up and maybe have somewhere to change for swimming.

By the time they reached Ephesus on the west coast of Turkey, they were feeling more relaxed. They walked along the cobbled road which goes from the harbour through the main part of the ancient town; they looked down from the Acropolis, and they saw the still-remaining shrines to the heathen gods worshipped by the people of Bible times. Most magnificent of all was the huge, circular amphitheatre built by the Romans nearly two thousand years before.

Standing high at the back on the top stone step, they all

looked down to the arena where some American tourists were experiencing the view looking up from below. Suddenly a voice rang out from among the group. 'Friends, Romans, Countrymen, lend me your ears!' came the strong American accent, echoing around the vast circle.

Mary, wondering at the amazing clarity of the sound reaching them at the farthest point of the arena, could not resist calling back, 'I come to bury Caesar, not to praise him!'

The American, not to be outdone, continued: 'The evil that men do lives after them ...'.

And Mary countered with 'The good is oft interred with their bones ...'

'So let it be with Caesar!' [1] sang out the American, and with this triumphant shout, the company rewarded the 'duet' with appreciative applause! It was a practical demonstration of the excellent acoustics of Roman amphitheatrical architecture.

A little later, on the way to see the ruins of the Temple of Diana, Michael was elated to be able to share the gospel with another American tourist, and he considered that it would have been in the same street where Paul would have stood to evangelise so many centuries ago!

There was now a lake within the area of the ruined temple, and they sat down to picnic beside it. As they ate, they talked about the formerly magnificent temple with its colonnades and ancient stone statues, and its altars to the worthless goddess. An element of sadness crept in as they noticed that even today, substantial livings are earned from the sale of statues of the goddess Diana, just as it was in the days of Paul.

'The spirit of the silversmith Demetrius still lives on,' said Mary, pensively.

---

1. William Shakespeare: *The Tragedy of Julius Caesar*, Act 3, scene 2

Following the west coast corner of Turkey, they stopped at Pergamum, and visited another magnificent amphitheatre and acropolis which they reached by a flight of stone steps.

As usual, Michael strode ahead followed closely by the ever-adventurous Ruth, with Mary and Sarah doing their best to keep up. The steps rose steeply with a low wall on each side to which Ruth clung, using it to press against as she eagerly climbed on and up behind her daddy.

Michael glanced around to watch her progress and suddenly froze.

'Stand absolutely still, Ruth,' he ordered. His stern tone caused the little girl to look up anxiously. Michael willed her to obey instantly and not to delay by asking 'why?' There on the wall just a little way in front of Ruth's hand was a two feet long very poisonous viper, nervous of the people around and ready to strike.

'Now Ruth,' said Michael, quietly but insistently, 'I want you to put down your hand, and walk to me in a straight line.'

Although she had no idea why she must do as she had been instructed, Ruth obeyed. She walked straight past the deadly snake and on to Michael where she was safe. Everyone breathed a grateful sigh, as they saw what the danger had been.

'You see now, Ruth,' said Mary, 'why it is that we have taught you to obey without argument. If you had questioned and walked on, you might have been killed. We are very proud of you for remembering that lesson.' She was hugged in relief, and from that day on the episode was brought out and recounted at any time when Sarah or any other younger children needed an example of the need to obey.

Michael had planned that they would take a ferry from Izmir (which was once Smyrna) across to Philippi, in

Greece, instead of their usual crossing at Istanbul. He had been given the name of an American Marine officer who was a Christian and who had been known by some of their missionary friends in Pakistan. They hoped they might find accommodation with him.

They were very glad to receive a warm welcome and as Michael was by now very tired after a gruelling, albeit exciting journey, they were invited to stay several days.

There were, however, one or two nagging problems. They had been travelling for seven weeks by now, and although Mary wrote regular letters home, it was not possible to make closer contact by telephone to let her parents know how far they had reached.

It could take a whole day's waiting to arrange an international call, and was therefore impractical, and it left them feeling somewhat cut off from home. In addition, they had to face the fact that once they crossed into Greece and therefore Western Europe, the cost of buying food would suddenly become much greater, and they were beginning to wonder whether their finances would hold out.

Their marine officer friend suggested another plan.

'Do you know that there is a Turkish ferry line which is a three day trip from Izmir to Venice?' he offered, eagerly. 'If you went that way you would get a three day rest from all the driving, and it would cut your journey considerably.'

Mary and Michael agreed that this would be a wonderful plan, but the snag was the fare. They just did not have the resources to pay for all four of them.

'I believe the Lord is telling me to pay half the cost,' went on the American. 'Does that help?'

'It certainly does, and we are very grateful to you and to the Lord for his provision,' said Michael. 'May the Lord bless you for your kindness.'

They went off to bed with light hearts that night, but before going to sleep, they prayed as usual. Ruth was first.

'Dear Lord Jesus,' she prayed, 'please make Grandma all better, or else take her home to be with you.'

Mary and Michael looked at each other. This was not Ruth's usual prayer. Every other night she prayed, 'God bless Mummy, Daddy and Sarah, and keep Grandpa and Grandma safe until we reach them.' Why had she suddenly changed?

They were strangely unnerved. Their long experience had taught them to be alert for the Lord's leading and direction, and this out-of-the-ordinary prayer might have significance. Mary's heart sank as she was forced to wonder if God might be preparing her for a deterioration in her mother's health. The remainder of the journey would now be rather more urgent.

They boarded the ferry for Venice the next day on May 18th, and since they could not arrive there faster than the ferry took them, they decided to relax and enjoy the rest which God had undoubtedly prepared for them. It proved to be a wonderful trip as they basked in Mediterranean sunshine and viewed the beauty of the Greek Islands.

However, had Michael and Mary known at the time that they were even further out of communication with the world, they might not have enjoyed their trip so much. Afterwards they realised that God in his love had allowed this so that the rest of the journey would not be fraught by anxiety.

At home in Tankerton, Mary's father was distraught. On the evening of May 17th, his wife had another massive stroke. He knew that she might not live through this one, and Mary needed to be found quickly. But he had no idea where the family were. He only had the information from their last letter several days before, and they would have moved on by now.

The minister of their home church in Tankerton, John Bishop, took a hand. There was only one way in which travellers such as Michael and Mary might be reached, and that was through the SOS service of the BBC. He contacted them immediately, and the same day, the 17th May, a message was broadcast on the World Service. 'Would Mary Cawthorne, last known to be travelling overland from Pakistan, please contact the Whitstable and Tankerton Hospital, telephone number - - - - - where her mother, Mrs Stella Bogg, is dangerously ill.' Then they all waited and prayed.

But Mary and Michael were by now on board the ferry travelling across to Venice, and although Michael had tried to tune in to the World Service as usual, the reception was so bad, he gave up.

On the 18th May, Mary's mother died.

Mary and Michael were fully refreshed on arrival in Venice, and now the urgency they had felt earlier returned. They determined to drive home as fast as possible, and would spend only four hours in Venice. But what an eventful four hours it turned out to be!

They toured the Grand Canal and visited a glass factory and St. Mark's Square, but then as they rested for a few moments in a cafe in order to sample the delights of Venetian ice creams, they were astounded to see a familiar face. It took a second or two to register that this actually was their friend, Floyd McClung, whom they had last seen at the Dil Aram - 'Heart's Rest' - Centre in Afghanistan!

After a few amazed greetings, Floyd invited them to join him and his young people at a 'Mission to Venice' open air meeting he was holding at the railway station. It was a rousing end to their brief stay in Venice.

That was to be the last respite to the urgency of the remainder of the journey. From now on, Michael drove almost continuously, going across the Austrian Alps overnight, and pushing on through Southern Germany and Belgium to Ostende with the minimum of stops.

They arrived in Dover on May 28th, and Michael went immediately to telephone home. He could not get through. They motored on to Canterbury, and there he tried again. When he returned to Mary, she could see that something was wrong.

'It's my mother, isn't it,' she said, all the gentle indications which the Lord had sent falling into place.

'She has gone to be with the Lord,' said Michael, quietly, and added, 'it is sad for us, but happy for her.'

The funeral, which had been delayed until their arrival, was held five days later on the 2nd of June, and although Mary had regrets that she had not arrived early enough to see her mother before she died, she was thankful to the Lord for his gentle preparation. She thought wistfully about the shawls she had been prompted to give to her friend in Kabul. God knew that Mary's mother would have no need of shawls in the beauty of her heavenly home. It was good to have passed the gift on.

In spite of the fact that it had been thought that Mary's mother might have died at any time after her first stroke seventeen years before, Mary's father took the death of his wife very badly. They had been very close - especially as he had provided much of the extra care she had needed throughout the years, and he found it very difficult to come to terms with her passing.

There could be no possibility, therefore, of Mary returning to Pakistan in the planned six months. She would be needed to help her father adjust to his new situation.

During this time, Michael responded enthusiastically to a request for his services. He was still a Lieutenant Commander with the RNVR, and from time to time he could be called by the Navy to undertake refresher exercises. He was therefore very pleased to be asked if he would go to Portsmouth to take part in a NATO training exercise. This was just the kind of activity he enjoyed most. He loved the sea and the Navy, the adventure and the danger involved, and was completely at ease with the organisation and authority it engendered.

It was, however, with mixed feelings that he consequently received an invitation to serve with the Navy again. The temptation was very great. The sea had been Michael's great passion for most of his life, and he could think of nothing he would like better than to spend the rest of his working life in the Navy. But now there was a greater love in his life. He was fully committed to his Lord, and his perfect will must be paramount now.

He prayed long and hard, searching for God's will for his future and preparing to accept whatever he felt God was saying to him.

The decision was a great sacrifice. He felt convinced that although other men might be able to do the job offered by the Navy, there were very few who could take the gospel to the Pathan people of Pakistan. So although he would love a life connected with the sea, he was compelled to refuse the offer in favour of continuing his missionary work.

If he was not to earn a living in the Navy, an income of some kind must be found elsewhere. When in Pakistan, they received a little regular support from the four church fellowships who were particularly interested in their work, plus occasional gifts from friends and family, but it seemed that when they were home on furlough, the gifts often petered out. There seemed to be an unconscious idea that when they were at home, support was not needed. It was necessary, therefore, to find a job while they were in England.

As usual, teaching came to the rescue, and Michael was again glad that God had led him to gain his teaching certificate some years before. He put his name onto the list of supply teachers, and was soon filling in for staff absences in local schools.

But the time sped by, and in January 1979, Michael was beginning to plan his return journey to Pakistan. Mary would not go back with him straight away as her father's recovery was very slow, and they also felt that a full year at school in England would give the girls a good basis for boarding school at Murree when they eventually returned. It was decided, then, that Michael would leave in March to drive overland, and Mary and the girls would follow him by air at the end of July when the schools closed for the summer holidays.

Michael's overland journey was not to be like any of those he had had before. The news from the Eastern countries was ominous. The prophecy revealed to their American missionary friends in Teheran had proved accurate. There had been a revolt in Iran and the Shah had been deposed. The 'King of Kings' had escaped, but he no longer had a realm over which to reign. The country was now a Moslem Fundamentalist State, and Christians were being persecuted as never before.

Stories filtered through of the pastors being arrested and tortured, and some were killed. Mary and Michael feared for their good friend, Haik Hovsepian, who had often been arrested and questioned in the past. He was a kindly man who had given them accommodation several times. His Christian witness was such that many Moslems had come to the Lord through him, including even some of the police who had arrested him. He would now be in great danger.

All this presented a great problem to Michael. He had to get the Land Rover back to Pakistan, and there was simply no other way to take it other than driving through Iran and Afghanistan, both of which were now in a state

194

of revolution. Then when he heard that the British Embassy discouraged any travel through either country, Michael got down to prayer.

The problem was debated by all four of the churches involved in Mary and Michael's support. Three of them felt that the journey was altogether too risky, but the Hempstead Fellowship offered a word of prophecy. They thought that Michael should go, and that 'he would be delivered even as Daniel had been delivered' (Daniel 6).

Mary rejoiced to hear this - until she remembered that Daniel had to be delivered from a den of lions!

Characteristically, Michael himself was convinced that God was telling him to go ahead, especially as it had already been arranged that Mary and the children would fly. However, he bowed to advice which said that he should not go alone, but take a willing passenger with him.

Charles had been one of the students Michael had met at teacher training college, and whom he had been instrumental in bringing to the Lord. They had kept in touch, and he had been the organist at Mary and Michael's wedding.

Charles had been under a great deal of stress at work, and had recently left his job, his doctor advising a complete change. So with his wife's agreement, it was decided that he would accompany Michael on his epic overland journey, staying in Pakistan for a while to teach before flying home again.

He might have known that he would be exchanging one kind of stress for another - but the excitement of the adventure proved too great to miss! And so it was that on March 21st 1979, Mary and the girls were driven by a friend to Sheerness to see Michael and Charles off on the easy part of their journey by the Olau Ferry across to Vlissingen.

16. East Into Danger

The first signs of trouble came as they were leaving
Bulgaria, when someone warned them that diesel fuel for
the Land Rover would be difficult to obtain. At the border
they were told there was no diesel, but a sympathetic
guard directed them to where some could be bought.
Driving on to Istanbul they were told that the diesel
supplies were being blocked by Iran, and here Michael
managed to get a phone call through to Mary, asking her
and the local church to pray. One hundred miles later in
Ankara they were able to buy some diesel, but realised that
this might be their last reasonably easy purchase.

Michael carried a large spare can in addition to his two
petrol tanks, and it was not until they had exhausted it all
and they had passed two garages where queues had been
waiting for days that he became really anxious. At the
third garage he was obliged to join the queue. It stretched
dozens of cars back from the pumps, and as he drove up,
other drivers in the line called out to him 'Impossible!
Impossible!'

They had not been there long when a man walked
down the line inspecting each car carefully. He stopped at
Michael. 'You are foreigners?' he stated, and without
needing an answer he added, 'come this way.'

Michael drove the Land Rover to the front of the queue
where the man filled up the tanks, waved him off, and then
turned to serve the rest of the queue!

Just before the border between Turkey and Iran the
tanks had run out once more. Wondering how they were
still managing to drive on, Michael made it to a garage he
knew. He drove into the yard only to find the pumps closed
and locked up.

Going to the office, Michael found the door open, went in, sat down and prayed. A few moments later a young man came in and told Michael to come back at two o'clock that afternoon.

At the appropriate time Michael and Charles returned to find out what would happen. They were taken by an older man to the back of the premises where they saw, mounted on stilts, a huge tank, fifty feet high, which was used for filling tankers.

'This is diesel,' explained the man, 'but I do not know how we can get it to your Land Rover.'

It took the rest of the afternoon to work out a way of using the foot-wide filler pipe to transfer the diesel to the Land Rover. Finally they hit upon the idea of getting a huge empty drum, and letting the pipe 'drip' into it. It took just one 'drip' to fill the drum! After that it was easy. They filled the tanks with a can, Michael thanked the man profusely and travelled on.

At the Iranian border Michael was not a bit surprised to experience trouble over his insurance. It happened every time. The authorities were supposed to accept his 'Green Card', but they always argued over it. Instead, they demanded a huge payment. Michael always refused, and he was always told that he could not pass through. After some insistent arguing, Michael would manage to win sooner or later.

On this occasion one of the border officials seemed particularly kind. After the usual attempts at obtaining payment, he gave up and told Michael that he could go on, but would have to join a convoy of lorries. Michael explained that this was impossible because the lorries went too slowly for his Land Rover.

'In that case,' went on the official, 'you can go with the convoy of Mercedes cars.'

Michael explained this time that the Mercedes went

too *fast* for the Land Rover, and added that he would be perfectly all right alone, he had travelled that way many times before.

'If you do that, you will have to sign a paper to say that you have gone at your own risk,' insisted the man.

This was not acceptable to Michael either, so he compromised. 'I will go with the Mercedes,' he said, 'but I will drop out of the convoy en route.'

This decided, he was allowed to leave, but not before he had been warned that there had been trouble the day before in Teheran, and that travel would be difficult.

They set off, and before many miles had passed, they had lost sight of the Mercedes convoy.

Signs of fighting were everywhere. Towns which Michael had known as beautiful cities full of spectacular gardens were devastated and burnt to the ground.

Some way into Iran Michael stopped to find a newspaper which might tell him what the state of things would be. The picture on the front was disturbing. It was a graphic photograph of the Prime Minister who had been shot. Michael kept his fears to himself.

They arrived in Teheran at about six in the evening, which would be early enough to risk a phone call to Mary. They drew up at a Post Office where some soldiers with guns stood by on guard. Parking the Land Rover near them and next to a large pile of sandbags, Michael and Charles both went inside to phone home. There was the usual wait for an international line, but when Michael finally got through, he heard Mary clearly.

'I'm fine!' he told her. 'Everything's going well. No problems at all!'

On their return to the car they saw the broken window. They had been robbed. A case which Michael had filled with presents for friends in Pakistan had disappeared, together with his camera and another case of clothes -

dirty clothes which he had been saving to take to a launderette! He felt under the seat. In relief he found the case which held all his official papers. His passport had been in his coat pocket, so had not been in danger, but he was glad that the thief had not had time to take more.

Angrily he turned to a guard standing near by and was immediately faced with a gun barrel.

'You were on guard,' Michael retorted, ignoring the gun, 'What happened?' His answer was something which seemed to indicate 'Go away'.

Furiously, he began to protest, but the guard pointed the gun more threateningly. Thinking this was not getting him anywhere, Michael turned to another man who looked very well-dressed. The man shrugged.

'What can we do?' he said helplessly. 'No-one has any power now. The youngsters are in control,' but then he added, 'You must get off the streets now, there is a curfew.'

This could be serious. People out on the streets after the curfew deadline would be shot. Michael and Charles got back into the damaged Land Rover and drove off. They would have to find somewhere to stay quickly. He drove down the main street past the old palace towards a district he knew well, but before they had gone far they saw a Jeep full to overflowing with young soldiers in field uniforms coming towards them.

'Slow! Slow!' they bellowed in Parsee at Michael's oncoming Land Rover.

By the time they shouted, Michael had passed them - and he kept on going. He chose to be a deaf, and uncomprehending foreigner! There was no way he would stop for a gang of hyped-up young soldiers looking for trouble. He turned down the first side road he came to and wound his way through the back streets looking behind him all the way. If they followed him, the likelihood of being shot was very great. He kept going until he came to the place where Operation Mobilisation used to have their boys' home.

He noticed that there were no lights in the house, and he switched off the car lights, too. Opposite the OM house was a palace which belonged to a princess of Iran. He remembered the beautiful garden and the guards which patrolled it. The length of the road could be viewed from the princess' garden, and the Land Rover would be seen easily. They must get it inside quickly. He got out to open the gate and felt for the lock.

'Are you all right?' asked Charles anxiously.

Michael steeled himself to calm down, and the lock turned easily. He drove inside, got out to shut the gate and then rang the door bell. There was no reply. He walked back to Charles and they prayed.

It was bitterly cold; they were exhausted with travelling and tense with anxiety. What should they do next?

After some moments of prayer, Michael mentioned quietly that he felt very strongly that they should stay where they were. They settled uneasily in their seats, totally unable to sleep.

Suddenly Michael tensed. In the darkness he sensed someone creeping around the grounds. They sat motionless, hardly breathing, aware that the figure was coming closer.

'Who's that?' barked Michael, terrified. The movement stopped. For some moments nothing happened. The silence went on and on. A strange, uneasy silence fraught with fear which seemed to encompass the Land Rover like a heavy black curtain. Michael was too frightened to say more. His instinct was to remain silent.

After a time which seemed to stretch their nerves to the limit, Charles could bear it no longer.

'What is it?' he asked in a loud whisper.

Tensely, Michael murmured back, 'I can't speak their language. I can't say anything.'

Suddenly a voice from the darkness said, 'Is that Michael?'

'Yes!' said Michael, his whole body relaxing with relief, 'but who are you?'

From the darkness, the voice came back, 'It's Ramazan, but keep quiet.'

'Ramazan!' exclaimed Michael, and whispered, 'what are you doing here?'

'Who is with you?' answered the voice, still a little nervous.

'A friend of mine,' said Michael. 'He's English,' and then he ventured, 'is there anyone else here?'

'No,' answered Ramazan, 'but I will take you into the house.'

They followed behind, but as they went in, Ramazan warned them. 'No lights. I am blind, so I don't need them, but you must manage without light.'

Skilfully, he led the two weary men down to the cellar, where he warned them again. 'You can have a light for a little while here, but make sure the curtains are shut tightly.'

Then, as they began to relax together, he welcomed them. 'This is indeed a miracle,' he smiled warmly. 'I was told by the authorities to stay in the house I occupy, but yesterday God told me to come back to this house. This is a very dangerous area, but I had to come.

'The day before yesterday soldiers went through every house in the next street, smashing everything and stealing whatever they could take. They stole even from the poor, and if anyone protested, they were shot. I didn't want to come here, but now I know God wanted me to look after you two.'

Charles and Michael praised God for the provision of

help, and they gratefully waited as Ramazan prepared a simple meal. He feared that the light might be seen, so turned it off very soon, and the two men sat patiently in the blackness, amazed that God had sent someone who had no trouble with cooking in the dark!

When they had eaten - still in the dark - Ramazan showed them where they could sleep, and they slept soundly. He woke them early the next morning.

'You must leave with all the trade vehicles,' he ordered. 'Many cars and lorries travel in and out of the city to and from the markets. You will not be noticed so easily. If you wait until later, they will stop you.'

Following his advice, they drove off, and went straight through the police checkpoint even though the Land Rover had GB plates.

Their next destination was to be Mashhad near the Afghan border. On the way they were stopped and questioned as to whether they had the right tyres and lights. This over, they went on until they reached a village not far from Mashhad. Michael had some post cards ready to be posted, so he pulled up at a Post Office. A crowd of people immediately surrounded the Land Rover.

'Americans! Americans!' they shouted threateningly.

Michael leaned out of the window and shouted back, 'No! British! We are British!'

'Are you Swiss or American?' they insisted.

'We are neither,' answered Michael firmly, 'We are British - English!'

'Good!' smiled the spokesman. 'We like the British. If you were American we would shoot you!'

'Then I am very pleased that we are British,' grinned Michael, and the crowd grinned back.

Then, seeing that Michael wanted to post cards, one of the men said, 'The Post Office is closed, but we will take the cards for you and see that they get through.'

Michael thanked him and handed over the cards, wondering if they would ever reach their destination. Several weeks later, Mary delightedly told him that the cards did arrive.

The next night was spent with their Pastor friend, Haik Hovsepian. Staying with him would be a great risk, but he welcomed them gladly. He later told them that the authorities had tried to burn down his house, but it had been saved by the Mullahs who stopped the marauding crowd.

They crossed the Afghan border without incident, but were told that there would be checking along the road. They managed to reach the outskirts of Herat before being stopped. Here they were told that they must not stop in the town, but must travel straight on to Qandahar. This annoyed Michael intensely. Qandahar was a drive of six hundred miles across the desert. He had no intention of setting straight off at night.

'We're going to Herat,' he told Charles firmly.

At the crossroads to the town they were stopped again. The police would not let them go any further. 'You must go round the bypass,' they directed.

Michael was now even more determined to go into the town. He followed in the direction the police indicated, but only beyond their sight. He then turned into a field, crossed it and drove into a housing estate on the edge of the town. He now made for the homes of some Christians he knew.

He found them very nervous. Two days earlier a community of Russians had been killed in retaliation for the killing of a number of Afghans. This had been followed by a bombing raid, when the children of the Christian couple had been playing in their paddling pool in the garden.

Hearing planes approaching the couple had grabbed the children and sheltered under the chimney breast of their house. When the planes had passed, there were bullet holes through the pool.

Their friends would rather that Michael had gone on to Qandahar, but it would be impossible to get out now because of the curfew - in fact, they could not understand how they had managed to get into the town in the first place!

The next morning, Michael and Charles left, taking the main road out of town in the hope that they would blend into the traffic. On the way, Michael recognised a little restaurant which had been run by some more friends, so he stopped to see if they could buy some food to take with them.

The father of the family was not there, but his son was pleased to see Michael, although he was afraid. In the trouble of the previous two days, five thousand people had gathered in the square to protest. They had all been machine-gunned and many had been killed. The son had received a flesh wound to his shoulder. Michael looked at it, and told the young man that he should really be treated in hospital.

'No,' he answered. 'All those who were injured and taken to hospital were shot. I cannot go there.' All Michael could do to help was to dress the wound from the first aid kit he kept in the Land Rover, and accepting advice from the young man to keep away from the mosque area where snipers shot at the worshippers or passers-by, they took their leave.

They were soon at the roundabout of the bypass, but now it was littered with field guns. Michael was forced to slow up, and as he approached he realised that a cannon aimed straight at the Land Rover. Suddenly shouting broke out, and the next thing he knew was that two rifles were pointed directly at him. He slowed even more, and wound the window down. One of the soldiers came up and rammed his rifle so roughly into Michael's chest that it ripped his shirt and tore off a button.

Instinctively, both Charles and Michael swung their hands above their heads.

The soldier said something in Parsee which Michael could not understand, so he quickly responded, 'I am English - British.' He felt the soldier relax slightly, but the gun remained pressed into his chest.

'Papers,' he demanded.

Michael didn't see how he was to show him their papers with his hands up.

'Take the gun away, and I'll get them,' he said.

The soldier tensed again and jabbed with the gun. 'Papers,' he said more roughly. Michael turned to Charles and indicated to him to reach for the papers under the seat. As he was doing so, another soldier came up.

'We are English - British,' Michael repeated again to him, and totally unexpectedly the rifle was removed and the soldier waved them on.

They headed off into the desert towards Qandahar. After about thirty miles they came to a roadblock. At gunpoint again, they were made to get out of the Land Rover and unpack it. Every single thing had to be removed. The contents of every case and each trunk were required to be taken out and set on the road side. When, at last, all their luggage was displayed for all to see, they were allowed to re-pack. It had all taken some considerable time, but the soldiers were in no hurry. Having got everything packed in once again, in relief the two exasperated men went on their way again.

Fifty miles later, the same thing happened again. They had to get out at gunpoint and unpack everything until the Land Rover stood empty, and then they were allowed to repack.

They had not seen the last of these checks. In all, they

had to undergo the same routine every fifty miles for the length of the journey to Qandahar, and the Land Rover was emptied and repacked twelve times. They finally arrived at their destination completely exhausted at one-thirty in the morning, instead of the intended six o'clock in the evening, but there was to be no respite.

Pulling up at a checkpoint, a huge tank swung round and forced them to stop. A soldier got out of a small Jeep beside it. He stood in the road with a rifle. His officer got out and came over to Michael and Charles, signalling to them to pull over to the road side. The tank gun turned to point at them.

'Why are you out so late at night?' asked the officer.

Frustrated, Michael explained that they had been checked and checked all the way there.

'You cannot go into the town,' said the officer, 'there is a 9 pm curfew. You will have to stay here.'

Michael's heart sank. They had been sitting in the Land Rover seats the entire day across the dusty desert, they had humped all their luggage in and out so many times they had nearly lost count, and now they were expected to stay sitting in the Land Rover for the remainder of the night. It was too much to bear.

'Can't you contact your officer on your radio and tell him what has happened so that we can get to our hotel?' asked Michael in desperation. 'We are going to the *Spogmai*.' This was the 'Moonlight' Hotel, where he had stayed before. He knew they would be welcome there.

'No,' said the officer, 'you must stay here, but I am going into the town. I will ask then.'

'Can't we follow you?' persisted Michael.

'Stay here,' ordered the officer, and went off. When he was clear, the tank started up again. It manoeuvred round and came towards the Land Rover. Michael's heart leapt as it bore down on them. He watched helplessly, thinking they were going to be crushed. Instead, the gun was lowered until it rested on the bonnet. They were trapped.

An hour later, the Jeep returned. 'You will follow us to your hotel,' ordered the officer, and gratefully, Michael started up the engine as the heavy gun swung away from them. As the tank rattled away, and they followed obediently, eventually reaching the *Spogmai* where the tank went on, and Michael turned into the garden forecourt.

It was not until he reached the front of the hotel and noticed that it was completely dark, that something jogged in his mind, and he remembered hearing somewhere that the owner had moved to another hotel several doors away.

Now he had a problem. Should he knock at this hotel at three in the morning and wake people he did not know, or should he risk turning out on the road again to find his owner-friend, and maybe meeting up with guns again? He looked around. The tank had gone, the road was deserted. He decided to risk finding his friend.

They backed out of the *Spogmai*, and drove three doors further down. The gates were locked and covered with corrugated iron, but Michael was sure it was the right one. He banged on it.

A moment later he heard a shuffling inside. Not wanting to bang again, Michael simply mentioned the name of the owner. 'Who is that?' came a voice.

'Michael - the Englishman,' he said eagerly. '*Ghirawallah* - the one with the beard.'

'Ah! I know,' the voice said, and the gate opened. 'Stay here,' he ordered excitedly, and ran off into the house. He returned a minute or two later, and said loudly, 'Azam[1] is not here, but you may come in.'

Michael and Charles were led in, and asked to wait in an inner room. Fifteen minutes later, the door opened and in walked the friend who was 'not there'. They greeted

---

1. not his real name

each other warmly, and Azam explained softly that there were unwelcome guests who might make trouble. He went on to say fearfully that the day before some of his friends and their wives and children had been killed, and the Mullahs were protesting. They wanted to be free to worship God, but the communists would not allow it.

When the two exhausted travellers finally lay down, they slept soundly, waking comparatively late the next morning. Their host gave them a good breakfast, and chatted with them while they ate. During the meal the newspaper boy called.

Azam told the boy to sit down, and then opened the paper. Out of it fell a small handwritten note which he read, shook his head, wrote on the back and handed it back to the boy, who put it in another newspaper.

When he had gone, Azam explained. Messages were passed from one to the other under cover of the newspaper. This morning, the shopkeepers had planned to protest about an order they had been given to drape their shops with red cloth. Some were going to defy the order and drape Islamic green instead. However, they learned that every shop not displaying red would be burned down, and putting out the fires would not be allowed. Then, if shops either side with red drapes were burned too, so be it. The protest had therefore been called off. It was too risky.

It was about this moment that Charles decided that he needed currency. Michael protested that it was too dangerous to go changing traveller's cheques, but Charles was insistent that he couldn't go home without taking gifts for his family.

Azam suggested that his servant could go on the errand, but he would need Charles' passport to take with him. Charles was horrified, and would not be separated from his passport, so he went himself.

On his very welcome return, he smiled broadly. 'It was

easy,' he said, 'everyone seemed so friendly towards me.'

Michael probed deeper. 'What did they say?' he asked anxiously.

'Oh, they were all very nice,' went on Charles, cheerfully. 'They asked me why I was here, and where I was going.'

Greatly alarmed, Michael spluttered, 'What exactly did you tell them?'

'Oh, I didn't say anything,' said Charles, trying to allay their fears. 'I said we were travelling to Pakistan.'

'Good,' said Michael, 'but did you tell them where you were staying?'

'Yes, I said *the Spogmai*.'

'Thank goodness,' breathed Michael. 'That's the wrong hotel! We would all be in danger if you had told them exactly where we are.'

It was time to move on very quickly. Their host would be seriously at risk if he was to be found harbouring them.

There were to be just two further incidents before they reached the end of their journey.

At a checkpoint, Michael was asked again for his papers, this time by two very scruffy looking Afghan soldiers. He showed them, but one said 'Visa.'

'That is my visa,' pointed out Michael in Pashtu.

'Visa,' said the soldier again, more insistently.

'This is the visa - look - can you not read it?' said the irritated Michael.

'What does it say?' asked the soldier in faltering English, and then Michael knew. The soldier must be a Russian dressed up as an Afghan, because all Afghans could speak either Pashtu or read Parsi. This soldier could understand neither. It was a great relief when the soldier gave up and waved them on.

They had no further trouble, except when Charles decided he needed more traveller's cheques changed when they finally arrived in Kabul. He had necessarily to pass the main square, and when he returned his face was white.

'What on earth's the matter?' said an alarmed Michael.

'They were all being shot,' he said, shaking. 'Many people - herded into the square - they were shooting them all.'

Badly shaken, they got out of the town as soon as possible and drove the last leg of their adventurous journey to Peshawar as fast as they could.

17. New Experiences

Arriving in hot, dusty Peshawar, with nowhere to live and no job to go to, seemed like entering the Promised Land to the two weary, stressed travellers after all they had experienced. Michael's first port of call would therefore be University Public School, to see if they needed one, or maybe two teachers.

As usual, Michael was welcomed since well-trained English teachers were few and far between in Pakistan, but not only that, he was asked if he would take the position of Boarding Master and therefore live in - just until Mary's return. The same offer was made to Charles for the duration of his stay, which would probably only be a month or so, and the two men accepted gratefully.

The innate Pakistani sense of humour soon vented itself upon the unwary Charles, who found himself on the receiving end of all kinds of jokes due to his inability to speak the boys' language. If he made the mistake of asking the boys the appropriate word for whatever he wanted to buy in the bazaar, he would inevitably find himself caught up in a struggle with a shopkeeper who would insist on trying to make him buy something he didn't want! Most embarrassing of all was the advice he got from the boys when he wanted to buy a present for Michael's friend, the Khan in Swat, who had invited them for a visit.

Charles thought that pomegranates would be a good and acceptable gift for the kindly Khan, and duly asked his students what the Urdu word was so that he could buy some. They told him the word for 'squash' - a kind of very common marrow which the Khan grew on his land and which he would harvest in cartloads! The unsuspecting Charles took himself to the market and came away with a large bagful of squash which the Khan eventually accepted with his usual grace and charm!

The time soon came for Charles to return to England, and when the University Public School closed for the summer, Michael went off for a refresher course at the language school at Murree for a time, looking forward to welcoming Mary and the girls when they returned from England at the end of July.

The plan was that since the schools in Peshawar closed for the summer, they would all go to Murree to enrol the girls in the Christian School, and then return to Peshawar when the schools reopened again in September, by which time they hoped to have found permanent accommodation.

Unfortunately they discovered that children could not be admitted as boarders until they were six-and-a-half years old, and Sarah was not quite six.

The Principal of the Christian school offered a solution. What did Mary think about helping them on the staff for a while? She could be allocated staff accommodation for herself and the girls, both of whom could then live with their mother instead of boarding, and then when Sarah became old enough they could both be admitted as boarders at the same time. This would go a long way to solving their problems, one of which was that as 'freelance' missionaries, the children's school fees could not be paid by a supportive missionary society, and so were beginning to be something of a burden. Mary's pay would go some way to helping in this respect.

However, it would mean separation from Michael when the University School reopened, but they decided that this couldn't be helped and they would content themselves with seeing each other for a weekend as often as possible.

The girls were happy to be back 'home' again in

Pakistan. They had loved their times with their grandparents in England, and it was fun to see all the wonderful shops and enjoy the luxuries of western living, but Pakistan was 'home', and they were glad to be back - especially with the brief reprieve from boarding, which was rather an unknown quantity.

However, their lives were to be not quite as peaceful as they had hoped.

Suddenly news came of an incident at the foremost Moslem holy place, the Mosque at Mecca, where many Moslems had been horrifically killed. An international outcry naturally followed and every advantage was taken to implicate the Americans.

Since Murree Christian School was American-based, the staff and children found themselves the object of possible recriminations. A guard was put around the premises, and all children and staff living out were obliged to travel to school with an armed guard. In addition, the school decided that every child must now possess their own passport rather than be included on that of their parents, so that should danger threaten, the school would be able to send each child directly to his or her home country without having to be dispatched to their parents first.

As it happened, the trouble died down, and the children were not threatened, but it highlighted the unstable conditions in which missionary children are brought up, and the sacrifice they, too, might have to make in order that their parents can be free to spread the gospel.

By Christmas, when Murree school closed for three months, Mary and Michael expected to return to Peshawar where they were to rent a small apartment near the University School. They arrived there to discover that the apartment was once again not ready for them, and that they subsequently had nowhere to live.

Immediately they were offered hospitality by their

friends from Chittral - the sugar farmers who lived in a small village some fifteen miles from Peshawar. Gratefully they accepted the offer on a temporary basis, since travelling to and from Peshawar on bumpy, difficult roads could not be undertaken for long. So for the next few weeks, the girls and Mary enjoyed the company of their friends, together with buffaloes, donkeys and heaps of sugar cane, while Michael tried to find them a permanent home.

Living in close proximity to their friends, Mary found it easy to share the gospel with them, and she was delighted when the family accepted a Bible in their own mother tongue of Parsi, and heard, some time later that the mother and daughters read it daily.

But this was not to be the only family who became interested to learn more about Christianity. As Christmas approached, Mary received a request to go next door and explain to the neighbours what Christmas was all about. One evening, therefore, she was led into a little open courtyard where the family were gathered to listen. They sat together under a starlit sky, and next to the stable where a donkey, buffalo and oxen were tethered. Here Mary told the story of God's own Son sent into the world, not to a grand palace, but to a manger in a stable just like the one in their own courtyard. The whole family listened spellbound, easily picturing the scene of two thousand years before.

But Mary knew that it would take many, many more visits before Moslems could become convinced that Jesus was alive and infinitely greater than their prophet, Mohammed.

Then on Christmas Eve, Michael found them a home. It would be impossible now to go back to living right inside the village as they had done before. The girls had formed a much greater understanding of their British heritage, and once they were installed at Murree School, their lives would become even more westernized. It would therefore be very unfair to place them back in a restricted culture. At the same time, Mary and Michael did not wish to cut themselves off from their friends in the village.

It was fortunate, therefore, that the house they had lived in before on the edge of the village, No. 1 Swati Gate, became vacant. It had since been divided into two separate apartments, and the landlord asked Mary and Michael if they would take one.

It was a little more expensive than they could afford, but after prayerful thought, and since it was the only option open to them, Michael took it that this was where the Lord wanted them to be. So on Christmas Eve, 1979, they moved back to Swati Gate. They were to remain there for the rest of their years in Pakistan.

In the following March, the girls began their first term as boarders at Murree. Unexpectedly, it was to be the shy, quiet Sarah who was to enter smoothly into the new experience. Ruth, the confident tomboy, found it threatening and traumatic. She was outspoken, brave and extrovert - just like her daddy - and the staff were at pains to know how to cope with her!

But at the age of ten, Ruth did not complain. In fact, Mary and Michael had no idea she was unhappy until some years later. It was due to her maturity and strength of character that she understood her parent's work would be jeopardised if they had to worry about her. She made it part of her own Christian commitment to suffer and persevere for the gospel's sake.

The incident at the Mosque in Mecca had left Pakistan under martial law. The army generals had always had great power and authority, but Mary was to find out that their influence became even greater now.

A two-and-a-half hour journey over the mountains from Peshawar was the town of Kohat, with its large army training centre. It was not a very popular posting with the army wives, however, since it was surrounded by tribal territory, and a long way from the more westernized cities of Lahore, Karachi or Islamabad.

The wives would complain that they were isolated and bored, and worse still, they had to remain in purdah in that Fundamentalist Moslem area. In the interests of a more satisfied personnel, therefore, the general in charge decided that a nursery for the younger children might help to give the wives a little more freedom.

Somewhere or somehow, he had heard mention of the name 'Montessori' in connection with excellence in nursery education, so he determined that he would find a teacher wise in the ways of the Italian educationist, Maria Montessori, who could train the army wives to run a model nursery school.

Mary, being the only western-trained woman teacher in Peshawar at the time and once more teaching at University Public School, soon attracted the attention of the general, and he came to question her with regard to her qualifications.

'Yes,' replied Mary, 'I do know about Montessori methods, but I am essentially a secondary school teacher and it has been a long time since I taught in an Infant school.'

Nevertheless, she was the general's only chance, and to know *something* of Montessori was better than nothing, so without more ado, the general gave an order to the Principal of University Public School.

For the next term, every Tuesday and Thursday, Mary was to be seconded by the army for the purposes of instructing the army wives in the setting up of a nursery school. A Jeep would be sent to collect her at six-thirty in the morning; she would teach at Kohat most of the day and be delivered home in the afternoon. The Principal had no choice in the matter, and he would continue to pay Mary's salary for the days she was not at school. He was obliged to co-operate because the general held the power. Any complaint could possibly mean a curtailment of any future career - or worse.

So for the next term, Mary's life included a new pattern. She would rise at the crack of dawn to be escorted to her job each Tuesday and Thursday, instructing the army wives in the finer points of water and sand play; the making of 'play dough' and the joys of finger painting; to return in the afternoon after a total of five hours' journey each day.

She enjoyed her time there, and at the end of the course was presented with a fine silver dish as a mark of their appreciation. But, Mary wondered, what might have happened if she had refused the general's request?

In the summer, Mary was obliged to uproot once more and go off to Murree. The Christian School had a strange system, but one which was no doubt beneficial to the children. Bearing in mind, in the first place, that it was better for the mothers to be up in the delightful warmth of Murree, rather than the intolerable heat of the plains during the summer months, they decreed that the children's usual boarding hostels would close for these months. Instead, the mothers were required to come to Murree, take up temporary accommodation - some of which could be supplied by the school - and receive their children to live with them instead of boarding.

Into this short time was packed all the events which normal schools put on for the parents - Sports' Day, concerts, second-hand clothes sales, prize-giving and even the Parent-Teacher Association meetings - all were condensed into a few months. The fathers could not be there, of course, as they could not usually leave their work, but they would travel the long journey to stay every other weekend or so, depending on the nature of their work and its distance from Murree.

The children loved this time of the year, and looked forward eagerly to having their mothers near and sharing in the fun of the summer. It was good, too, for the mothers, who could socialise together after their often isolated work away from their own nationals or English speaking friends.

At the end of the summer, when the girls went back to boarding, Mary would return to her teaching at the University Public School together with Michael, and they both continued their Gospel outreach as they shared ideas and took tea in the homes of the hospitable Pakistani teachers and pupils. But there was to be another excitement which the girls looked forward to in particular.

Now that Grandpa Bogg lived alone and did not have the responsibility of his invalid wife to care for, there was nothing to stop him going out to Pakistan to visit Mary, Michael and the girls. The fact that he was by now eighty years old and had never been out of England before did not deter him at all! Besides, it would be far more economical to pay the one fare for Grandpa to come to Pakistan, than the four fares for the family to fly to England.

So in November 1980, Grandpa arrived for a stay of around two months, acclimatising to his completely unfamiliar surroundings and strange food, before the girls came home for the Christmas holidays.

He loved the flight and his stay, having lots of fun with his little granddaughters, but he particularly enjoyed the unexpected honour he received from the local Pathan people because of his great age! In a country where sixty or seventy years would be quite old, he had only to mention that he was eighty, and ask to sit down for a moment in any of the fascinating little shops in the bazaar, to be instantly primed with tea and attention as to his welfare! Neither was he ever pressed for money or to buy anything he did not want! It was refreshing to discover that the Pathans venerated old age, and treated him like a king at every opportunity!

He was not so happy with the treatment he saw meted out to the little donkeys who carried such heavy burdens in the streets, or with the constant calls to prayer by the Mullahs in the mosques five times daily, and seeing the people bowing down in the dust to pray. He found all that very hard to bear.

He had also been rather worried when he caught a touch of 'flu and realised that with no health service, treatment could be sparse. It did not reassure him over much to point out that a western-trained doctor probably could be called for urgent cases, because even he would have to be paid for his services!

Grandpa's eyes were further opened when his daughter and son-in-law took him on a visit to the mission hospital at Bannu, a long day's journey over the mountains way beyond Kohat. The hospital was founded by one Doctor Pennell, a young, wealthy Victorian who had given up everything to become a missionary.

The large mud brick, comparatively luxurious house he had built for himself amongst the poverty of the surroundings still stands, and the present missionary staff still occupy it. The primitive hospital also still provides good medical care in spite of the lack of equipment and facilities. But Grandpa could not come to terms with the conditions under which the staff were forced to work.

The hospital was divided into two parts, the maternity department and wards set around a courtyard - muddy or dusty according to the weather - on one side of the main street of the town, while the men's wards were on the other side of the street. In addition, the spartan operating theatres were only to be found on the ladies' side of the road.

Therefore, whenever a man had to have an operation, it had to be performed on the ladies' side, and directly afterwards the poor patient would have to be trundled back on his stretcher to the men's wards - his drip or blood transfusion bottles carried or pushed alongside. The accompanying nurses would have to run the gauntlet of the traffic with their patient - bullock carts, cycle rickshaws, donkeys, lorries or cars, not to mention the weather and the crowds - all hurrying to their destinations! Grandpa made a mental note that he would never again complain about the long waits to be endured at the clinics in England.

When the time came for him to fly home, the girls were very sad. It would be a long time before they saw him again, but he promised that he would return to stay with them another time in the not too distant future.

They drove home unhappily, but worse was to come. They went into the garden to feed their pet rabbit, and found to their distress that he had died. Their tears flowed freely. It was too bad.

There were some workmen there at the time making the garden wall higher in accordance with custom, and they were very upset to see the two little girls so distressed. One of them went to Michael and explained that he had a friend with an English dog who had just had puppies. There were two female puppies for which it was difficult to find homes and did Michael think he would like them for the girls, to take the place of their dead rabbit?

Michael agreed readily, although they already had a male dog, and the two puppies were duly installed and quickly named 'Pinka' and 'Ponka'. It was made quite clear, however, that it would not be possible to keep both puppies for good - especially as they were both female, and that as soon as they had decided which of them would make the best pet, the other would go to another home.

So, true to their word, when Ponka was eventually judged to be the most affectionate pet because when called, she rushed to be petted instead of going straight to her dish as the unfortunate Pinka did, there were no tears. Instead, it was decreed that since Pinka had been Sarah's dog, she would now take over ownership of their existing male dog, 'Bhalu', (which meant 'bear'). Ponka proved to be a good choice. A time was to come when she would earn her keep in her new home.

In March 1981, after the girls went back to school, Mary and Michael were visited by a friend. The friend's skin glowed bright yellow, showing every sign of jaundice. However, he felt well, and reckoned that there was no reason for him to remain in bed. Two days later, Mary arrived home from school feeling ill. Before long she was too ill to stand and a diagnosis of hepatitis with pancreatitis was soon confirmed.

This time they were not able to call in a friendly medical student who could administer a drip for Mary, and she had to be subjected to daily painful injections. In addition, the Pakistani lady doctor forbade her to do anything - including reading or, she insisted, even *thinking*! Mary was to have complete rest, and must not worry her head about any problems at all.

At first she had been too ill to want to do anything, and it was only as she improved that the ban began to take effect. When Sarah and Ruth came home from school for half-term in April, they found a very poorly mummy lying on a charpai under the orange trees in the garden, trying to enjoy enforced relaxation. They did their best to fuss her and aid her recovery.

By the middle of April she was obliged to return to her teaching, although she was far from well, and as the doctor had encouraged her to go to Murree as early as possible this year, she made arrangements with the Principal to leave school at the earliest opportunity.

Once out of the heat and into the cool warmth of the hills, she began to feel better, and after a couple of weeks' rest, the inevitable call from the Christian school came again. They had children with special needs who would benefit from extra help. Often the children of missionaries missed out when they returned to their home countries on furlough with their parents, and would have to catch up on important work when they came back. Mary could help with this, and she began with a will.

The work went well, and Mary's contribution was appreciated by all. It was so well received that the Head Teacher asked if it would be possible for Mary to remain until December instead of returning to the University Public School in September. They had applied to America for another teacher, but there was no hope that he or she would arrive before the Spring. It would be a great help if Mary could stay at least until Christmas. She promised to discuss the proposition with Michael and that they would pray about it.

Teaching 'special needs' meant that Mary would not keep the regular school hours. Her pupils were required to attend normal classes at first in the morning, and then would have additional help later.

This involved Mary in walking alone to school from her accommodation, instead of with other teachers. For greater safety, she used to take Ponka the dog with her and leave her tethered to a tree in the school yard while she worked. The friendly little dog was well loved by the children, many of whom fussed her shamelessly at play-times.

But Ponka could show another side of her character if necessary. One afternoon when Mary was walking alone round the mountainside to her apartment, she saw a man approaching. He looked at her, and she instinctively clutched her handbag closer. The man did not turn away but came nearer. His eyes were on her bag, and he glanced around to see if they were alone.

As he took another step towards her, Ponka, a nine-month-old puppy, bristled. She stopped, stared at the man and gave a low growl. The man hesitated, but did not turn away. Now Ponka began to snarl menacingly, her tail erect and still, and her head stretched out low. With her eyes fixed on the man, she continued to growl and snarl. The man retreated and Ponka stood her ground.

Just at that moment, around the corner came two more teachers. The man fled, and Mary relaxed. Ponka had never had so much fuss made of her! Mary would never feel so vulnerable again while she had the brave little dog at her side.

After praying about asking to be released from University Public School for a few months, both Mary and Michael felt that it would be right for her to remain in Murree. Michael could argue that a Pakistani teacher could continue Mary's job in Peshawar for a while, whereas there would be no-one to take over her work at Murree.

It was therefore up to Michael, as the head of their household to discuss the problem with the Principal of University School. It came as a surprise, then, when the usually accommodating Principal refused. In fact, the refusal was so adamant that Michael was informed sternly that he should see to it that his wife obeyed him and returned to Peshawar immediately.

This tone of voice piqued Michael. No-one told him what he had to do, especially when it came to giving orders to his wife!

'I'm sorry,' he retorted, 'I truly believe that it is God's

will for her to remain in Murree, and beside that,' he continued equally sternly, 'Christian men do not make their wives do anything which is against their conscience.'

Now it was the Principal's turn to get angry. 'In that case,' he said, 'you can either order your wife to return, or you can consider your own job here ended too.'

There could be absolutely no chance of Michael succumbing to pressure such as this, and he informed the Principal that he would therefore leave.

He was sorry to have to leave, and the parents of many of the boys expressed their regret too. Although he never preached at his boys, there were those who had inquired about his Christianity, and some showed positive interest. It was sad to be leaving at a time when some were close to the Kingdom of God.

18. New Beginnings

In October 1981 it was necessary for Michael to find a job of some sort. Mary could return to Murree where she would stay for the whole of the Autumn term, but Michael could not remain at home without making some attempt to provide for his family.

He had long been hankering to help the boys who came from poor and crowded homes and did not have room to study. They had no books and no-one to explain their work to them. Maybe this was the opportunity to do something about it.

Very soon he had turned one of their rooms into a study, found some tables and chairs to put in it, and for a very small fee, boys came to do their homework in peace and quiet, but with the advantage of a teacher to explain what they needed to know. Some boys were disappointed to find out that Michael was not actually going to do their homework for them, but he soon set them straight!

One of the boys who came to him for help was an Afghan refugee called Saeed Noor - *Noor* meaning *Light*. Another descendent of Mohammed, he came from a well-to-do family, but they had been devastated by the war. Saeed Noor had been a second year medical student and his father an eminent judge in Kabul when the war began, but it had not been long before his father was arrested and thrown into prison.

The family had taken food and clothes to him, but were never allowed to see him. Then they were told not to bring anything any more. That could mean only one thing, and soon some prisoners who managed to escape confirmed that the judge had been shot.

Being a wealthy man, Saeed Noor's father had taken

four wives. Each wife had her own apartment and furniture, but such was the understanding and fairness of their husband, that all the wives got on well together and lived in harmony.

But the war ended all that. Some of their sons were killed in the fighting, and other children and two of the wives were shot when Russian planes strafed the streets with machine gun fire. In fear and desperation, the remaining two wives, three sons and several sisters escaped to Peshawar by walking for eight days over the mountains.

Saeed Noor now came to Michael to improve his English, but it was difficult for the family to afford the fee. As it happened, Michael's servant, Shah Nawaz had left to learn a trade as a tailor, and Michael himself could do with some help. So Saeed Noor became a kind of personal assistant - a position which would be more suitable to one who was high born - rather than the usual kind of servant.

Before the study classes began, Michael used to have an optional Bible Study for those who cared to come. Some of the boys would attend, and Saeed Noor was one of these. He listened avidly, and it was not long before he became a radiant Christian. When Mary and the girls came down from Murree they were delighted to meet the sensitive, charming young man, and he became a great favourite with them all.

But his story was not to have a happy ending. Many of the young Afghans felt obliged to return to their country to fight the communists, and Saeed Noor was no exception. It was only a couple of years later that he went off to serve as an officer in the Afghan army, and Mary and Michael were very sad to learn that after fighting courageously, he was killed.

In July 1981, the church in Pakistan decided that having just two dioceses for the whole country was not enough. In order to improve the situation, therefore, seven new bishops were created, including a Bishop of Peshawar. His diocese included the whole of the North West Frontier Province, a huge area. There was no cathedral, of course, but in Peshawar there was an excellent garrison church which had been built by the British in the days of the Raj. It was quite large, and would pass adequately as a cathedral.

So Bishop Khair ud Din, a quiet, godly man, married to an English wife, came to take up the work, aided by just nine ordained clergy for the whole area. He was in his sixties, and the job was hard and not a little dangerous in a diocese which included mostly tribal territory ruled by tribal chieftains.

He had not been installed long before he met Michael at the cathedral services, and heard about his work background. This was just the kind of person he needed to help with his administration of the huge diocese, and so it was that when the study centre closed down for the summer, Michael went each day to help the Bishop in his office by the cathedral.

In September, Michael intended to reopen his study centre, but the Bishop was alarmed. He could not envisage finding anyone else who could cope so well with the diocesan work. Whatever would he do without him?

Michael would be happy to remain, but the problem of money intruded once more. The Bishop was not able to offer a salary, and they had to earn their keep somehow. But the Bishop and Professor Michael Close, who had known Mary and Michael in their first days in Pakistan, were now involved in another educational project about which they had already formulated a plan. A well-paid job for Mary would probably leave Michael free to work for the Bishop.

The Bishop and Michael Close knew that the police force had long been piqued by the fact that the army and the air force both had schools for the children of their personnel. Apart from the fact that they enjoyed the prestige such a school engendered, it was also necessary to help the mothers left at home when their husbands were away on duty, since often they could not control their growing sons.

The Inspector General, Dil Jan Khan, whose name, appropriately enough, meant 'kind-hearted', was determined to do something about the problem. He concerned himself with the welfare of his men, and also with trying to stop the corruption which was rife throughout all layers of society. He had already dismissed some corrupt officers, although he understood the temptation to accept bribes when they were so poorly paid. He could not do much about that, but he could try to improve their lot in other ways, and maybe educate a whole new generation of boys. A school for the sons of the police was, therefore, long overdue, but since he intended that their school should be the best, he would, naturally, need a Western-trained former head teacher to set it up. Perhaps the Bishop of Peshawar would know of a likely candidate.

The Bishop did, indeed, know of a highly qualified lady teacher. He was sure she would be delighted to help out. It might also be of mutual benefit since a favour given would be a favour returned, and he could expect the police to assist his secretary, Mr. Cawthorne, as he travelled around on official diocesan business.

And so, with a little liaison between the Bishop, Professor Close in his capacity as educational advisor to the police, and the Inspector General, it was soon decided that Mary should be appointed to the position of Principal of the embryonic Police Public School, plus being made an honorary member of the police force with the exalted rank of superintendent.

A huge, new building was provided, together with a

large office and desk, but that was all. She now needed to arrange for appropriate furniture to be designed and made, since none could be bought ready made; she had to search for and buy all the equipment she would need; interview, train and appoint the staff, and design a uniform and school badge. Ruth came into her own here, for, as Mary could not draw, she called upon the services of her talented twelve-year-old daughter, and an excellent badge and uniform was the result!

Before long Mary had appointed her staff of mainly lady teachers, but also added four graduate police officers who were on loan from the police force to teach the subjects in which they had graduated.

The furniture proved more of a problem. It began well. Mary took into account the fact that the architect who had designed the building had included what he considered to be an inspired improvement on the usual dull flight of stairs between the floors. He had proudly included instead, a stylish, wrought iron spiral staircase.

So the eight science laboratory benches Mary therefore ordered, each with appropriate gas and electricity points, plus lightweight stainless steel sinks, could be made in sections and assembled in situ.

A craftsman was found, designs were made and promises of delivery were given. However, the first snag arose when it was discovered that the craftsman had 'improved' on the designs for the laboratory benches.

He could clearly see a much cheaper way of achieving the same results - he would, of course, not reduce the price to his customer, he considered the extra profit his due - so he altered the specifications. He would make four benches twice as long, and instead of the stainless steel sinks, he would substitute far more substantial glazed china clay sinks. He also forgot the bit about making them in sections.

When the huge benches were delivered, Mary could

see the problem straightaway. Apart from the fact that her entire male staff of twelve could not even lift one of the benches between them, she was forced to a wry smile as she looked at the spiral staircase.

She contacted the Deputy Inspector General for advice.

There was only one thing to do as far as he could see. He would send a coachload of police cadets, who together might be able to manhandle the monster benches up the spiral stairs.

It was some considerable time and effort later that the exhausted young men triumphantly achieved their aim. All that remained was to send for the recalcitrant craftsman to repair all the chips and cracks in the benches, plus the damage to paintwork, caused by his 'corner cutting'!

Mary hoped there would be no further problems, but she became increasingly worried when chairs for the lady teachers were not forthcoming. Several times she rang the shop manager, but although he assured her that everything was under control, still the chairs did not appear. In the meantime she learned that the manager had a grievance against the police, and that his delaying tactics were simply aimed at getting his own back.

Two days before the school was due to open, Mary rang her friend, the Deputy Inspector General once more.

That evening, when Mary returned from a ladies Bible Study she attended each week, Michael told her that there had been several frantic calls for her and she was asked to ring a certain number as soon as possible.

She could not help a tinge of smugness to discover that the manager had been imprisoned and would have to remain there until Mrs. Cawthorne gave orders for his release!

'Do you give your permission for his release?' asked the caller.

'Not until I get my chairs!' grinned Mary.

The next day the chairs all arrived promptly and soon after, police officers presented themselves in Mary's study together with their repentant prisoner, to ask if permission for his release could now be given!

The school proved very successful and received unexpected notoriety through its exalted connections with the hierarchy of the police force. Mary, as superintendent, often invited the Inspector General to attend the school's Sports Day or Prize Giving, and since he was such a public figure, the television cameras came too. What excitement there would be when she got home to find that some of her friends had seen her and the school on television! Mary herself never saw it - they did not possess a television!

Michael's work as the Bishop's secretary now went ahead most efficiently. In fact, so efficiently that the Bishop talked to Michael with regard to taking steps to secure the position on a more permanent basis. To this end, he suggested that Michael really ought to think about joining the Church Missionary Society.

Up until this time, it had been part of Michael's principles to be as self-supporting as possible, inasmuch as their minuscule Pakistani salaries would allow. He did not wish to be a burden to anyone, and included the established missionary societies in this view. However, the Bishop had a point, and although a missionary's pay would not be a lot, it would at least be guaranteed, and therefore very welcome. At the same time, it was becoming increasingly difficult to find the fees for Ruth and Sarah's education, and affiliation to a missionary society would help considerably.

As usual they prayed about the proposition, but it did not take long to agree that joining up with the Church Missionary Society would be a sensible and logical move - if the society would have them. Negotiations were soon begun, and before long they received a visit from the

Home Secretary of the Church Missionary Society. He extended a warm welcome to them together with temporary on-the-field membership until they went home for their next furlough, when they would need to go before the selection committee for official approval.

By December 1983 they had not been home since Mary's mother died five years before. The Police School were not too happy about losing Mary for a long furlough, but they eventually agreed to three months unpaid leave. Michael and Mary arranged to be back at the end of March ready for the new term in April.

This time they went home by air and, as required, met with the selection committee. The Church Missionary Society would have liked them to attend the usual compulsory term at their college in Selly Oak for three months, but as this was impossible, it was decided that the refresher course would be fulfilled on their next six month furlough. They were therefore accepted as 'Partners' - the term 'missionary' being now old fashioned, and the Bishop would become their Field Director.

From now on, the churches who had so faithfully helped to support them would send their gifts direct to the Church Missionary Society. But now it would include ten or eleven Anglican Churches who would help and watch their progress with interest.

Some of these they were able to meet during the furlough, and one of them was the church which Michael had attended when a child. They had asked to be linked with a missionary - a 'Partner' - and knowing the connection, the society readily agreed to them being linked with Michael and Mary.

Going home also gave Mary the chance to get treatment for the hepatitis which still had not completely cleared up. Gratefully she saw a doctor who soon saw to it that she felt much better.

Just before they were due to fly back, however, Michael's mother was rushed into hospital. She had an operation which was announced to be successful and given a clean bill of health. Michael and Mary went to say goodbye as she recovered in a nursing home, and then prepared for their flight back to Pakistan. They did not know then that this was to be the last time they would see her, for she died suddenly in 1984 while Michael was flying home specifically to see her.

He was just too late, in the same way that Mary had been just too late to see her mother. Michael was comforted, however, by a message left for him by his mother. It assured him of her faith and trust in God.

19. All Kinds of Help

Michael was now officially designated as secretary to the Bishop, and with a greater freedom to get to grips with the task ahead of him.

There had also been changes at home. By this time Saeed Noor had gone to fight in Afghanistan, sadly never to return, and Shah Nawaz, who could not manage completely on his tailoring work, returned on a part-time basis to help in their home.

Then Mary resumed her position as Principal of the Police Public School. She received a warm welcome from her staff and pupils, but an especially warm welcome from the school accountant. He offered her gifts - a sari, a box of fruit, flowers. Somewhat embarrassed, she refused them as politely as she could.

It was not until she got to looking carefully at the books that she began to suspect the reason for the gifts and to be extremely glad she had instinctively refused them. There seemed to be something wrong. Somehow she could not make the totals tally. Large payments of fees seemed to be missing.

Mary's first step was to call in Professor Michael Close. As educational advisor to the police perhaps he could see what had happened and give advice. He looked at the books and agreed with Mary that it looked like a case of embezzlement.

The next move was to call in two trusted police officer graduate teachers, and together they confronted the accountant. Immediately the man accepted that he had been caught. He pleaded for mercy and promised to repay the debt. However, Mary was now required to call the superintendent welfare police officer, who took the man away for a decision on his future. But Pakistan was still under martial law. The matter would have to be passed on to the military court.

As the court case approached, it became apparent that things had changed. The accountant had sought advice and the services of lawyers who responded to his 'gifts'. The case now took a sinister turn. They would try to prove that their client was innocent, and that he had taken the money at Mrs. Cawthorne's request and with her full knowledge. Now Mary was called to court to answer a countercharge.

The intimidating affair became a matter of prayer to all Mary and Michael's friends. The situation could be very serious. To begin with, bribery permeated every strata of society and there could be no automatic guarantee that justice would be done. Then there was Islamic Law. This decreed that the word of a Moslem was worth twice the value of a non-Moslem, and the word of a man was worth twice the value of a woman. A Christian woman, therefore, in any court case needed four times as many witnesses to speak up for her if she was to plead her case adequately.

In addition, nothing would be recorded as it would be under British Law, so no-one could really prove anything. Also, the accused accountant and his lawyers were allowed to sit through the entire proceedings, but Mary was obliged to remain outside, hearing only the part in which she gave evidence. The case was heavily loaded in favour of the accountant.

When the time came for Mary to be called in, the major asked her to take the oath on the Koran.

'I'm afraid I cannot do that,' said Mary, 'because I am a Christian.'

The major spoke to Mary in English, but to the court in Pashtu. As Mary spoke Urdu, she could not understand anything he said to them. He turned to Mary.

'Will you take the oath on the Bible, then?'

'I would prefer not to,' Mary risked, 'because it says in the Bible that we should not swear by heaven or earth or anything else. Your 'yes' should be 'yes' and your 'no' should be 'no', and that should be good enough. 'But,' she asked politely, 'would it be acceptable if I were to give you my word to speak the truth, the whole truth and nothing but the truth as a Christian?' she asked with a deep breath.

To her surprise, the major agreed. He then started to ask Mary lots of questions which had been given to him by the crooked lawyers of the accountant. Most of these did not seem to Mary to have any bearing on the case, so she ventured a question of her own.

'If you please,' she began, 'would you give me permission to tell you in my own words exactly what happened? After that I would be willing to answer any questions.'

Once again to her surprise, the major agreed, and Mary explained everything as clearly as she could.

Mary's case was further hampered by the fact that Professor Close had not been called as a witness. She was obliged to rely totally on her account being believed by the major.

Then the accountant was allowed to tell his story - while Mary was sent outside. She could do no more than wait for the verdict.

When it came Mary had yet another reason to praise God. The major had simply believed her story against that of the accountant. The man was sent to prison.

He remained there only about a month. Again, his bribes were accepted, and he was released.

By 1985 Michael had acquired three separate jobs in his capacity as secretary to the Bishop. Apart from the inevitable secretarial work, he also headed the work of the development office, dealing with all the buildings in the far-flung diocese, but in addition the Bishop had made him Headmaster of the English speaking section of the prestigious Edwardes' High School in Peshawar. This school had been set up in the early days of the Raj, and tried to offer a British education to poorer Pakistani boys.

Michael enjoyed the work, but found it impossible to cover everything he had to do. The Bishop frequently sent him around the diocese to check on buildings which, if unattended, might be looted or taken over by squatters, but this could take several days each time, and all the while his other work at Edwardes' High School was being neglected. He really needed someone to take over when he could not be there.

To this end he wrote a letter to CMS, the Church of Scotland, and the United Society for the Propagation of the Gospel, asking if they knew of any young men volunteers who would like to take a year out before going to University or immediately afterwards, and who would appreciate the opportunity of teaching in an English speaking school in Pakistan. He explained that he would value the help of any such young man who could look after the teaching while he travelled for the Bishop.

It was some time later when Michael's request had receded into nothing more than a fading hope, that Mary arrived from a morning at the bazaar with Ruth and Sarah, to discover a young man in the sitting room. He had been plied with tea by the cook during their absence and settled to await their return.

Mary was mystified. Young men appearing from nowhere unannounced and finding their way to Swati Gate were very rare, and as she greeted him she asked what had brought him there.

The young man was equally mystified. He had been teaching in Kashmir for six months, and due to trouble between India and Pakistan his visa had not been renewed.

The Church of Scotland had therefore directed him to help Michael in Peshawar for the remaining six months of his year out, and he thought that they would have long since informed Michael of his imminent arrival.

Michael had heard nothing, but received his helper, Will, gratefully. Before long Will settled into life in Peshawar, becoming a great help to Michael, and an elder 'brother' to Ruth and Sarah who would cajole, tease and talk him into taking them on outings at every opportunity!

Most of the time the family did not think much about the dangers of wild life which could lurk in and around their home. The children always had to be careful where they walked in the garden, of course, for scorpions were common, and Michael had been bitten very painfully several times. Small, deadly snakes might be found there too, but mercifully they would not attack unless provoked.

It was all the more terrifying, therefore, when Mary woke in the middle of the night to hear Ponka whining eerily, and making a half-bark, half-gurgling kind of noise. She knew immediately that something was wrong. Ponka was in trouble. She woke Michael to go and look. He went quickly to the verandah where Ponka spent the nights.

There he saw the little dog jumping up and down and keeping a three-foot cobra at bay. The deadly snake was raised up and displaying its distinctive hood in a threatening pose. Ponka sensed the danger and was managing to keep it from entering the house.

Quickly Michael picked up the nearest available thick stick and felled the cobra swiftly. In relief, Mary, the girls and Will petted brave little Ponka, without whom the story might have ended far more tragically. They were all shaken, however, and more than one of them took a look under their beds before getting back to sleep that night!

They were still nervous the next morning. Michael had been sent off for the day by the Bishop to one of the further outposts of the diocese and would not be home until late. He was not there to call on, then, when Will, still vigilant after the scare, spotted the end of a reptilian tail disappearing behind the fridge as they all sat down to a meal.

'Don't look now,' he began, his face draining of colour, 'but there's something scaly just going behind the fridge.'

Mary and the girls looked nervously. True enough, they could see the tip of the tail poking out ominously.

'Right,' said Will, taking charge in the absence of their regular intrepid hunter, Mike. 'Everybody out! I'm not a snake killer like Mike - we'll all have to keep out until he comes home!'

So, trying to be brave, they all moved out onto the verandah, and remained there nervously for the rest of the evening, hoping that the cobra in the dining room would stay where it was until their relief arrived.

Michael was welcomed more warmly than usual when he eventually appeared. They explained what they had seen, and stood back, waiting for him to go into action.

Their hero went into the dining room and, as four pairs of eyes watched from the safety of the verandah, with great care Michael moved the fridge. There, enjoying a rest in the shade was a small *gekko* - a harmless little lizard of the kind which often frequented houses!

A sigh of relief came from the verandah, but it would be difficult to live down the fact that they had all cowered, terrified, for a whole evening because of a small, harmless gekko!

It was very good to have Will to help in the work, but although the problem of cover for Michael was solved, it did not provide him with more free time. He still continued the three different, taxing jobs which no-one else could do, and Mary worked from seven in the morning until three or four in the afternoon. This meant that they spent less and less time together, and inevitably found themselves missing the companionship they had once enjoyed.

The problem was an all-too familiar one to missionaries, most of whom throughout the ages have found themselves pressured and with little time to build relationships with those they love. There never seemed any time to share their various problems, joys or sorrows, or simply to relax in one another's company. The problem spread itself into unexpected areas of their lives.

Their servant, Shah Nawaz was a great help to Michael who had known him since the lad was a boy of about thirteen. Michael had had many opportunities to share the gospel with him, and over the years a rapport had grown up between them. Now he became a companion on the necessary journeys Michael had to undergo throughout the diocese, since it was not safe even for a man to travel alone in the tribal areas of Pakistan.

In spite of the fact that Shah Nawaz was still officially in Mary and Michael's employ, the fellowship he and Michael enjoyed naturally changed from that of servant/master to that of friends, and Michael hoped that sooner or later the young man might come to know the Lord as his Saviour.

But a conflict inevitably began to arise when Mary asked the young man to do something.

He no longer considered himself to be the usual kind of servant, and Mary found herself treated in the same subservient way that Moslem men treated their womenfolk. The young man's position in the family had blurred, and he could no longer relate to Mary as an employer.

Sadly, there never seemed time for Mary to explain to Michael what was happening. They were always coming or going, and discussions were edged out. The situation became very tense and neither could understand the attitude of the other.

Eventually Michael was forced to decide upon a compromise. He did not wish to lose or alienate the young man, so decreed that his orders were the only ones Shah Nawaz need obey, his work being confined to the garden when not out travelling, and that Mary would deal only with her cook. This would hopefully keep him largely out of Mary's way and restrict the conflict. He hoped that the problem could be held at bay without it jeopardising his chances to influence the young man for the Lord.

The arrangement went some way to alleviate the situation, but it formed a barrier between husband and wife which might have been better solved by having more time to communicate and discuss mutual concerns. The missionary's three-way problem of the pressures of evangelisation, culture and overwork had taken its toll. It was to be several tense years before pressures of work eased and conditions relaxed giving them time to be together and rebuild their relationship.

Certainly, for the next three years or so, the house was to become so full of people that 'togetherness' took on an entirely different meaning.

In the summer Will's time came to an end, and he had to say goodbye. However, he had written to his school in Scotland and encouraged someone else to take over. So in August Douglas arrived, prepared for a stay of one year.

By this time Mary and the girls were all in Murree, so Douglas went straight there, and was delightedly greeted by the teenaged Ruth and Sarah. Handsome elder 'brothers' had excellent uses in a culture where females could not go out unprotected by a male, and he was instantly seconded to 'chaperon' not only Ruth, Sarah and Mary, but about a dozen of Ruth's admiring friends too!

But poor Douglas was to discover that escorting a bevy of young ladies had its disadvantages - especially when one of them was fluent in the language of the country and it was necessary to depend on her for communication when out together.

With their male escort, Mary and the girls could now visit a little restaurant in the 'Mall' - the main bazaar of the town. Often they would stop for a cup of tea on their way home or just for an afternoon's break. But the girls would inevitably be in high spirits and Ruth teased Douglas unmercifully.

It was during his first visit to the restaurant that Ruth could not resist the temptation to take advantage of him. He had asked Ruth to find out where the toilet was, and she duly spoke to the waiter.

What Douglas could not know was that she had not only asked the waiter to show Douglas to the toilet, but she also informed him that Douglas was very mad and would need careful watching! Poor Douglas could not understand why several waiters looked very strangely at him and waited nervously for him until he came out!

It was not to be the last joke played on the hapless Douglas, who endured all the practical jokes stoically, but there came a time when he was glad of the sheer audacity of his attractive persecutor.

The family's dogs also benefited from Douglas' advent for the two of them enjoyed a sudden burst of walk-taking! The dogs provided a measure of protection for the girls, since any brigand or thief would think twice about attacking if there might be the possibility of catching rabies from an angry dog.

However, when one day on the mountainside the two pets were in danger of attack from a whole pack of wild dogs, Douglas did not see what he could do to help.

The frightened girls looked at him for salvation, but sadly, Douglas did not consider one eighteen year old to be adequate odds against a snarling pack of dogs.

Suddenly, Ruth took control. If Douglas was not going

to do anything, then she would. She stepped out fearlessly towards the pack and demanded, 'Go away - in Jesus' Name!'

To Douglas' astonishment, and that of all the others - and probably Ruth herself - the pack of dogs obediently sloped off! Douglas looked at her in a different light from that time on!

By the end of September, Douglas understood not only what he was up against where Ruth was concerned, but he had got used to his new surroundings and the strange culture, and was ready to start work with Michael. It was now time for the girls to bid him a regretful goodbye and for him to return with Mary to Peshawar.

On arrival at Swati Gate, Mary was once more surprised to see another young man ensconced in her sitting room. She soon discovered that George had been sent by the United Society for the Propagation of the Gospel in response to Michael's request. They could not know that the Church of Scotland had already responded by sending Douglas, so now Michael had two helpers.

The two young men had hardly settled into their work before a young geology graduate arrived - also sent from the Church of Scotland. Alick was a postgraduate student, well qualified to teach at Edwardes' School.

This required a little reorganisation in the household arrangements. There was only limited accommodation in the house, so now Ruth and Sarah would have to share a room when they came home, and two of the young men would go into the room which had been Michael's study centre.

Although grateful for the help, Michael began to have trouble finding places for all the boys, but he did his best. It was something of a puzzle, therefore, when a week or two later, a fourth young man, Alistair, arrived on the doorstep! He turned out to be from a rival school to

Douglas', a fact which ensured much friendly competition - once the two lads in Michael's study room had squashed up to make room for one more.

By the time the fifth young man, Kevin Huggett - the son of Joyce Huggett the well-known Christian writer - arrived, Mary gave up and appealed for accommodation to Mr. Williams, the Principal of Edwardes' High School! Kevin was to remain in Pakistan for three years, staying at first with the Williams and moving into Swati Gate when all but one of the others had gone home.

But that was not to be the end of the stream of helpers. One more pushed the occupants of Swati Gate to the limit of available space. He was Rev. John Royds, an elderly clergyman who had also, before his retirement, been the Headmaster of a prestigious public school in England. He wanted to offer CMS a few years of service, and he was sent out to join the throng!

Now the study room held three young men, the room which had belonged to one of the girls contained the fourth, and John was placed in a little-used room at the back of the house! There were now four 'brothers' for Ruth and Sarah to tease when they came home from school, and they took every opportunity to exploit them!

Living in close proximity in a foreign culture, the boys had to learn to get along with each other, and Mary and Michael were grateful to John Royds who provided something of a stabilising influence on his young compatriots as they struggled to come to terms with each other's idiosyncrasies.

All four of the younger men were capable and willing, and the mix of different strengths, weaknesses and characters made for some lively discussions. However, Douglas was now able to put into practice something of what he had learned at the hands of Ruth, the practical joker, and the accident-prone Alistair became a likely target.

Alistair was the kind of unfortunate young man to whom accidents just seemed to happen! If he slammed a door, the glass would break, or if he boiled a kettle, it would blow up! He never intended such things to happen - the accidents just seemed to wait around for Alistair to turn up so that they could stage the spectacular in his presence!

He thought he had had a reprieve one evening when some friends of Mary and Michael's invited him to supper. During the evening there was the inevitable power cut. These were quite common, and everyone had a collection of strategically placed candles for use at these times. In the candlelight, Alistair took himself off to the bathroom, and returned minutes later to sit down for the meal. About an hour later, there was a spine-chilling crash from the bathroom.

Everyone rushed to see what had happened, only to find that a candle which Alistair had moved to a more convenient position below a glass shelf, had consequently heated up the glass to shattering point! All the toiletries which had been on it were spread liberally on the floor amongst the broken glass!

In spite of his reputation, Alistair was unconcerned about the inevitable approach of April 1st. In fact, he was so unconcerned that he was totally unaware when it arrived. The rest of the group were all set ready to stage their jokes and pitched in with a will.

First Alistair found his pyjamas sewn up. He took it in good part, but since he still did not realise the date, the group tried something else. When Alistair came in to breakfast, he found salt in his tea instead of sugar. Still he did not give them the satisfaction of knowing he had been 'April Fooled', so the jokes went on.

Gradually the time came for each one to leave for their respective work. Mary had left earlier for the Police

School, Michael and the Edwardes' School contingent set off in good time, and John Royds went off to the Bishop. Even the cook took his daily trip to the bazaar.

Unfortunately, all the tricks which had been played on Alistair made him rather late, and he was the last to leave. That is, he attempted to leave, for he came to realise that everyone else had gone and he was locked in!

The cook had been very efficient. There were no such things as 'Yale' locks in Pakistan, and security had to be assured by the use of padlocks. The cook had secured each of the doors, confining Alistair to his room and the verandah from which it opened. The verandah was also well covered by mosquito wire, so there could be no escape! Poor Alistair was mysteriously absent from school that day!

When the others came home they found him pacing up and down like a caged lion, and not a bit amused at the cries of 'April Fool!' It seemed to the rest of them that the best joke had been the one which they had not planned, but Alistair knew ruefully that the score was once again 'Accidents - 1, Alistair - 0'!

20. Anxious Times

It was clear after a few months that John Royds was not well. Michael arranged for him to see the mission doctor who suspected malaria, but there were some worrying symptoms which he felt ought to be properly investigated in England. This caused something of a problem because John had come out to Pakistan at his own expense to serve CMS, and had even bought himself a small Suzuki car to help his work. Now it was felt necessary that he should be flown home, and it would be too expensive to take his car with him.

The problem was solved in a typically generous way. John had noticed that Mary often needed transport to get to her school and frequent meetings, and that relying on public transport or others to ferry her around could be very frustrating. His answer was to leave the car with Mary, bearing in mind the distinct possibility that he would never be back to Pakistan to claim it again. Mary was overwhelmed by his generosity, and gratefully accepted the gift which would substantially change her life. So for the first time in all her years in Pakistan, Mary found herself with independent transport just at the time when women were becoming accepted as drivers in the restrictive society.

The news which finally came out from England regarding John Royds, was at first not good. He was diagnosed as having leukaemia and tuberculosis, and underwent extensive treatment. However, prayers for his recovery were answered and Mary and Michael were thrilled to hear some time later that the leukaemia had been cured, and although some of the tuberculosis remained, he eventually went on to serve on the staff of Salisbury Cathedral.

Mary began to enjoy her new state of independence. She already possessed a British driving licence, although the restrictions on women had never allowed her to drive in Pakistan before. If she had not held a licence, however, there would probably not have been too much difficulty in getting one.

Being British, her qualifications would undoubtedly be accepted without having to complete the written question paper supposedly necessary, but in fact everyone knew that any kind of official document could be obtained by offering an appropriate bribe. From driving licences to University degrees, all could be easily acquired with money.

Kevin Huggett had applied for a licence to drive the diocesan motor bike soon after he arrived. He had gone to the authorities, but since he was British and looked an honest young man, he had only been required to answer one question. He was asked, 'What would you do if you approached a traffic light which showed red?'

Answering this correctly, he was then presented with a licence which allowed him to drive not only a motor bike, but a car too!

After the arrival of the band of young men helpers, visits to the Rest House at Gala by the Tarbela Dam became a particular treat. As it was only supposed to be for family use, Mary and Michael did not think they could take more than two young men at a time, so a strict rotation had to be insisted upon.

It was therefore decided that for the 1986 visit, since Alick had finished his year of secondment and was about to return home, he would be allowed to go to Gala with George, whose turn came next, and the rest of the Cawthorne family.

But as a farewell party had been arranged at Edwardes' School for Alick, he could not travel earlier on the Friday with Mary, George and Sarah. Instead, he, Michael and Ruth, who had been helping Michael in the school office, would travel later after the party. Mary packed the little car with food and supplies which they would need for their weekend stay, then in piled George, Sarah and Ponka, and off they went.

On arrival they found that although the house had been pre-booked, someone was already there. Mary spoke to the cook whom they knew from past visits. Apparently the Frontier Constabulary had commandeered the house together with all the other available guest houses in the area. Something very secret was going on.

Now what was Mary to do? She had no way of contacting Michael or the others, and in an hour or so they would all be arriving, expecting a meal to be ready for them. Just as she was wondering what to do next, the Frontier Constabulary Officer came in.

He recognised her immediately as the Principal of the Police Public School, and listened as she explained the dilemma.

'Well, I am only occupying half the house,' he told her, 'and providing you will promise not to let anyone know what we are doing, you are welcome to stay if you can manage with the reduced accommodation. I will be out most of the day, so will not disturb you.'

Mary agreed readily, and later when Michael arrived, he too, was recognised, and the officer explained what was happening. It seemed that a previous Governor of Peshawar had waged war on the growing of illicit opium, and had sent the army in to destroy all the poppy fields in the Jamrud area near the Khyber Pass. The intention had supposedly been to replace the poppies with other acceptable seed and try to reduce the drug trade.

However, the action had not been as righteous as it had seemed, for everyone knew that the Governor himself had poppy fields which earned him vast amounts of money - most of it stashed away in bank accounts in America - and the fields he had destroyed had simply been those of his rivals. In the process he had also killed or injured a lot of tribal people.

The officer explained that now the Governor had been deposed, the Police could step in. A very careful campaign had been planned which included police being stationed in every spare nearby house, and now the day had come when all the ex-Governor's poppy fields were to be destroyed.

So it was that Alick and George became the envy of their fellows when they returned after the weekend to describe the exciting 'cloak-and-dagger' operation for which they had been sworn to secrecy - the vow lifted now that the event was over, of course - and they delightedly described the blazing poppy fields and the ensuing mayhem seen from the safety of the other side of the dam.

By now Mary had already given notice to the Police Public School that she would be going home for six months furlough in 1986, and that when she returned she would need to work with the various diocesan schools, all of which needed a lot of help.

By rights she should have been working for CMS since coming under their auspices, but they had agreed that she should not leave immediately but give plenty of notice to PPS. So Mary began to wind up her work at the school, and prepare for the coming furlough.

Meanwhile, a major change approached in Ruth's life. After her end of year examinations in May she would need to leave Murree Christian School and return to England for sixth form college or university, since she needed 'A' levels not offered by the school.

So following discussions with CMS it was suggested that when Mary and Michael came home on furlough, they should look at King Edward's School in Surrey, a highly recommended school for which CMS would be prepared to pay two-thirds of the fees. Mary and Michael could cope with the remainder from a trust fund left by Michael's mother specifically for the education of the two girls.

The coming furlough was planned to be something of an event. The girls were anxious to take the overland route, and so see the sights which they could hardly remember from their last overland trip when they had been very little. Michael always enjoyed travelling overland, so planned it eagerly.

At the same time, Will, who had been their first volunteer but had gone home some time previously, had contacted them when he learned of their plans. An overland trip was something he had always wanted to do, so he asked if Michael would take him along as a co-driver. If so, he would fly out specially for the trip.

There was just one problem. The Iranian border had now been closed to tourists, but there had been some talk of it being opened again. Michael planned optimistically. He applied for the appropriate visas and waited.

As it was no longer safe for them to sleep in tents, some time earlier he had also exchanged the Land Rover for a Volkswagen Camper Van for the journey. Will arrived and everything was packed.

A week before they were due to leave, the visas had still not arrived. Michael pestered the authorities constantly, but was always told that 'they were being processed'.

It seemed strange because Will had received his visa with no problem, so it could not be that the borders were closed. Now Michael went to Islamabad to see the Inspector General who had been Mary's police chief when she worked at Police Public School. He was now a member of the government as Minister of the Interior. He knew both Michael and Mary well, of course, and tried his best to find out what the problem could be.

Another string to Michael's bow was the British Naval Attache´ whom he knew well because of his naval connections. Both men tried to acquire the vital visas, but eventually were forced to report to Michael that no visas were being issued to anyone connected with the church. Tourists were allowed them, but as Michael and Mary's occupations stated 'Diocese of Peshawar', they would not be granted a visa.

There was just one slight chance left. The authorities in Quetta, near Karachi in the south, might give them a visa there if they explained that they would only be travelling through.

So during the worst weather of the hot summer, the van set off with its occupants to drive the first leg of their journey to Quetta. They were to remain there for several days trying desperately to persuade the authorities to grant the visas, but finally they had to admit defeat. Without the visas, there could be no overland journey.

All Michael could do was to arrange for Will to join another group travelling overland, and they parted sadly.

But then he was obliged to sell the camper van and store all their belongings with a Christian family living in Karachi until they could retrieve it all again. There followed a further two week's wait in Karachi in stifling weather until an appropriate flight to England could be arranged.

In spite of its inauspicious beginning, the furlough proved to be a successful time on all counts. Having seen King Edward's School, Sarah asked if it could be possible for her to begin there with Ruth, instead of waiting the remaining couple of years until she reached the right age for leaving Murree. A shy girl, she would feel more confident if she had the support of her sister, since by the time she reached the usual age of transfer, Ruth would already have left. CMS agreed, and the arrangements were made.

Then there was much deputation work to do for CMS as Michael and Mary travelled around to the various churches who were supporting them, this time in and around Bradford. This would be the first time they had met this group of churches and they built up a mutual appreciation and understanding of each other.

Then there was also the term to be spent at Selly Oak on their missionary 'Training' course. Michael loved this time, particularly because he had never had the opportunity to go to Bible College before. Now he could spend the one term doing Biblical Studies and Mission Studies for his own enjoyment and edification, plus the joy of having fellowship with other colleges round about - of which there were several.

They both enjoyed sharing some of their experiences with the students, and explaining what it was like to be a missionary in the twentieth century. They emphasised the importance of being a 'Mission Partner' and not a missionary in the old sense, pointing out that nowadays Pakistanis do not expect the expatriates to behave like officers of the British Raj, giving them orders, but to share in the work - as 'partners'.

In addition, they reported gratefully, the Overseas Personnel Department of CMS was excellent. It took a great deal of trouble to care for the Mission Partners, providing all the help, advice and counselling they could possibly need.

They both testified to the continued support received since joining CMS and spoke of the high regard in which they held the organisation.

In September the girls would start the first term at their

new school, and Mary was glad that she would be on hand to see them settled in before having to return to Pakistan in January 1987. She could also take time to find an appropriate person who could act as guardian to the two teenagers in the absence of their parents. A couple whom Michael had known from his West Runton Camp connection lived a mile or two from the school, and they generously agreed to take on this important task.

The final half-term before the end of the furlough was to be specifically for the two girls' benefit. There would only be one more short weekend before their parents returned to Pakistan, and it would seem a long while before they were to meet again. So Mary and Michael wanted to give them a time to remember.

First they went to Chard where they stayed on a farm which they had visited when the girls were very young. They all had a lovely time relaxing together in the peace of the countryside before going on to Stratford-upon-Avon where they saw *Romeo and Juliet* performed in modern dress at the Shakespeare Memorial Theatre.

The final weekend after Christmas proved to be somewhat traumatic. In spite of the fact that the sixteen year old Ruth, and thirteen year old Sarah had spent a lot of time in boarding school in Pakistan, they were all aware of the vast distance which would be between them until the next holidays. Pakistan was essentially the young sisters' home, and they would be far from it for a long time. It was true that CMS would pay for the girls to have two holidays in Pakistan during each school year, but the long times between would seem endless to begin with. Mary, especially, who had spent the summer months of each year at Murree with the girls, knew that she would find the parting traumatic.

When the time came, they parted tearfully, the separation proving to be a great wrench, and they covered it with promises to write regularly. The return flight was a sobering, reflective journey and not as optimistic as former flights had been.

In spite of their natural anxiety for their daughters, Mary and Michael fell back into their work in Pakistan, refreshed from the furlough.

Mary would now begin working with the Christian schools of the diocese, all of which had been instigated at the time of the Raj, and were largely ignored now by the Moslem authorities; and Michael returned to his work with the Bishop and as Head of the English section of Edwardes' High School - but now his job was officially recognised.

Mary had originally thought she would be working at Elizabeth High School For Girls, the equivalent prestigious school to Edwardes', but instead, she was contacted by the Finnish Mission who also did a lot of work in the diocese.

Their missionary who had been looking after the church schools for poor Christians was going home on furlough, and they wondered if the Bishop would appoint Mary as co-ordinator of these schools. All the schools were in poor condition and needed upgrading, and although the Finnish Mission were willing to finance improvements, they needed someone with educational experience and qualifications as a Head Teacher to lead the work.

It was also suggested that as tolerance to expatriates was tenuous, it would be necessary to train up a Pakistani teacher to take over the work in case missionaries should become eventually unwelcome.

So Mary found herself suddenly busy with five schools for poor Christians to oversee, plus helping occasionally with Edwardes' and Elizabeth's High Schools, Edwardes' College and another school further south over the mountains near the hospital at Bannu.

In addition, the Finns and the United Dutch Reformed Church had been instrumental in starting a training college in Lahore for Christian teachers from all over Pakistan, and it was not long before Mary and her assistant were asked to run some training courses for the students. Their involvement with the college later increased to helping with refresher courses for teachers already in service, and also helping to assess teaching practice. Mary particularly enjoyed helping with teacher training, especially in the very valuable Christian college.

The usual system allowed just two places at any state training college for students from the minorities - Christians, Hindus and others, and since most Christians could not afford a public school education which would give them top examination marks, there was very little chance of getting into a college at all. The Christian Teacher Training College, therefore, provided a lifeline for those who would otherwise have no opportunity of becoming a teacher - but teaching skills were not all the students learned.

The general attitude of the Moslem population towards Christians left them with a very low self-esteem, and many had to discover a new awareness of their own worth before they could take their place as leaders. They would never before have had to give orders, but only take them, and all this had to be reversed if the teachers were to develop successfully.

Little by little, the staff built up in the students a confidence in their own ability, and they loved to see the young people blossoming into self-assured and mature teachers able to pass on their new-found confidence to their pupils. Mary considered this to be arguably one of the greatest services given by the missionary societies to the poorer people of Pakistan.

One of the schools apportioned to Mary was at Mardan,

some fifty kilometres from Peshawar. It was supported by a Danish Mission Society, who also supported the nearby technical training centre and the Chapel of the Corps of Guides.

This chapel had become famous through the writings of M. M. Kaye in the novel *The Far Pavilions*, and most of the incidents and places described in her novel were based in and around Mardan, where her husband, the Officer-in-Charge of the Corps of Guides was stationed.

The assistant whom Mary appointed to train into the work was Mrs. Talat Peters who was the daughter of an unusually well-educated Christian family. She had spent most of her childhood in Lahore where she learned to speak excellent English, going on to gain a Masters degree in Maths and to become a Bachelor of Education.

Most of the Pakistani teaching methods were totally antiquated. They consisted mainly of teaching from a book which the teachers first, and then the children were expected to learn by heart. Mary and Talat, like the excellent Finnish missionaries before them, aimed to change all this, showing their teachers a new way of presentation which involved originality and self-expression. Many teachers and students were amazed at the idea of making lessons *interesting* to the children! It had simply never occurred to them before that such a thing could be possible! Mary and Talat showed them how to make visual aids including charts and pictures, and how to bring drama and vitality into their lessons. The work was not always readily accepted. Many would rather take the easier option of learning the book and repeating it 'parrot-fashion'.

Michael did not find his work quite so satisfying. He increasingly found himself travelling around the diocese reclaiming properties which had been taken over by squatters or vandalised.

Before the new generation of Bishops had been appointed, it had been quite impossible for the former two Bishops to oversee all the properties handed over to the church by the British Raj. Consequently, many of them were considered by the local population to be abandoned and therefore fair game, and had been looted, used as cattle sheds, taken over in some other way or simply left to deteriorate.

It was now Michael's job to reclaim the lost properties and try to put them to rights. It often involved him in rebuilding them himself, sometimes with a little local help, but in the meantime his more interesting work teaching at the school had to wait.

And then a more sinister situation arose which threatened to split the diocese.

Some money had been sent to the diocese for a specific use. When a representative later arrived to inspect the project, no work had been done and no trace could be found of the donation. Only two people could possibly have had access to the money, and the people of the diocese began to take sides. Michael, being closer to the situation than most, was convinced of the innocence of one of the two, and felt naturally obliged to defend him. It was to place him in a very difficult and uncomfortable position.

At the same time, the Bishop was approaching the age of retirement, and there were those who thought he should retire in favour of a younger man. However, Pakistan supported no adequate pension schemes, and unless one had private means, retirement held a grim prospect. The diocese began once more to fall into two camps, and its former unity disintegrated into controversy.

And then, amid all this, Michael and Mary heard disturbing news from England.

It appeared that a house mistress in Sarah's section of

the school had been teaching the girls about animal rights, with the consequence that many of them became vegetarian. This would have been fine if the girls had been registered officially as vegetarians and could receive a properly balanced vegetarian meal, but instead they simply dropped meat and animal related products from their diet. This left them with a meagre diet deficient in protein and unenhanced by extra vegetables. The result was that now Sarah had become very thin, and her guardians, horrified at the minute quantity she ate, feared that she might be anorexic.

Mary's instinct was to get home to Sarah as fast as possible, but the cost of the flight was prohibitive, and anyway, it would not be very long before Sarah was due home in Pakistan for a holiday.

When she arrived, Mary and Michael were horrified. Sarah was indeed very thin and white-faced. There could be no doubt that she was not eating enough, but she claimed vehemently that she was not anorexic. Someone whom Sarah would trust needed to talk to her, and Mary thought she knew the right person.

As it happened, Sarah was due for a checkup on a minor operation she had had some time before, and so Mary arranged for her to go to the hospital at Bannu. The surgeon there was the highly-esteemed Ruth Coggan, the daughter of a former Archbishop of Canterbury, and a good friend of Michael and Mary. She gladly agreed to have a talk with Sarah.

Her findings were that Sarah was a 'borderline' anorexic, and Ruth Coggan told her clearly about the use of protein and vitamins and why she must make sure of having a good, balanced diet. Sarah was responsive, but her health was to remain a matter of concern for the next two years.

21. Doors that Open - Doors that Close

Ruth seemed to be the only member of the family whose problems were few. In fact, she had only one - large though it loomed - the need to raise £1,800 for a very special project.

She had seen an announcement in the National Geographic Magazine saying that there was to be a British Schools' Exploring Society Expedition to the Himalayas, and that young people eligible could apply for a place on the team.

Ruth's heart leapt. She had spent a lot of her time at Murree looking out at the hills and wondering what it would be like to explore them properly, but she had never had the chance. Perhaps now ....

She looked at the closing date on the advertisement. Her bubble of enthusiasm burst. The date had passed a week or so before. Nevertheless, she wrote to the organisers, telling of her background, pointing out that she was studying Geography at 'A' level and that such a trip would be invaluable to her course. She also mentioned that she could speak fluent Urdu into the bargain, and begged them to consider her application if possible.

After a very comprehensive interview, the reply was that the places were full, but that she would be added to a reserve list. Since it was inconceivable to Ruth that anyone would want to pull out of such an experience, she was astounded and delighted eventually to receive a letter informing her that she had been allocated a place on the team. However, to take it up, she had to have the backing of £1,800 in addition to buying her own equipment, and once more, her bubble of enthusiasm was pricked.

It took her some time to raise half the required sum.

She saved all she could from her allowance, and was given some help by various relatives, and then, just when she thought it would be impossible, she was amazed to see a new entry in the credit column of her bank statement. Someone had paid in more than half the amount she needed! She never found out who the anonymous donor was. She could only be profoundly grateful and make sure she put it to good use.

The expedition was everything Ruth had hoped. The Himalayas were every bit as wonderful as she had thought, but in addition, the Geological group of which she was a part were exhilarated to discover two previously uncharted lakes which would be reported to cartologists for inclusion on future maps.

However, when in the region of Ladakh on the border of Tibet, she found herself profoundly disturbed by seeing the people worshipping idols. Even in Pakistan the people were monotheistic - although they did not accept the work of Jesus Christ in taking the punishment for the sin of the world. But she had never before come across anyone who actually bowed down to inanimate idols. The impression upon her was very great, and from that moment she determined to go into full-time Christian service as soon as God opened an appropriate door.

The expedition company included more than twenty Indian students who, although Hindi-speaking, discovered they could adequately converse with the Urdu-speaking Ruth. It was not surprising, therefore, that she made friends with them all, and was willingly included in their trips to the local bazaars where they tucked into hot, spicy curries which the rest of their English colleagues were too nervous to try!

The climax of the tour was a television appearance in Delhi, when a few of the group were interviewed by the Indian Prime Minister at the time, Rajiv Gandhi. Ruth was naturally chosen as one of the spokespersons for the English contingent, and she was delighted to receive compliments as to her excellent Urdu with its absence of any foreign accent! The happy memories of the trip were later to be tinged with sadness when Rajiv Gandhi was assassinated in 1991.

In spite of the difficulties besetting the diocese of Peshawar, there were some encouragements. The village where Mary and Michael had lived amongst the people for three years, now sported a small, struggling group of Christians who were meeting in one of the houses. Also, to their great joy, Moslems for whom they had been praying for a long time were beginning to openly confess Christianity, and thoughts of a church building began to be discussed.

The group of new Christians included a family who had become some of Mary and Michael's dearest friends. The mother and her daughters had been reading the Bible for a long time, and were now believers, and although such a radical profession of faith might mean extreme hardships for the family, even the father began to show interest. They wanted to join a church fellowship, but at this stage they preferred a lower key venue than that of the cathedral. Mary and Michael recommended them to the little fellowship in the village, and they were subsequently able to attend sometimes.

On the occasions when Michael was not travelling around the diocese, he tried to catch up with his paper-work in his office beside the cathedral. To his surprise, one day a military jeep drove quietly up the drive and its driver got out and looked around nervously. Satisfied that he had not been seen, he went into the office, and asked if Mr. Cawthorne was alone. Michael indicated that he was Mr. Cawthorne and that he was, indeed, alone. The driver then went back outside and opened the door of the jeep for his passenger, an officer in the Pakistani Army. Again, glancing around, the officer went into the office, and took a small Bible from his pocket.

'I would be grateful if you would explain this passage to me,' he said. 'You know that I am not allowed to mix openly with Christians, but when you are alone sometimes, would you mind if I came to ask you about some of these things?'

Michael assured the captain that he would be delighted to discuss the Scriptures with him, and from that day on, from time to time the military jeep would appear, and the officer would slip discreetly into the office with his little Bible.

There was another completely unexpected surprise for Michael and Mary in January 1989.

They had often thrown out invitations to the folk from their various supporting churches over the years, assuring them that if anyone would ever like to visit them in Pakistan, they would be greatly welcomed. So far, in the eighteen years of their work, no-one had ever taken them up on the offer.

Now, suddenly, a couple from the Tankerton church asked if they could come. It was an exciting time for them all as Mary and Michael gave David and Helena Rogers an overview of their work, from visits to each of Mary's five schools for poor Christians; Edwardes' High School, and the cathedral, where David was asked to preach at the early Sunday morning services; the hospital at Bannu, and to some of the schools and buildings which Michael looked after.

They were totally unprepared for what they saw. The drastic change of culture was to profoundly influence their future attitudes and thinking as they saw the conditions under which Christians were not only living, but *pleased* to live. They humbly expressed that their attitude towards possessions must now be permanently affected, and would necessarily influence how they conducted their lives when they got home.

A highlight of the tour was a visit to a school for handicapped children which was in one of the buildings for which Michael was responsible, but where Mike and Christine Miles of CMS were the experienced missionaries in charge of the project. David and Helena were shown the workshop where callipers and various other aids for weak limbs were made.

As they watched, a young man produced a calliper for a five year old boy out of odd bits of metal and pieces of cast-off perspex. Then they watched awestruck as the little boy, who had never yet stood or walked alone, patiently submitted to the calliper being strapped to his leg, and was lifted to his feet. The visitors watched with bated breath as he took his first ever few steps holding the hand of a teacher, and then they gasped as he let go and walked alone before tottering and being caught by willing hands. His joy was great as the whole company applauded his efforts with cries of '*Shah bash! Shah bash!*' - 'Well done!'

As a former Head Teacher herself, Helena gazed in disbelief at the total lack of what schools in the West would consider essential equipment, and they both stood in silent wonder at the hardships suffered by Doctor Ruth Coggan and her staff at the Bannu hospital, as they struggled to care for patients and perform operations with minimal equipment in appalling conditions.

The visit was mutually beneficial to both parties. The Rogers' commented to Mary and Michael that in their opinion if every Christian in the West could spend a little time in countries such as Pakistan and be similarly challenged, the momentum of the consumer society would probably change overnight!

From Michael and Mary's point of view the visit was an expression of care from their supporters, and they appreciated the fact that someone from their home church had taken the trouble to make the long, expensive journey just to stay with them and take an interest in their work.

It was also good that the Rogers' were able to take first hand impressions back to the people in England, together with a video film which could be passed around the churches.

Mary's father was now nearly ninety and finding it difficult to look after himself alone, especially as cataracts rendered him almost blind. He was grateful for Ruth's help for a time when she left school to go to Canterbury college to take a course as a Personal Assistant, but the problem remained on Mary's mind.

At the end of her course, Ruth got an excellent job in London, and continued to live in the upstairs flat of Grandpa's house from which she commuted to London each day. During this time she very efficiently saw to all the arrangements which enabled Grandpa to go to Tunbridge Wells for a cataract operation by the same opthalmologist whom Mary and Michael had known in Pakistan.

After the operation, Mary went home at her own expense to visit Grandpa and see that he was all right, but at the same time she was able to take Sarah to interview for the sixth form college at a school in Canterbury. When CMS heard this, they decided that this was a necessary visit, and refunded her fare. It was another example of the very caring ethos of CMS.

It was also necessary for Sarah to have another guardian since she lived now in the Canterbury area, and a friend from the Tankerton church, Ruth Peevit, who had been a missionary and a school house mistress, kindly agreed to take over.

But in 1990 Mary and Michael were due for their official furlough, and it was to spark even more radical changes.

They decided to go on a week's course on the use of drama in worship run by the 'Riding Lights' drama group, based at Scargill House Christian Conference Centre in Yorkshire. Michael found himself particularly interested because he had taught the two founders of the group, Paul Burbridge and Murray Watts, to climb during West Runton Camp holidays. Since it was in holiday time, both the girls came, but as Ruth had had one or two disappointing experiences in relationships previously, Mary prayed that she would perhaps find a young man with whom she could relate in friendship - at least for the length of the course.

By the end of the week, Mary had to admit that there had been no answer to her prayer. However, on the last night, the team leaders invited one or two of the younger members of the group to a final evening out.

To her surprise Ruth discovered that one of the young men had, like her, spent a lot of his school days in boarding schools as his father was in the RAF, but he was now about to move to Blackheath, near London, to train as a Church Army Officer. Since he knew no-one in the south, and Ruth would be travelling to and from London each day, they agreed to meet again.

Just before Mary and Michael returned to Pakistan, the young man, Roy Hollands, spent a weekend with them all in Tankerton, and it was no surprise to Mary when several months later, Roy asked Michael's permission to marry Ruth. Once more, God had more than answered the prayer from an anxious mother.

When the time came to return to Pakistan, Mary found herself leaving with some anxiety. Her father may have been able to see rather better, but she was not at all confident about his ability to look after himself now. She tentatively suggested that she would feel happier if he went into residential care, but the old man was fiercely independent and quite naturally preferred his own home.

She was therefore obliged to leave him, having arranged for various friends to call in from time to time to make sure he coped, and assuring him that she would return immediately if he really needed her.

But anxiety now spread to Pakistan as the Gulf War took hold. To begin with Pakistan entered the war on the same side as Britain, but declared that they would not fight against fellow Moslems, so would take the stand of a peacekeeping force. However, many Pakistanis were not happy with this situation, and it was eventually decreed that if Israel retaliated to the missiles sent over by Iraq, then Pakistan would change sides. All this had repercussions for the expatriates who became targets for abuse.

A butcher was in the habit of setting up his shop directly outside Mary and Michael's house in Swati Gate. The 'shop' consisted of a three-sided shed and a tree trunk 'table' where he would chop up the meat, hanging the joints around the roof on hooks. On one day each week he would slaughter a buffalo, letting the blood flow freely down the street, and then chop it up ready for sale. Dogs would hover waiting for scraps, and in the summer the meat would look black with its coating of flies.

During the war, his 'shop' was covered with posters and anti-foreigner slogans, and he would wave his meat cleaver around threateningly. Mary and Michael were forced to keep a low profile and only go out in their safer Mitsubishi Pajero, sticking strictly to the curfew instigated on all foreigners for their own safety.

A glimmer of light in a dangerous time was the appointment of a new Bishop. The one Mary and Michael had known decided to retire eventually, and moved with his English wife back to England. He had done his best under difficult conditions, and had never been afraid to defend his Christian faith in the face of fearful odds.

The new Bishop had the effect of bringing the diocese together once more as the war placed all the Christians on one side and the Moslems on the other. These were the kind of days when trusting God became an everyday necessity rather than a holy aim.

Mary now had to think about whether she should return home again to visit her father. Michael could not leave because he had been made Head Warden for Peshawar and needed to be in constant communication with all the expatriates.

He was naturally concerned for Mary; and she for her daughters and father in England, should anything happen to herself and Michael.

Then Mary and Michael's dilemma found its uneasy solution. They received a phone call from home telling them that Grandpa had been taken into hospital for a gallstone operation. It was not considered necessary for Mary to rush home, but they thought she ought to know of the situation. They promised to let her know immediately if it deteriorated.

Mary was not happy, however. She knew that it would be very doubtful whether her father would be able to manage when he came out of hospital, but she was reluctant to leave Michael. There was only one thing to do - as always - she prayed about it.

She felt that she needed a definite sign if she was to take the very expensive and even dangerous step of flying home. Even getting to the airport held risks for a foreigner. She prayed that the sign would be a phone call from someone at home specifically requesting her to return. Having committed the problem to the Lord, she went to bed, exhausted, at ten o'clock that night.

Michael had to remain awake most of the night to

maintain telephone contact in four hour shifts, so he was awake when the phone rang at midnight to say that Mary should come home. The next day was spent in urgently arranging for the earliest possible flight.

It was very difficult for Mary to leave Michael under such circumstances but he assured her that at least he would not have her safety added to his responsibilities. She arrived home not knowing what the future would bring.

Grandpa actually recovered well, but was grateful to have Mary at home to care for him. In spite of his protestations about being able to look after himself, he had to admit that it was good to have someone to cook his meals and to see to the many tasks which were becoming a burden to him.

Mary, however, was still employed by CMS, so she suggested that she write a handbook for her in-service teachers in order that they would be able to continue their studies - just in case she should not be able to return to Pakistan.

They decided that Talat would translate it into Urdu, before distributing it to the schools and then the college, so that it covered both languages. Mary laboured at this task for seven months while Michael remained in Peshawar; the Gulf War having ended.

Ruth and Roy were glad that Mary had come home. They had planned on getting married in perhaps two years' time, but suddenly everything changed. The Church Army College announced a move from Blackheath to Sheffield, which meant that Roy would be in the north while Ruth remained in the south. However, when Ruth was made redundant from her work, there seemed little to stop her going north with him.

They discussed the situation with Mary, and she agreed to write to Michael suggesting that Ruth and Roy should get married in the summer of that year so that they could be together. It seemed a sensible solution, and in August, CMS allowed Michael to fly home for the wedding.

It was a wonderfully happy time for the two young people who were particularly pleased to have several of their Pakistani friends coming to England to share in the day, together with another special guest, the Rev. Geoffrey Peters, Talat's brother-in-law who lived in England. As Michael and Mary said goodbye once more to one of their daughters, they were satisfied that Ruth and Roy were beginning their married lives on the best possible basis as they set out in a life of dedication to the Lord.

Now it became Michael's turn to wonder about his future in Pakistan. It became increasingly evident that Grandpa could not manage alone, and the possibility of remaining permanently in England had to be faced. The thought was not a happy one to Michael. He believed God had called him to Pakistan, and he would not leave until he received guidance from God. At the same time, his work for the diocese was changing, and it could be that his part in it was coming to an end. What was God's will for him?

The solution to the problem was forced upon him. He heard from CMS that, in common with all other enterprises, they were experiencing financial difficulties and after much prayer would have to make some changes. One of these was that they were going to retire a number of personnel abroad who were administrators. Michael would be one of these. God was leading him into new pastures. He would obey trustfully and await further orders.

Postscript

Michael has since returned to Pakistan several times, for three months or so at a time, staying with his many good friends, and being no longer a church 'official', he is able to reach out and teach in many new spheres.

The first of these visits included the whole family when Ruth and Roy came out for a *valima* following their wedding. Traditionally the bridegroom's family hold this gathering so that their friends can all meet the bride's relatives and friends. Mary and Michael reversed the situation so that all their friends could come and meet Ruth's new husband, and more than two hundred came to celebrate with them.

It proved to be a dual-purpose gathering because it turned out to be a farewell for Mary and Michael too. The happiness for Ruth and Roy was tinged with sadness that after more than twenty years of service and the building up of many friendships, the time had come to say 'goodbye'. However, many agreed to keep in touch, and carry on the good work.

They left Swati village with the news that the little Christian fellowship was beginning to thrive, and that plans were being drawn up for a small building where they could meet together. Money would be needed to finance it, but they are trusting God to provide this need so that they can worship freely.

One terrible tragedy has since overshadowed the fond memories of the work. Mary and Michael, and many of their friends and colleagues, were devastated to learn that Mrs. Talat Peters and her husband, together with one of their daughters and Talat's sister were all killed in a horrific head-on road crash in Peshawar.

It was very difficult to come to terms with such a senseless tragedy, but Mary and Michael could only leave their grief in the hands of their Heavenly Father, who knows all answers.

Two other good friends were also to die tragically. Azam, the friendly hotel keeper of the *Spogmai* in Qandahar was executed as a counter-revolutionary, and then in February 1994 it was reported on the BBC News that the body of Haik Hovsepian, Evangelical Church leader in Tehran, had been found in a street. He had been stabbed many times.

They will always be remembered with gratefulness and love, and as those who gave their lives for the cause of the gospel.

Back in England at the time of writing, Mary and Michael are now as busy as ever with work for the local church at Tankerton and other voluntary service for CMS and societies such as the Red Cross, in addition to looking after Mary's father.

Roy is now a Church Army Officer, and he and Ruth are in full-time Christian service in Leicester, but have not ruled out the possibility of maybe working in Pakistan one day.

Sarah is in her third year at Hull University, and Grandpa Bogg still insists he can look after himself - at ninety-four years of age!

No Christian ever really retires from the Lord's work, and so long as they are able, Mary and Michael will still be looking to God for further instructions.